Contemporary American Poetry

D1531110

Here is what teachers have said about each poet's contribution to *Contemporary American Poetry*:

Kim Addonizio
"Addonizio's commentary is an excellent example of how one might discuss technical decisions. I like very much her focus on forms, which is the way I prefer to introduce poems to beginning students."
—Alyce Miller, Indiana University, Bloomington

Dick Allen
"I especially appreciate Allen's splendid use of forms and his ability to find the music of slants. His feel for narrative, for image, his sense of history and of place—these are foundations upon which to build mighty poems."
—Miles Garett Watson, Arkansas State University

David Baker
"David Baker's essay is brilliant, insightful and honest."
—Porter Shreve, University of North Carolina, Greensboro

Robert Bly
"Very useful, and, as usual, his comments are interesting. His remarks on assertions could provide a whole new way for students to look at their poems."
—Bruce Williams, Mt. San Antonio College

Michael Bugeja
"Jealousy—*I cannot avoid it when I think of Bugeja and what he has been able to do with sonnets and sequence. Here is a voice we can all learn much from, a voice students can lean on, a voice they can trust.*
—Miles Garett Watson, Arkansas State University

Wanda Coleman
"Perhaps some will be offended by her honesty, but that, and her grit, makes the commentary so tremendous. Thanks for including her."
—Kathleen West, New Mexico State University

Billy Collins
"Billy Collins' commentary addresses the surprise of what he calls 'the happy accident' and I think there is much merit in that idea, particularly for beginning writers who fear 'making mistakes'."
—Alyce Miller, Indiana University, Bloomington

Denise Duhamel
"A good series of poems. The commentary presents a good story about the genesis and publication of the poems."
—Susan Swartwout, Southeast Missouri State University

Stephen Dunn
"I've long admired Dunn for the way he crystallizes the writing of his poems, makes the process understandable without losing sight of his own human, common, ordinary flaws. His prose piece is marvelously illuminating. . . . Dunn writes for the love of language first and last. . . . This will be a joy to teach."
—John Wylam, Bowling Green State University

Stuart Dybek

"I like the way Dybek begins the commentary with the confessional sense of a man who knows he's being read. This makes the reader feel, I think, that he's right there, ready to respond."

—Beckie Flannagan, Francis Marion University

Ray Gonzalez

"Excellent job of explicating his process in a way that takes the reader deeper into their own kivas, their own layered vastness."

—James Bertolino, Western Washington University

Bob Hicok

"Hicok is an incredible poet. His defense of the 'finished' poem is interesting and worth discussing."

—Susan Swartwout, Southeast Missouri State University

Jane Hirshfield

"These poems are important in the tension between general observation and personal experience."

—Danielle Dubrasky, Southern Utah University

David Lehman

"Very useful, especially the numerous suggestions, like keeping a notebook and giving yourself assignments."

—Bruce Williams, Mt. San Antonio College

Timothy Liu

"Liu's own poems are edgy, sure, and yet they remember the history of poetry and never turn their backs on what's gone on before . . . a good reminder of how the best writers are reservoirs of history at the same time they 'add to the stock of available reality'."

—John Wylam, Bowling Green State University

Adrian C. Louis

"I love 'Indian Summer' . . . it is terrific for talking about long poems and narrative poems."

—Susan Swartwout, Southeast Missouri State University

Campbell McGrath

"McGrath's commentary is fabulous. He not only talks about his work in an accessible and clever way, he also makes useful comments about poetic form, lines, influence, construction, and the value of the specific."

—Beckie Flannagan, Francis Marion University

Peter Meinke

"A brilliant and exceptionally useful commentary. I especially liked how he discussed the tension between 'formal' and 'free' verse."

—Kyle Torke, Elon University

Lisel Mueller
"This intimate memoir about a life-embedded poem is beautiful."

—James Bertolino, Western Washington University

Sharon Olds
"A strong, influential voice. [Her poems are a] good model of strength and craft for students."

—Kathleene West, New Mexico State University

Lee Ann Roripaugh
"The use of concrete details, the simplicity of language, etc., the consistency of voice, and so on, are all exemplary."

—Alyce Miller, Indiana University, Bloomington

Kay Ryan
"The most important thing they [students] will get from Ryan is the commiserating notion that until we stumble across our own individual sound, or 'voice,' we really aren't going to have a clue what we're doing."

—John Wylam, Bowling Green State University

Vivian Shipley
"She does a wonderful job of putting us within the mindframe of the poem's time period."

—Susan Swartwout, Southeast Missouri State University

Elizabeth Spires
"A useful look at the impetus to write and the revision process."

—Beckie Flannagan, Francis Marion University

Virgil Suárez
"Powerful poems and studies in prose poems."

—Bruce Williams, Mt. San Antonio College

Ron Wallace
"Wallace is teacher Par-Excellence. His commentary touches upon so many issues: the inspired poem/the culmination of experiences. The truth/the invented truth. The political/the personal. And he's generous with his explanation of the initial exploration impulse. . . . "

—Susan Swartwout, Southeast Missouri State University

Afaa Michael Weaver
"The commentary is engaging throughout. I like the way Weaver introduces visual art in the discussion. Sometimes students show a reluctance to engage with visual art. Weaver breaks down this barrier with apparent effortlessness."

—John Wylam, Bowling Green State University

Miller Williams
"I very much like Williams' discussion of lineation."

—Alyce Miller, Indiana University, Bloomington

Contemporary American Poetry

Behind the Scenes

Ryan G. Van Cleave

Longman

New York • San Francisco • Boston
London • Toronto • Sydney • Tokyo • Singapore • Madrid
Mexico City • Munich • Paris • Cape Town • Hong Kong • Montreal

Vice President and Publisher: Joseph Terry
Acquisitions Editor: Erika Berg
Associate Editor: Barbara Santoro
Senior Marketing Manager: Melanie Craig
Supplements Editor: Donna Campion
Media Supplements Editor: Nancy Garcia
Production Manager: Joseph Vella
Project Coordination, Text Design,
and Electronic Page Makeup: Thompson Steele, Inc.
Cover Design Manager: Wendy Fredericks
Cover Designer: Laura Shaw
Cover Illustration/Photo: Fred Otnes, "Time with Alesso," Collage Painting.
Fred Otnes is represented by Reece Galleries, New York.
Manufacturing Buyer: Lucy Hebard
Printer and Binder: Courier Corp.
Cover Printer: The Lehigh Press

For permission to use copyrighted material, grateful acknowledgment is made to the copyright holders on pp. 359–362, which are hereby made part of this copyright page.

Library of Congress Cataloging-in-Publication Data

Contemporary American poetry : behind the scenes / [compiled] by Ryan G.
Van Cleave.-- 1st ed.
p. cm.
Includes index.
ISBN 0-321-09578-2
1. American poetry--21st century. I. Van Cleave, Ryan G., 1972-
PS615 .C655 2002
811'.608--dc21
2002030091

Copyright © 2003 by Pearson Education, Inc.

All rights reserved. No part of this publication may be reproduced, stored in a retrieval system, or transmitted, in any form or by any means, electronic, mechanical, photocopying, recording, or otherwise, without the prior written permission of the publisher. Printed in the United States.

Please visit our website at http://www.ablongman.com

ISBN 0-321-09578-2

3 4 5 6 7 8 9 10—CRS—05 04 03

Contents

Preface to the Instructor

Art is not something you can take or leave,
it is a necessity of life.
—Oscar Wilde

During the past 20 years, aspiring poets seem to have taken to heart the attitude that personal experience rather than experience with literature should be the catalyst for creative endeavors. Many writing teachers now lament how student poems often rely almost *exclusively* on their life experiences. The reasons for this are many, but often it's that students fear "corrupting" their own creative impulses by reading other works. Literature teachers have similar difficulties in finding a text that features and discusses diverse modes of writing and, above all, gets students excited about poetry.

Contemporary American Poetry: Behind the Scenes is designed for both the aspiring poet as well as the student of literature. This anthology invites readers to experience poetry selections from 28 of America's best poets—selections that the *writers themselves* have picked as some of their best works. These poets then provide the "behind the scenes" information—original commentaries—that demystify the poets' own creative choices and explain how they negotiated many of the craft issues that can confound student writers. Taken individually, each poet's selected poems and commentary offers a glimpse into one successful writer's life. Taken together, these 28 sections offer a rich diversity of poems and discussions on the creative process.

Unlike other poetry anthologies, this text offers a student-centered, process-oriented approach that makes it a flexible, inclusive, and useful anthology suitable for literature or creative writing classes.

What Was Asked of the Contributors

The poets featured in this book were chosen not just because they are accomplished, award-winning poets, but also because they are experienced *teachers*. It seemed particularly appropriate to ask these writers to begin a conversation with students about all of those rarely talked-about issues that help make some writers successful, and others much less so.

The poets were asked to select examples of their best work—or the work they felt close to in a way that they could talk constructively about it—and then discuss the genesis of the poems. They were asked to speak from their own experiences and beliefs as makers of art and to endorse their own particular artistic values, while answering such common student questions as:

- How do I know exactly what to change as I revise my poem?
- What is the value of form poetry today? And how do I keep it from sounding "hokey"?
- What is the relationship between line length, line breaks, and meaning?
- What makes a "good" poem title "good"?
- How do I know if something is worth writing? Are you ever surprised by what works or doesn't work? What do you do then?
- What is the place of rhyme in contemporary poetry?
- From where do the best poem ideas come?
- How do I develop my own poetic voice?
- What's the most useful writing advice you ever received?

The responses came in a flurry, and more than a few highly qualified poets declined to contribute, often with a reason similar to this, "I'm a little uneasy about arguing as to which of my poems are the best ones. Some of the poems left out might get offended." So it's no surprise that the poets included here are by no means a *comprehensive* grouping of America's best poets, but are instead a representative grouping of accomplished writers who have experience teaching student poets how to write better—which is the primary goal of this book.

In effect, *Contemporary American Poetry: Behind the Scenes* invites its readers behind the curtain, revealing some of the "tricks" behind the magic of today's top poets. This text shows, perhaps, that there aren't secrets so much as there are choices—some easy, some hard, some blind, some nerve-wracking—and a great deal of guesswork and determination in the writing process.

Organization of the Text

In the interest of flexibility the poets are listed alphabetically by last name in the table of contents. This structure allows for creative frisson by juxtaposing differing attitudes, styles, voices, and concerns. Since insights can be gained by studying these poems in relation to their stylistic characteristics and elements as well, Appendix E provides suggestions on how poets can be grouped according to their writing style and the form of their poems.

Distinctive Features

- **Student-Oriented Approach** This text lets well-known and respected contemporary American poets choose favorite poems from their own repertoire and discuss what makes these poems so successful. Because all of these poets have significant experience teaching poetry, their selections were chosen with an eye towards providing models of different types of truly first-rate poems. In short, these are highly "teachable" poems from which readers can learn, both inside and outside of classrooms and between formal programs of study.

- **Advice from the Masters** Each poet offers the "behind-the-scenes scoop" on serious poetic issues such as voice, style, structure, revision, audience, publishing, and other topics. In addition, each poet offers advice to aspiring poets on how to develop and improve upon their craft in a clear, process-oriented style. This pragmatic approach engages students in the aesthetic views, personal ideas, and rarely shared practical advice from some of the masters of contemporary American poetry.
- **Writing Suggestions** Following each poet's commentary is a sequence of exercises. These exercises encourage students to reflect upon the advice offered in the commentary and then employ this advice directly into their own writing. The exercises also contain a research question that asks students to "go into the field" to examine the life of the writer in the wider culture, to experience advances in technology that call the nature of poetry into question, and to further their "conversation" with the 28 contributors by seeking out more of their work. A CD icon, , is placed next to writing suggestions that refer to, or in some way draw upon, a poetry reading or interview that is included on the audio CD that accompanies this text.
- **Quotations** Each section of the text includes inspiring quotations by a host of published poets beyond the 28 contributors. These quotations amplify, expand upon, and enrich the discussion of poetry begun in each commentary.
- **Sidebars** Pithy, useful insights from each commentary are featured in sidebars for easy reference.
- **Introduction by Edward Hirsch** The enlightening introduction by one of most respected, award-winning poets in the United States offers students a contextual and historical framework for understanding and appreciating contemporary American poetry.
- **Extensive Appendices** The text offers five appendices to help students further develop and strengthen their appreciation for and writing of poetry. Appendices include biographies on the poets featured in the text, suggestions for further reading, references to other writing resources, Web addresses to useful Web sites, and sample poet groupings. The text also includes a glossary of definitions and examples for terms mentioned or discussed throughout the commentaries.
- ***The Voices of Poetry: Selected Readings and Interviews*** (ISBN: 0-321-10761-6) This audio CD contains 22 "live" readings by poets featured in the book, as well as short interviews with two poets on specific craft issues. The CD offers students the opportunity to hear poetry and focus on each poem's sound, tone, and rhythm. This CD is available free when value packed with *Contemporary American Poetry: Behind the Scenes*. To order, use value-pack ISBN: 0-321-16143-2.

Additional Resources for Instructors and Students

For Instructors

CourseCompass Site. Resources for Introduction to Literature, Fiction, Creative Writing, and Drama, Second Edition (Access Code Card: 0-321-14311-6; Blackboard Content: 0-321-14313-2)
This site includes a wealth of resources to help students analyze and write about fiction, poetry, and drama, and conduct research on-line. Also included is a journal for responding to literature and a journal for creative writing as well as a guide to teaching literature on-line and teaching multicultural literature. Available free when value-packed with *Contemporary American Poetry: Behind the Scenes.*

Teaching Literature On-Line, Second Edition (0-321-10618-0)
Concise and practical, *Teaching Literature On-line* provides instructors with strategies and advice for incorporating elements of computer technology into the literature classroom. Available free to adopters of *Contemporary American Poetry: Behind the Scenes.*

For Students

A Student's Guide to Getting Published (0-321-11779-4)
This clear and concise "how-to" guide takes writers of all genres through the process of publishing their work—including the considerations of submission, how to research markets, the processes of self-editing and being edited, how to produce a "well-wrought manuscript," as well as other useful and practical information. Available free when value-packed with *Contemporary American Poetry: Behind the Scenes.*

A Workshop Guide to Creative Writing (0-321-09539-1)
This laminated reference offers suggestions and tips for students to keep in mind in a workshop situation—both as a participant and presenter. Blank space is provided for students to record additional guidelines provided by their instructor. Available free when value-packed with *Contemporary American Poetry: Behind the Scenes.*

The Longman Journal for Creative Writing (0-321-09540-5)
This journal provides students with their own personal space for writing. Helpful writing prompts and strategies are included, as well as guidelines for participating in a workshop. Available free when value-packed with *Contemporary American Poetry: Behind the Scenes.*

Responding to Literature: A Writer's Journal (0-321-09542-1)
This journal provides students with their own personal space for writing. Prompts for responding to fiction, poetry, and drama are integrated throughout. Available free when value-packed with *Contemporary American Poetry: Behind the Scenes.*

Glossary of Literary and Critical Terms (0-321-12691-2)
A handy glossary includes definitions, explanations, and examples for over 100 literary and critical terms that students commonly encounter in literature and creative writing classes. Available free when value-packed with *Contemporary American Poetry: Behind the Scenes*.

Acknowledgments

This book and its editor owe a great and sincere debt to Erika Berg's patience, faith, tact, and editorial astuteness, as well as to the help and assistance of so many fine and generous people at Allyn & Bacon/Longman (Barbara Santoro, Michele Cronin, Beth Strauss, and many others). I am also indebted to friend and mentor Virgil Suárez, whose teaching fueled my interest in pedagogical issues. Thanks, too, to Andy Speth and Nicholas Marto at the University of Wisconsin–Green Bay Media Center for their help in making the audio CD.

Also, a special thanks to the many instructors who have reviewed this book during its various stages of development and offered many helpful comments: James Bertolino, Western Washington University; Debra Bruce-Kinnebrew, Northeastern Illinois University; Cathleen Calbert, Rhode Island College; Carol Ann Davis, The College of Charleston; Beckie Flannagan, Francis Marion University; Clarinda Harris, Towson University; Colleen J. McElroy, University of Washington; Alyce Miller, Indiana University; Jeff Mock, Southern Connecticut State University; Porter Shreve, University of North Carolina–Greensboro; Susan Swartwout, Southeast Missouri State University; Kyle Torke, Elon University; John Wylam, Bowling Green University; Bruce Williams, Mt. San Antonio College; and Kathleene West, New Mexico State University.

A huge thank you goes to the many instructors and teachers of creative writing—far too many generous souls to mention—who assisted in the testing and development of the many exercises listed herein.

Finally, and most importantly, I thank the many students who diligently worked through the exercises, writing prompts, and research projects, and offered valuable feedback at critical times in this endeavor. Without them—and Adam Houle, my student assistant and part-time typist—this book would have been impossible.

—Ryan G. Van Cleave

The editor welcomes suggestions, ideas, concerns, or comments via his Web site, www.ryangvancleave.com, which contains poetry resources and information beyond what is included in this text.

Introduction by Edward Hirsch

"The experience of each new age requires a new confession," Emerson writes in his key essay "The Poet," and it is this confession that I find energizing in *Contemporary American Poetry: Behind the Scenes*. What is crucial is the range, the veracity, the depth, and the diversity of this enterprise. There is tremendous value in the very multiplicity—an American idea in and of itself—of the poetic voices represented here. Yet, delving further into the poems in this anthology, we also find the way in which these contemporary poems combine, merge, and react to the ideals, styles, and subjects central to the poetic movements that preceded them.

Writing in the 1800s, the Transcendentalists believed in a philosophy that stressed the value of intuition, the importance of thinking for oneself, a self-reliant individualism, and the original power of nature. They felt that the American spirit was essentially hopeful and affirmative. Emerson, for example, liked to write in what he called "the optative mood," and he praised American literature that was fresh, energetic, volatile, and rapturous. What we find among the poems in this anthology is a way in which that affirmative spirit has turned into a struggle to be reborn, to save one's soul.

This struggle to be reborn—to be renewed—can be explained partly as a vying with the complexities of the modern world, and partly as a reaction to the generational despair and negativity of T. S. Eliot's defining poem "The Waste Land," published in 1922. Stylistically, "The Waste Land" is far different than any poetry that came before it. It is an open structure of fragments, a poem without a fixed center, and it has no single interpretation or truth, no single narrator or narrative thread to hold it together. It contains scenes and vignettes from a wide variety of times and places: agitated scraps of conversations, parodies, unattributed and often broken quotations, strange allusions, a medley of foreign languages, a disturbing cacophony of voices. The result is a poem with the feeling of a nightmare. Indeed, much of the potency of "The Waste Land" was in its bleak message to the readers of 1920s America. It seemed to sum up the European and American sense of despair and tragedy following the first World War. Eliot's poem suggested that modern society lacked a vital sense of community, a spiritual center.

Yet it can be seen that most of the poets included in this book are heavily influenced by Eliot's contemporary, William Carlos Williams (1883–1963), who felt that "The Waste Land" had set American poetry back twenty years. Williams struggled to create a new art form rooted in the locality that nourished it. In contrast to Eliot, Williams' poems focused on the dailiness of life and the experiences of ordinary people. Like Williams, the poets in *Contemporary American Poetry: Behind the Scenes* are compelled to respond to the past, react to the present, and look to the future. In doing so, they also inherit the quest of Hart Crane (1899–1932), who sought to absorb Eliot's techniques and assemble them "toward a more positive, or . . . ecstatic goal." Crane's incendiary recognition was that after Eliot's "perfection of death" a spiritual resurrection was both possible and necessary, and nowhere was this more evident than in his major work, the book-length epic poem "The Bridge."

In the 1940s, Emerson's message "The quality of the imagination is to flow, and not to freeze," went unheeded by a generation of so-called New Critics who taught us the precepts of "close reading," but whose formal method of reading poetry ended up purifying and freezing the text. The methods of New Criticism enriched American poetry by a scrupulous attention to the linguistic structure of the poem itself, but impoverished it by banning authorial testimonies, denying the value of the personal, and excluding social, political, and historical information of great relevance. The result was a poetry—and a way of reading poetry—that treasured cold perfections.

Part of the quest of contemporary American poets has been to redress Modernism, and, in particular, the despair that permeated Eliot's poems as well as the sterile methodology that some say obsessed the New Critics. At the same time, contemporary American poets seem to be re-absorbing the Transcendental messages from Emerson and Whitman as deeply as they first absorbed us, even—or perhaps especially—in a dark time. The poets in this text accept Whitman's challenge to abandon ourselves to the present moment. "What is known I strip away,/I launch all men and women forward with me into the Unknown," Whitman declared. He challenged us to embrace an empathic democratic poetry, a truly inclusive democratic society.

Randall Jarrell (1914–1965) was one of the first post-World War II poets and critics to rescue Whitman from his detractors. His voice is driven by an eager imagination that helps point the way to a more humane American poet. "But I identify myself, as always / With something that there's something wrong with, / With something human," he wrote in "The One Who Was Different." One also takes heart from Muriel Rukeyser's ferocious poetry of engagement, and from Robert Hayden's formal poems that investigate the nature of freedom ("America," he writes in "American Journal," "is as much a problem in metaphysics as / it is a nation.") I particularly identify with John Berryman when he cries out to Whitman in his poem "Despair" from *Love & Fame* (1971):

> Walt! We're downstairs,
> even you don't comfort me
> but I join your risk my dear friend & go with you.

Many of the best contemporary poems at the start of this new century—a good deal of them on display in this anthology—join hands with Whitman and take the Whitmanian risk: to engage, to examine, to elate, and to create original modes of expression.

The poems in *Contemporary American Poetry: Behind the Scenes* follow up on the humane breakthroughs in American poetry in the past decades, such as the prophetic utterances of Allen Ginsberg, the highly personal poetry of Robert Lowell and Sylvia Plath, the descriptive clarity and scale of Elizabeth Bishop, and the intimate spirituality of Theodore Roethke and James Wright. What contemporary American poetry offers us today is a poetry that is more wide ranging, more connected, and more human.

Contemporary American Poetry: Behind the Scenes is a much-needed book that takes the poet's side. It reveals the writer's viewpoint. It throws open the doors and windows; it lets fresh air into the house. It follows up on the anthologies of previous generations by instigating a great range of poets to choose and engage their best work. These poets insightfully discuss their own process of working, their key influences, their formal and spiritual concerns. We read their poems and listen to their undersongs. We become privy to their considerations, their dark anxieties and bright hopes. We engage their ideas of the American poetic project itself. Poetry is a stubborn art, and the poet is one who will not by reconciled, who refuses to vanish—to let others vanish—without leaving a verbal record. These poets are makers who have been struggling to create a testimony that lasts. We are equal participants in their quest to make meaning out of experience. We launch with them into the Unknown. And we let our imaginations flow.

—Edward Hirsch

Kim Addonizio

First Poem for You

I like to touch your tattoos in complete
darkness, when I can't see them. I'm sure of
where they are, know by heart the neat
lines of lightning pulsing just above
your nipple, can find, as if by instinct, the blue
swirls of water on your shoulder where a serpent
twists, facing a dragon. When I pull you
to me, taking you until we're spent
and quiet on the sheets, I love to kiss
the pictures in your skin. They'll last until
you're seared to ashes; whatever persists
or turns to pain between us, they will still
be there. Such permanence is terrifying.
So I touch them in the dark; but touch them, trying.

Onset

Watching that frenzy of insects above the bush of white flowers,
bush I see everywhere on hill after hill, all I can think of
is how terrifying spring is, in its tireless, mindless replications.
Everywhere emergence: seed case, chrysalis, uterus, endless
 manufacturing.
And the wrapped stacks of Styrofoam cups in the grocery, lately
I can't stand them, the shelves of canned beans and soups, freezers
of identical dinners; then the snowflake-diamond-snowflake of the
 rug
beneath my chair, rows of books turning their backs,
even my two feet, how they mirror each other oppresses me,
the way they fit so perfectly together, how I can nestle one big toe
 into the other

like little continents that have drifted; my God the unity of everything,
my hands and eyes, yours; doesn't that frighten you sometimes, remembering
the pleasure of nakedness in fresh sheets, all the lovers there before you,
beside you, crowding you out? And the scouring griefs,
don't look at them all or they'll kill you, you can barely encompass your own;
I'm saying I know all about you, whoever you are, it's spring
and it's starting again, the longing that begins, and begins, and begins.

The Way of the World

We know the ugly hate the beautiful,
and the bitter losers are all seething
over bad coffee, washed in the sleazy fluorescence
of fast food restaurants. We know

the wheelchairs hate the shoes,
and the medicines envy the vitamins,
which is why sometimes a whole bottle
of sleeping pills will gather like a wave

and rush down someone's throat to drown
in the sour ocean of the stomach.
And let's not even mention the poor,
since hardly anyone does.

It's the way of the world—
the sorrowful versus the happy,
and the stupid against everyone,
especially themselves. So don't pretend

you're glad when your good friends
get lucky in work, or love,
while you're still drifting through life
like a lobster in a restaurant tank. Go on,

admit it: you'd claw them to death
if you could. But you're helpless,

knocking futilely against clear glass you can't
break through. They're opening champagne,

oblivious of you, just as you don't notice
how many backs you've scrambled over
to get this far, your black eyes glittering,
your slow limbs grimly and steadily working.

Night of the Living, Night of the Dead

When the dead rise in movies they're hideous
and slow. They stagger uphill toward the farmhouse
like drunks headed home from the bar.
Maybe they only want to lie down inside
while some room spins around them, maybe that's why
they bang on the windows while the living
hammer up boards and count out shotgun shells.
The living have plans: to get to the pickup parked
in the yard, to drive like hell to the next town.
The dead with their leaky brains,
their dangling limbs and ruptured hearts,
are sick of all that. They'd rather stumble
blind through the field until they collide
with a tree, or fall through a doorway
like they're the door itself, sprung from its hinges
and slammed flat on the linoleum. That's the life
for a dead person: *wham, wham, wham*
until you forget your name, your own stinking
face, the reason you jolted awake
in the first place. Why are you here,
whatever were you hoping as you lay
in your casket like a dumb clarinet?
You know better now. The sound track's depressing
and the living hate your guts. Come closer
and they'll show you how much. *Wham, wham, wham,*
you're killed again. Thank God this time
they're burning your body, thank God
it can't drag you around anymore
except in nightmares, late-night reruns
where you lift up the lid, and crawl out
once more, and start up the hill toward the house.

The Magical Glass: Addonizio on *Duende* and Desire

First Poem for You

I had been writing and calling myself a poet for a while when it occurred to me that I knew very little about traditional forms. I'd been writing free verse, but had little sense of the tradition of poetry that had led up to it and that was, in fact, still being practiced by a number of poets. I got interested particularly in sonnets, and spent a summer literally thinking in iambic pentameter—the five-beat line wore a groove in my brain, and I wrote sonnet after sonnet, most of them not very successful. But I got excited by the effect this kind of writing had on my language. I discovered that rather than being a constriction or restraint, having to rhyme a word or follow a rhythm for a line pushed me to be more creative and imaginative. I liked the compactness of the sonnet, too: only fourteen lines to say something interesting. When a sonnet works, I find, it's a little burst of energy. And, of course, sonnets have traditionally been love poems, so when I fell in love I wanted to write one. I wanted to talk about my love's tattoos as symbols of permanence while considering the impermanence of past relationships. His tattoos happened to be images that seemed important to describe, to add to the resonance of what I was concerned with: the lightning bolt that is love's realization; the waves, the serpent and dragon—water and earth and fire, the unconscious and knowledge and danger.

This was, as the title says, the first poem I wrote for this person. Shortly afterwards we married, then divorced, and are now, years later, together again. Things both turned to pain between us *and* persisted, something I didn't expect. The poem has been published in an anthology that's widely used to introduce students to poetry, and I've received a number of e-mails from students who find they can relate to it. I like hearing that people respond to it, and I like the fact that it's about tattoos and shows people that sonnets can still be an exciting form to work in, and can, really, talk about anything.

Onset

"Onset" is what I call a "radical revision" of an earlier poem. The first poem had some pretty images and talked about all the lovely little insects among the white flowers, and ended with the cells of someone's body "humming, preparing to rise." In its tone and language it was a rip-off of Mary Oliver; its ending was a trite and easy epiphany; and it didn't express what I'd really thought and felt when I saw those insects hovering over the bushes one sunny afternoon. That first version of the poem was published in a pretty good journal, but I knew it was a lie, and I didn't like it much.

About five years later, I came across the journal and thought again about how I'd failed with that poem. It hadn't come from a deep enough place; it had no *duende*—no mystery, no awareness of death. It was involved with surfaces but not with what was underneath. I took myself back to the opening image of the insects in the original poem, and started the one that became "Onset." I stopped trying to be a version of another poet. I stopped trying to make something lovely. I tried to access my original perceptions in order to articulate them. I remember particularly working on the words that follow "Everywhere emergence:"—I wanted to get the right things, in sound and meaning, to express that idea. It was the utter impersonality of it all that struck me, the *processes* of spring that involved new life, but not, it seemed, individuality. The poem is a succession of images that try to elaborate on that idea, and I worked to find the images that would be suitable examples.

"About five years later, I came across the journal and thought again about how I'd failed with that poem. It hadn't come from a deep enough place; it had no DUENDE—no mystery, no awareness of death. It was involved with surfaces but not with what was underneath."

The repetition of "begins" at the end is meant to bring that home, as well. The poem uses a lot of imagery to make its meaning, but rhythm and repetition are a part of it, too. It's important to really listen to your language, to the cadences of it, as you write and revise. Every comma, every period, is important. Punctuation is another way to control rhythm. The middle part of this poem is one long sentence, deliberately so, to reflect the narrator's sense of terror at the idea that she's just one of a series, that she's in so many ways exactly like everyone and everything else, that the natural world is in some sense this awful machine. Well, that's not everyone's vision, or even mine on certain days, but it was on this one.

For quite a while, the title of the poem was "Likeness." I thought that was adequate, but it didn't really satisfy me. "Onset" seems to me more accurate to the poem. One definition is a beginning, a setting out, a start; but "onset" also means an attack, an assault, and the narrator here is feeling a bit assaulted by it all.

The Way of the World

The first line of this poem popped into my head one day. I was thinking about the natural human tendency to envy the good fortune of others, even, sometimes, our closest friends. For a while the title was "Misanthropic." Is it really true that we only pretend happiness over our friends' luck? Probably, for most of us, it's mixed. But this poem wants to look at that dark side of human bitterness. It wants to make categorical statements, to see it all in black and white. I knew the poem couldn't proceed from abstraction to abstraction—ugly, beautiful, losers—so I hit on metonymy, using an associated thing to stand for the original, as a way to avoid saying that the old or disabled hate those who can walk, or that the sick envy the healthy. Medicines and vitamins led me to sleeping pills and thinking about suicides. Then it seemed okay to go back to some abstraction again: poor, sorrowful, happy, stupid. Then, a turn my poems often seem to take: addressing the reader. Of course, in this case, you might also wonder if the speaker isn't talking about himself, or herself, feeling like he or she is drifting through life, trapped like that lobster. I spent a lot of time trying to find that lobster image, brainstorming and dead-ending. Why did it show up? I suppose because I'd first seen live lobsters in the grocery store as a kid and had never gotten over that image of all of them piled on top of each other in the murky water, helplessly waiting to be eaten. Here was a place to use that memory as a way to make concrete the idea I was working with. Once I arrived at the image of the lobster, I stayed with it, looking for correspondences between a lobster in a tank and a person who is consumed with bitterness and envy.

I worked a lot on the rhythms throughout and wanted the similarity of sounds at the end of the poem, the "O" sounds of "notice" and "over," the endings of "glittering" and "working," to unify the ending and give it that feeling of real closure. It's a good technique, when you want a clear sense of finality, to rhyme a word somewhere in the last couple of lines of your poem with the very last word. I guess the theme of this poem is: Every lobster for itself.

Night of the Living, Night of the Dead

Every Halloween, I seem to find myself alone and deciding to rent a horror movie. The other thing I seem to do every Halloween is write a poem. October 31 is also Keats's birthday, so maybe I do it in his honor. Anyway, one year I rented George Romero's *Dawn of the Dead,* which wasn't very good, and it got me thinking about his earlier film, *Night of the Living Dead,* and I wrote the poem based on that. I began with simple observation—"When the dead rise in movies they're hideous and slow." But shortly I found myself, as I imagine most writers do, thinking my way through the poem as I wrote. What I mean by that is not that I thought things and then wrote them down, but that the writing itself was a way of thinking. I would say that writing is a way of feeling, as well—a mode of thought and perception.

I often use this poem as a litmus test at readings, to see what kind of audience I've got. Sometimes people receive it in silence. But if they have a certain sensibility, they're laughing. The poem is meant to be funny. It's difficult, I think, to write humorous poetry—it can end up being only funny and jokey, rather than what I find more interesting, which is to use humor the way Lenny Bruce used it, the way other comics have used it—as political commentary, or existential commentary. Humor has always been one way to cope with the horrors of life. And irony is often essential.

The poem is about depression, about addictive behaviors—not being fully alive. Wanting to get out of your body and be completely dead. But the contrary impulse is there, too, the one that keeps you staggering forward. I was happy to have found a way to talk about that, to use another story, not to be autobiographical. I love the confessional, the intimacy of that, but I get tired of it, too, and I like it when I can take my personal experience out of the poem, yet talk about something that is very personally important to me. It becomes a story and allegory, rather than "Hey, this is what happened to me last night."

Writing Suggestions

1. Write your own poem about love, but tell it in the voice of someone unexpected. The young bartender who's working days as a law clerk and observes two people in love from afar; the serial monogamist who wishes they weren't; the grandmother sipping seltzer water with a grandchild while waiting for the bus. Let the specific setting details that this person notices reflect his or her mental state. Revisit "First Poem for You," "Onset," or "The Way of the World" for inspiration.

2. Write a poem that approaches the body on a very intimate level. Use a liquid or liquids somewhere in the poem as metaphor: for example, a poem about Catholic Communion might talk about blood and wine; sweat might be compared to rain. That's right: blood, sweat, tears, bile, urine, pus, mother's milk. Also skin, cell, liver, follicle, tissue, DNA, vertebrae, clavicle, tendon, ankle, neuron, and so on. The poem should be about the body, at the level of the body. Try to get close to your subject—as close, as one blues song puts it, "as white on rice." Think about both surface and interior.

3. Take a poem that you've already written and give it Addonizio's "radical revision" by doing one (or more) of the following: change the voice drastically, reshape the structure, add end rhyme, or alter the tone. Which version(s) do you like better? Does changing one element force you to reevaluate (or rework) the poem in other ways?

4. Listen to Addonizio read "Night of the Living, Night of the Dead" on the audio CD. Now write your own poem about a subject you never thought you'd write about: the dead coming back, finding a live dinosaur in your bedroom, exploring a moon crater, experiencing a movie while blind. Let your mind run wild, the way Addonizio did. Challenge yourself to come up

with specific, concrete details purely from your imagination. See how far you can push the limits of your poem.

"The poem is never a put-up job, so to speak. It begins as a lump in the throat, a sense of wrong, a homesickness, a love sickness. It is never a thought to begin with."

—Robert Frost

Dick Allen

Veterans Day

You were the soldier shouting at the rain
Who walked the college campus with a puzzled look,
Brought back, without parade, from Vietnam.

Once I hated you, your uniform, your name,
The way you hunched with buddies in an open truck.
You were the soldier shouting at the rain.

I was the marcher with a cause to claim,
Jailed so many times I thought I'd crack.
We wanted no more deaths in Vietnam.

But the helicopter war went on . . . and on—
A country ravaged when green locusts struck;
You could hear them coming through the rain.

A child could kill you, or a crippled man.
You trusted nothing; you got high for luck
And stared through burning eyes at Vietnam.

I burned my draft card with a lighter flame.
I marched on Washington. You marched the jungle muck.
Necessity? Or madness. *Who can stop the rain?*
We were young men in the days of Vietnam.

Cities of the Fifties (A Glose)
for Frederick Feirstein

Cities were harmonies, vast orchestras
You could spend a whole day walking through
Among thin upper tones and deep down gutty basses,

Up Beggar Street, down Bullet Avenue.
Providence, Schenectady, and Denver
Drew us to their notes, their weaves
Of rich and poor, the Malamud grocery store
Shopped by a millionaire,
Flag-draped bridges, bargains you would not believe,
Glimpses of white bras
Between blouse buttons of a thousand Eves.
We wore our hearts upon a thousand sleeves,
Hoots and catcalls mixed with our applause:
Cities were harmonious, vast orchestras.

Dayton, Boise, Memphis, Santa Fe—
Each had a different sound and resonance;
In one, a love triangle, a piccolo café,
While in another cymbals turned to clay.
Each evening ended in a ballroom trance.
But every city we took Trailways to
Turned out a different audience,
A regional accent, strange cop beats, a tribal dance,
A long Chicago sob, New Orleans hullabaloo
You could spend a whole day walking through.

Day and night we wandered them alone:
Uptown, downtown, across the railroad tracks
Into their pits, then up their high trombones,
Flutes and oboes to the old brownstones
And civic monuments—to hear the trumpets
Of Seattle, Albuquerque's drumming paces,
To lie in New York's fields of clarinets,
Or pluck Miami strings, press thumbs to Pittsburgh frets,
And find, dear God, those still-believing faces
Among thin upper tones and deep down gutty basses

Sheet music rain of Bangor, street corner Hays violins,
Patches of foggy oboes and bassoons,
Harps in Charleston's tenements, the tuba taxis spins
Past Little Rock's gray window mannequins,
Cincinnati restaurants, Atlanta afternoons:
The riot wonderful . . . . And in the news
A mix of minor dissonance and whistling tunes

Preludes, overtures, immigrant tycoons,
Conductors bowing, pigeons flying, Old welcoming the New
Up Beggar Street, down Bullet Avenue.

BEING TAUGHT

Once a novelist showed me how a whole life might be caught
in a single brief sentence: *She was a woman*
who never walked in rain. Or, *Imagine a trumpet*
hanging from a willow branch. Creating lives, he said,
is half a game and half such desperate feeling,
it would be a mercy to go deaf and dumb and blind,
sometimes. *When he lit candles,*
he always thought of an Edward Hopper painting,
but which one it was, he could never tell his wife.
"Your life, for instance," he told me,
"how might you sum it up—or would you want to?"
If I lie in bed too long I feel my hands
will never stop shaking. "Japanese poets
do a similar thing with haikus," he said. "In fact
the whole of Japanese art can be explained
by mountain passes, butterflies,
robes left untied,
a swordblade misted with blood." We were walking
through a large Chicago mall
littered with cardboard. I watched a salesman
using only his left hand to tie a shoe, a girl
who swore at a mannequin as though it hated her
and all of her friends. *If I'm honest with myself,*
I'll disappear. He said every year or so
he had to concentrate on colors, blue especially,
the iceblue of an Adirondack lake
when it first freezes over, blue North Dakota ranches,
fishscale blue, the powder blue an evening snowstorm casts
in a car's headlights. But then he'd see someone
and the sentences would come again to him unbidden:
He was a man who loved to row dark waters . . . .
. . . . Without intention, she dressed to be undressed . . . .
All their houses smelled like smoke and beer . . . .
He had a habit of shrugging more than normal,

as if a jacket or a cape upon his shoulders
would never quite settle. We stopped to eat
at one of those cheap steak places where they serve
catsup automatically with fries. Our waitress
hummed to herself and looked like she was biting her lips
even when she wasn't. *Animal, vegetable, mineral,*
which am I? Scissors, paper, rock. I looked around,
and all the faces, all the clothes beneath the faces,
the shapes and gestures of bodies
were turning into one-line stories and I couldn't
stop summoning them, it made me dizzy:
all these lives that we were taking unawares,
confetti, heads of bobbing swimmers,
a sentence for each life. *Please, when mine is read,*
make it raw and beautiful at once.
                                        After lunch, we parted.
"Work," he said. "My work is a ship that sails away
and I'm on a wooden pier, hobbling, reaching out."
A boy at the bus stop corner glanced at him
vaguely . . . and I could swear that in this glance was how
the boy would see his entire life:
figures on glass surfaces, insubstantial, passing.

LOST LOVE

You're in the City, somewhere. I suppose if I stood
On Times Square a year or two I'd find you,
Face pleasant and older, coming out of the subway crowd,
Or studying poinsettias in a florist's window.
A flicker—that would be all. Both of us
Looked so much like others, which of us could be sure
We were not others? Once, we met in a glance.
So too, in a glance, should both of us disappear.

But I'm lying. Often on West Coast or East,
I'll be at a movie before the lights go down
And Beauty flees through the meadows from the Beast
Or the boy steps out of a throng to claim his crown,
When far down the aisles and rows I'll see you there,
Your body still young, your eyes, your taffeta hair!

The Cove

Something was out there on the lake, just barely
visible in the dark.
I knelt and stared, trying to make it out,
trying to mark

its position relative to mine,
and the picturesque willow, moon-silvered diving board
on the opposite shore. I listened hard
but heard

no sound from it, although I cupped one ear
as I knelt in the cove,
wondering how far I should take this, if I should seek
someone to row out there with me. Yet it didn't move

or grow darker or lighter. Most shapes,
you know what they are:
a rock-garden serpent, a house in the mist, a man's head,
an evening star,

but not this one. Whatever was out there kept changing
from large to small.
The mass of a wooden coffin surfaced,
then the head of an owl,

a tree limb, a window, a veil—
I couldn't resolve it. I ran one hand through my hair
as I stood up, shrugging. I had just turned 50
and whatever it was that might be floating there

I didn't want it to be. Too much before
that came unbidden into my life
I'd let take me over. I knelt again and stared again.
Something was out there just beyond the cove.

Then

What came through the fields was a white horse
galloping toward us:
a white horse with red eyes,

snarls of black flies
swirling about it. What came
through the fields had blood on its mane
and blood on its forelocks—and blood
splattered its loins. We stood
watching it come. We said prayers
that it might swerve. We put our hands to our ears
to block out its whinnying.
We did everything
but run. A coven of sparrows rose
from the grass and settled again. Across
the fields lay the broken swath
of weeds its slashing hooves left
bowed in their wake. No god
to protect us! No road
of words we might take—the white horse
galloping across the fields toward us.

DIGNITY

Remington's almost oriental picture of the Indian
Seated on a horse and looking out
Across blue snowy plains to where the stars lie leveled
Like coals in a campfire doused in heavy snow
May express it: that single muted figure
Half-wrapped in blanket and a long doomed ride ahead.
Who would not wish, or seem to wish
Such an ending for the human race: cold wind
And suffering accepted. In the posture
He is drawn in, and his frozen stature,
It's as if the world he lived through was entire;
He felt no shame, confusion, anguish
For being nameless in it, leaving no
Explanation of the snow squall, buried grass
And dreams of heavy bison and the hawk
Falling through the moonlight of a winter sky.
He probably was not much. But for a time,
There upon that ridge we can imagine, if we wish,
Not the pain to follow, not the horse gone lame,
The struggling cries of man and beast alone,
Their rotting bodies sprawled against a hillside,

But the tightening of muscle to be tried,
The lifted, blood-marred head,
And in that wish, our glory
Or delusion. Either brings us down.
Who would imagine man is more than this
Brushed figure on a horse above the plains.

Still Waters

No matter how deeply they run, no matter
  how you have been led here beside them,
watching the crow's shadow, the water-skeeter's ride
  across their filmy surface; no matter
how many have drowned in them, thinking their lily pads
  green stepping stones upon the face of time,
no matter. You are at their banks now,
  sketchpad discarded, the sound of rapids
so far behind you it is deer feet on the leaves
  in an old maple forest. No matter
who you have loved, or stolen from, or murdered,
  rest here. The cradle of Moses
lies hidden in these rushes, Monet's muted palette
  drifts within reach—and the frog prince sleeps
on that glittering log. If you look down
  through your reflection, knowing it is false,
you may see the dragon stretching out its claws
  that rake heaven for rain, or Ophelia's tresses
golden among the weeds. Or you may find
  nothing but minnows nosing in the sunbeams' latticework,
a turtle coming up for air, its reptile's head
  in almost blind swaying. No matter. Take off your sandals,
like on your back, breathe deeply, but with no
  purpose in mind. You are a sparrow's wing,
you are a psalm. Beside the still waters,
            you will be restored.

Allen on Form Poetry and Natural Speech Patterns

Two of the goals I've set for my poetry are to try and bring to traditional form the natural speech patterns of free verse, and bring to free verse deepening shadows of form taken from traditional verse. In my favorite poems, I hope I may be coming closer to doing this—using slant rhyme, colloquial language, lines of varying feet, and the like. After what William Carlos Williams showed us about American speech, I haven't wanted to use in usual ways the elevated rhythm and tone of traditional short prosody. I much prefer crossover or jazz. Often, purposefully, I change initially exact rhyme to slant rhyme and exact meter to irregular or broken meters until the future rhymes and meters of the poem follow their lead. Yet I want the bass beat, the iamb, to be underlying, for it's the root of our language. And I strive for a touch of artifice, rather than a diary or journal entry poem. Yes, I want to Americanize and reinvigorate the old forms, at once using them and transforming them.

> *"I want the bass beat... for it's the root of our language... I want to Americanize and reinvigorate the old forms, at once using them and transforming them."*

"Why?" my conservative friends ask. "Why not classical formalism?"

Because I believe all generations have their own sounds, and I want to capture the unique sound of our American language at this hugely important time in history. I want my poetry to sound like we sound now—partially timeless but also partially singing in our own late 20th- and early 21st-century chains.

Most important to me is that the poem not be "confessional," that the poem be fiction and relate directly to a wider audience even while containing some personal elements. What's most worth writing about, I think, are the significant events of our time, the Cold War, the resignation of President Richard Nixon, computers and the Internet, the changes in consciousness that have resulted from modern and contemporary science and technology. There are thousands of other worthwhile subjects, there is awe and wonder, although as Faulkner has said, much of everything comes down to "the problems of the human heart in conflict with itself," as well as "courage and honor and hope and pride and compassion and pity and sacrifice."

What's not usually worth writing about—or at least not more than once or twice except to criticize (but who knows?)—is trivia, especially commercial trivia. Also not usually worth writing about are one's actual mother, father, sister, brother, aunt, uncle, grandfather, dog and cat, *ad nauseum,* in poems relating only to the poet's sorry self, unless they can be transformed into symbolic or representational figures. See Christopher Smart's "For I Will Consider My Cat Jeoffrey" or Sylvia Plath's "Daddy" for how to do it right.

In a narcissistic age, I've constantly tried to avoid writing a sin sistic poem. When my poems start to become self-pitying or too self-consc , or want to turn into home movies, or are more interesting to those who know me personally than to strangers, I abandon them, for I have failed to listen to the world and to write at my best.

Since my poetry is obsessively concerned with what it felt like in the last fifty years of the century at the end of the old millennium and how it feels at the start of the new century and the new millennium, my favorite poems tend to be the ones that incorporate a sense of this place and time in American history.

My own "transitional generation"—the Silent Generation, ironically—functioned as "explainers" or "translators" of our Lost Generation parents and our 1940s and early 1950s older brothers and sisters to our Baby Boomer younger revolutionary generation brothers and sisters, and vice versa. We were, at once, the last of the old guard and the beginning of the new. In form and content, we were caught in the "war" of the Beats and the Academics, never firmly aligned with either T. S. Eliot or William Carlos Williams, Richard Wilbur or Allen Ginsberg, but learning from all schools, trying to create a new synthesis. The seeing of both sides is key.

Thus, "Veterans Day" is a villanelle which tries to capture the ambiguity so many felt during the Vietnam War. The narrator is a war protestor, but he burns his draft card with "a lighter flame" and who knows what that war was? When I found the villanelle's last line, it seemed to sum up everything exactly. But I've had '60s people from both sides scream at me after I've read this poem, still hating each other.

Each year, I choose a traditional poetic form to write a poem in, and try to bring to this form contemporary content and sensibility. I write scores of bad poems in this form, light verse that has little but rhyme and meter, throwaway poems, until the form seems to seep into my body and ghost my consciousness. Finally, a subject that wants the form comes along and pours itself into the form. That was the case with "Cities of the Fifties."

But without personal content, without strangeness, a poem would be just another exercise. "Cities of the Fifties" reflects my own hitchhiking around the USA when I was nineteen and in search of the Beats, when I wandered many American cities night and day—something I wouldn't do now that they're much more dangerous, and so many streets and avenues have turned, literally, into "Beggar Street" or "Bullet Avenue." As the poem evolved, the cities took on strange lives and musical personalities I hadn't expected. I found myself researching books on music in order to find enough instruments for the cities. This was fun. Also, I love American place-names. I love saying them aloud: "Cincinnati," "Bangor," "Albuquerque"!

"Without personal content, without strangeness, a poem would be just another exercise."

"Being Taught" starts off true and this is one of those poems that seemed to write itself as I followed it along, a few lines behind, just listening and transcribing. I like to hear people other than the poet in a poem. Here, I like transforming my novelist friend into the man who teaches, and I hope I've made it seem as if he's real. I also like information or pseudo-information in a poem, especially from another culture. Thus, the Japanese culture getting into the poem pleases me.

Sometimes a poem begins with a phrase or observation that may or may not remain after the poem is written. For years, I'd wondered about the truth of the New York City saying that "If you stand on Times Square long enough, sooner or later every person you've ever met will pass you." Then one day near Times Square I glimpsed an old acquaintance from years away and thousands of miles away who I'd never dreamed I'd see again. This poem resulted. It was a year of writing sonnets, so she appeared in a sonnet. I like the miracles that occur in the sestet of "Lost Love," and I very much like that Howard Moss printed the poem in *The New Yorker*. I like thinking that many a "Lost Love" will have known it was about her.

"The Cove" is a blend of reality and an imagined situation. Poets, like others, tell lies about themselves so convincingly and so constantly, they start to believe them. I seem to have actually had this experience at Thrushwood Lake, but I didn't. My persona did. However, of course I turned 50 and have grown tired—as we all have or will—of adjusting to the unrelenting responsibilities the world asks us to assume. The poem, it has later seemed to me, is my version of Robert Frost's "Stopping By Woods on a Snowy Evening," though my poem doesn't have the image purity of Frost's.

At some point in composing a poem, there's that "click," that absolutely true and right and completely unexpected phrase or image or simile or metaphor that gives the poem a true vividness. If this doesn't occur, the poem never quite works, and is often abandoned to drawer or wastebasket. For me, this "click" in "The Cove" was with "Most shapes/you know what they are:/a rock-garden serpent, a house in the mist, a man's head . . . ." These images come into the poem from that place into which I can only see darkly.

Likewise, images just appeared in "Then," the white horse starting to rear up on my clipboard one day, the first two lines, and since they rhymed themselves ("horse"–"us"), the rest of the poem wanted to be couplets and that's what happened. I like to think of this as a rhyming couplet poem where the reader or listener doesn't recognize the rhymes upon first hearing, unless they're pointed out. And this poem continues to frighten me because, like all my poems I like best, I almost but don't quite understand it. What's coming in this new century? *Almost anything.* Donald Hall has said that every really fine poem contains some quite bad line or phrase, and I think every really fine poem also contains something unanswered, strange, unaccountable. The idea is to try and hold that strangeness in a web of near-familiarity or story.

Much poetry is tribute, "Rühmen, das ists!" as Rilke wrote, and "Dignity" is my tribute to what Frederic Remington did with this painting of the Indian scout. I've traveled to the Stirling and Francine Clark Art Institute in Williamstown, Massachusetts many times to see the painting (*The Scout: Friends or Enemies*). The isolated figure, the isolato, the hermit, the recluse, the monk have always attracted me, and I hope I may have caught and held in a small cameo his loneliness and a sense of calm acceptance of obscurity.

In a frantic and chaotic time of unrelenting immersion in future shock, I've also tried to portray calm in a lifelong series of poems based upon the 23rd Psalm. I like the tranquillity of "Still Waters," how readers have written to tell me they turn to it in times of troubles, how the rhythm of the poem seems to me perhaps nearly as calm as the dissolution of matter which is "no matter" at all.

What I've written may give the romantic impression that most of these poems just "happened." That's not at all the case. All of them took scores of drafts, and in some cases over fifty drafts to reach their present shape. But that may be what an author's "best" or "favorite" poem also is: a poem that can be worked at, brought as close to perfection as possible (but never perfected) without the working with it destroying it. Weaker poems crack, splinter, disintegrate, get warped completely out of shape in revision, especially in those dangerous classroom group workshop sessions that so often tear out their hearts and guts. A strong poem, compelled by personal commitment and infused with content relating to more than the poet's Self, with certain form and mystery, can sustain the assault to emerge even better—and, strangely, sometimes even more raw and blesséd than before.

Writing Suggestions

1. Along with figurative language, rhythm, and sound, poetry makes good use of tone. Just because a poem is about a specific subject doesn't mean that the writer must utilize a prescribed attitude towards that subject. Write your own poem that takes an unusual/unexpected tone towards one of the following: divorce lawyers, death, the Vietnam War, God, nature, the President, botany, or dropping out of college.

2. Leaf through a good art book and find a painting that catches your attention. Meditate on it for a few minutes, then quickly write a draft of a poem in response. Once you've written your poem, go examine the ekphrastic poems—poems about paintings—other writers have done. Look at Brueghel's "Landscape with the Fall of Icarus" paired with W. H. Auden's poem "Musee des Beaux Arts" or William Carlos Williams's poem "Landscape with the Fall of Icarus." Look at Duchamp's "Nude Descending a Staircase" paired with X. J. Kennedy's poem of the same name. Look at van Gogh's "Starry Night" in conjunction with Anne Sexton's poem of the same name. Williams and Kennedy pretty much describe the painting without comment, letting language repaint the picture. Auden does some

art criticism, interpreting the painting, and he uses it as a way to state a truth about human experience. Sexton uses van Gogh's painting as a metaphor for her psyche. Consider all the possibilities in the idea of "poetic response" before you go back to revise your own ekphrastic poem.

3. Retype one of Allen's poems, but as you do so, remove every noun and replace it with a _________. After you're through, go back and fill in the blanks with your own words. How is your version different than the original? Has the tone and voice changed? (Variation: Work with a partner and exchange poems so you each won't have seen the original. Does this alter how you fill in the blanks? Does this make it easier or harder?)

4. Like Allen, many writers use memory as a source for their most powerful poems. In a quiet room, relax and close your eyes as you listen to Allen's selections on the audio CD, then write your own twenty-line poem where each line begins with "I remember _________." The more specific and vivid your memories, the better you'll be. Next, cut out most (or all) of the "I remembers" and see how well the poem coheres. Is what you have left more vivid than your usual first draft of a poem? Does it seem more spontaneous? Go back and revise as needed.

> *"[Poetry is] like the ancient mariner, I suppose, who grabs you and says, 'Listen, I have to tell you something. I have to explain myself.'"*
>
> —Gerald Stern

David Baker

STARLIGHT

Tonight I skate on adult ankles across the blue pond
sifted with snow, back and forth across ice lit
as if from underneath by moonlight and many stars.
As I sweep and turn, the wind warms itself
inside my collar and rings the cattle's crystal bells
where they huddle over ranging fields. *Starlight*,
she whispers, *bright stars*, though the tiny
woman I have always loved can't see them.

What is it like to drift between your life and your life?
Needles dot her arms, nurses rub their cotton cloths
like clouds across her face. Like melting ice
the fluids drop down trickling to their tubes.
When I take her hand, and off we go, our skates slice
lightly in the rippled ice, her hair blown-frost
and tangled. She tugs my arm and sings *I wish*.
Brittle tree limbs crackle in sudden gusts

and so she leaves me, skating ahead with surprising grace,
called to by something else. Once I watched her
pile of precious scraps become a quilt.
Once she pulled it to my chin and in my first sickness
I kicked it off. The fragile ice, blue-floured ice
we cut across, groans and gives, grows weaker.
Each time we pass in time. Once she wept when
her child's children, sullen in their hand-me-downs,

scuffed early home from school and wouldn't speak.
In this grown place, across blue sheets, we swing
until my ankles tire and ache. Who can finally reach her
where she whips beneath the trees? She pirouettes and floats,

she spins alone in spray, her body lifting luminous and whole
like song, now like a prayer. So this is what we are.
On she glides when I have stopped. On she sails when I have
laid me down and under starlight closed my eyes.

Patriotics

Yesterday a little girl got slapped to death by her daddy,
   out of work, alcoholic, and estranged two towns down river.
America, it's hard to get your attention politely.
   America, the beautiful night is about to blow up

and the cop who brought the man down with a shot to the chops
   is shaking hands, dribbling chaw across his sweaty shirt,
and pointing cars across the courthouse grass to park.
   It's the Big One one more time, July the 4th,

our country's perfect holiday, so direct a metaphor for war
   we shoot off bombs, launch rockets from Drano cans,
spray the streets and neighbors' yards with the machine-gun crack
   of fireworks, with rebel yells and beer. In short, we celebrate.

It's hard to believe. But so help the soul of Thomas Paine,
   the entire county must be here—the acned faces of neglect,
the halter-tops and ties, the bellies, badges, beehives,
   jacked-up cowboy boots, yes, the back-up singers of democracy

all gathered to brighten in unambiguous delight
   when we attack the calm and pointless sky. With terrifying vigor
the whistle-stop across the river will lob its smaller arsenal
   halfway back again. Some may be moved to tears.

We'll clean up fast, drive home slow, and tomorrow
   get back to work, those of us with jobs, convicting the others
in the back rooms of our courts and malls—yet what
   will be left of that one poor child, veteran of no war

but her family's own? The comfort of a welfare plot,
   a stalk of wilting prayers? Our fathers' dreams come true as nightmare.
So the first bomb blasts and echoes through the streets and shrubs:
   red, white, and blue sparks shower down, a plague

of patriotic bugs. Our thousand eyeballs burn aglow like punks.
America, I'd swear I don't believe in you, but here I am,
and here you are, and here we stand again, agape.

Benton's Clouds

The background is clouds and clouds above those
the color of an exhaustion, whether
of field hands stacking sheaves, or the coiling,
columnar exhaust of a coal engine.

It is eighteen seventy in nineteen
twenty-seven in nineteen ninety-eight.
The colors of his clouds express each new
or brooding effluence felt elsewhere as

progress, no matter which foreground story,
no matter the gandy dancer contoured
as corn field, no matter Persephone
naked as herself, as a sinew of

rock ledge or oak root yet pornographic
under the modern elder leering down.
The background is everywhere telling.
In the present moment, in the real air,

what we saw above the lake was an art—
gulls and then no gulls, swirl of vacation
debris twirling in funnels from the pier
though the wind rushed in wilder off the surge,

clouds, then not clouds but a green-gray progress
of violences in the lowing air, waves
like a bad blow under water. We stood
at the pier railing and watched it come on.

It is too late to behold the future,
if by future what we mean is the passed-
over detail in the painting which tells
where the scene is destined to lead—Benton's

brilliance, beside the roiling billowy
cloud banks blackened as battlefield debris,
beside the shapely physique of nature
on the move, its machinery of change,

is history in an instant. How else
infuse his Reconstruction pastorals,
his dreamy midwifes, sod farmers, dancing
hay bales wrapped in billows of sallow light,

with an agony befitting the sometime expatriate Modernist Wobbly
harmonica player he was. Who else
could execute such a beautiful storm,

whipped white, first a color on the water
like a wing or natural improvement.
When the Coast Guard boat swept by us waving,
it was already too late and too close.

The storm took down the big tree in seconds.
Though we were running, swirl of muscle, bales
and billows of fear like the wind breaking
over each swell with the force of a hand,

though we cleared the first breakwall and elm grove,
it was only accident the baby's
carriage was not crushed by the linden bough
sheared off, clean as a stick. We were standing

in the grinding rain, too soon still for tears.
It was too soon to tell what damages
there would be, though we knew, as in his art,
as though before the last skier had tipped

into the lake, there was peril ahead.
We could see it all in an instant's clear
likeness, where the future is not coming
but is already part of the story.

Forced Bloom

1.

Such pleasure one needs to make for oneself.
She has snipped the paltry forsythia
to force the bloom, has cut each stem on
the slant and sprinkled brown sugar in a vase,
so the wintered reeds will take their water.
It hurts her to do this but she does it.
When are we most ourselves, and when the least?
Last night, the man in the recessed doorway,
homeless or searching for something, or sought—
all he needed was one hand and quiet.
The city around him was one small room.
He leaned into the dark portal, gray
shade in a door, a shadow of himself.
His eyes were closed. His rhythm became him.
So we have shut our eyes, as dead or as
other, and held the thought of another
whose pleasure is need, face over a face . . .

2.

It hurts her to use her hands, to hold
a cup or bud or touch a thing. The doctors
have turned her burning hands in their hands.
The tests have shown a problem, but no cause,
a neuropathology of mere touch.
We have all made love in the dark, small room
of such need, without shame, to our comfort,
our compulsion. I know I have. She has.
We have held or helped each other, sometimes
watching from the doorway of a warm house
where candletips of new growth light the walls,
the city in likeness beyond, our hands
on the swollen damp branch or bud or cup.
Sometimes we are most ourselves when we are
least, or hurt, or lost, face over a face—.
You have, too. It's your secret, your delight.
You smell the wild scent all day on your hand.

Snow Figure

1.

A humble night. Hush after hush. Are you listening?
That's what the snow says, crossing the ice.

And the blue creek out back—where my love and I came
early one morning to remember nothing but blue

and the muffled joy of a far night's nothingness—
the blue creek, teasing, wild beneath its ice,

says hush. Snow whiffs around on its glassine surface.
Why did we wish so hard to walk where it deepens?

Why did we want to hold hands here?
My love and I came to learn how to love

the little that skates on the surface,
the nothing that flies, fast and fatal, beneath.

2.

I have put in a poem what has fallen from my life
and what I would change. Are you here?

We left a slender pathway of tracks. It led nowhere
if not to our bodies, and filled in our emptiness.

What I want most to say is what I never told her.
Don't trust me. Trust me. How could I lie?

3.

A figure of speech is where desire forces a crisis, a crossing—
one world and its weather suddenly brilliant with meaning.

My love and I came out early one morning to forget
the humble, one night when the snow came down

and we filled each other's body with our own.
So the old snow burns crystal in the sun. So the ice

slipping the creek's edges keeps teasing to be tried—
trust me, it brags, black, thrilling, or empty.

Why do we wish so hard to listen to what isn't here?
Here, the snow says, as if in response. My love was here.

My Suspicious Best: Baker on the Double-Exposed Narrative

Walt Whitman is my hero. Actually I have many heroes, but Whitman is my idea of a great American poet. Passionate, heartening, daring, sensual, inclusive—he projected the vast Romantic hope of nineteenth-century America. And despite the poor sales and paltry reviews of the first printings of his masterwork, *Leaves of Grass*, he *knew* he was making great art, poetry that was lasting, brilliant, and public. He was speaking for himself, but more so for America, when he wrote in "Song of the Open Road": "I am larger, better than I thought, / I did not know I held so much goodness." That's confidence. He knew he was the best of the best.

> *"Whitman also felt a heavy accompanying doubt about himself and his achievement. He further knew that such doubt—even shame—is one of our most deeply shared characteristics. Doubt binds us as much as hope."*

Yet Whitman also felt a heavy accompanying doubt about himself and his achievement. He further knew that such doubt—even shame—is one of our most deeply shared characteristics. Doubt binds us as much as hope. In "Crossing Brooklyn Ferry," he saw the "dark patches" over us all, and he confessed his own self-skepticism:

It is not upon you alone the dark patches fall,
The dark threw its patches down upon me also,
The best I had done seem'd to me blank and suspicious,
My great thoughts as I supposed them, were they not in reality meagre?

I freely admit to doubt as I write this commentary on my poems. Sometimes I am proud of what I've written, fulfilled, confident. Sometimes I feel "meagre" and ashamed, like Whitman. I read the great poets and the many, many good poets; then I look at "the best I had done" and wonder if anyone else can see my failings.

These contradictory feelings are true for every artist I know. We are driven by a mixture of confidence, passion, and uncertainty. In fact, such contradictions and conflicts are fundamental elements to every artist's imagination and work.

I do appreciate the opportunity to show you my work. And yes, I have personal favorites among my poems. Some of them sound better than others when I read them in front of people, while others work better on the page. Often I am wrong about all of this. So, instead of claiming the title "best" for my selection of poems, let me say instead: I have chosen five poems to illustrate something I aspire to do, or something about which I have a long-lived curiosity. "Starlight" and "Patriotics" are more than fifteen years old, while "Benton's Clouds" and "Forced Bloom" are quite new. "Snow Figure" comes right in the middle.

I vividly remember writing "Starlight." My grandmother died in 1985, and I wasn't there to say goodbye. I tried for the following year to write a poem suitable for her, a tribute, a memorial. But try as I might, my poem just didn't work well enough. It was an elegy, and it took place in a quiet, blue hospital room. The speaker of the poem sat with his grandmother until she died. It was tender enough and its grief was true, but it wasn't good enough. It was too flat in places, and self-indulgent. One late night as I tinkered again, I focused on a single image in the poem, where the hospital bed—with its icy stillness, its white flat surface—was like a sheet of frozen water. And with that single phrase I started over again, throwing away the rest of the poem.

My grandmother's life was vivid, active, and gently powerful. She lived most of her life in the country or in very small towns. So I extended the image of the frozen water into a fuller landscape—a rural scene, wintery, where the speaker and his grandmother are skating together on a farm pond. She's teaching him to skate, and she seems very alive, if also a touch otherworldly. Now, the magic—or the magic I aspired to—is the connection between the hospital scene and the pond scene. I wanted the details of one to carry into the other so that eventually a third kind of story or feeling results.

"No single position is ever sufficient to articulate our lives, but rather we are ALWAYS in several places at once. Photographers call this technique the double exposure. Take a picture, don't wind the camera, take another picture. The details of one bleed into and take part in the details of the other. Two individual scenes literally become a third and different scene."

I feel strongly that no single position is ever sufficient to articulate our lives, but rather we are *always* in several places at once. Photographers call this technique the double exposure. Take a picture, don't wind the camera, take another picture. The details of one bleed into and take part in the details of the other. Two individual scenes literally become a third and different scene. In fact, I ended up blending not only the two narratives (the hospital and the pond), but small pieces of several others, as you'll note especially in stanza three. Memory is full of quick, jumpy associations.

I am still pleased with the resulting poem, especially with its graceful tone. I think the very long lines here may contribute to its gracefulness, the fluidity of its movements like the fluid skating of the old woman. And its final irony—that the dying grandmother seems endowed with movement and power, while the grieving speaker closes his eyes in a sympathetic act of dying—captures the complexity of the event.

I wrote "Patriotics" during the same period as "Starlight," but this poem is much more social and vernacular where "Starlight" seems intimate and pure. Notice, though, the strategy of blended scenes again, the double-exposed narrative. Here the speaker and his friend (it was my wife, Ann) have come to celebrate the 4th of July in a little Midwestern river town; the place is busy with commerce and the smoke of bratwursts grilling and the bleats of the band. But something else haunts the festivities, for they find out that only the day before the celebration, a local father had murdered his daughter. Again, I hope the tension or pressure that comes from such opposite scenes might produce a dramatic, figurative effect. The poem, like the people, seems bitter, critical, or stern, but it also still wants, like the people, to be capable of praise or celebration.

It's hard to write a political poem without becoming pedantic or pious. A good poem must contain its own doubts; it must be of two minds, or more, always, and not merely single-minded. Here too, in "Patriotics," I wanted to capture something of the paradox of being American. We are full of hope and good will, ready to celebrate ourselves and sing ourselves, to paraphrase Whitman again. But we are violent and warlike as well. We love a good spectacle. We feel full of pride and love (*agape*)—of country, family, prosperity—while we feel ashamed of it all, too. A single small death may be able to represent our grief and loss more vividly than a whole battlefield of soldiers.

These long lines are more ponderous and troubled than those in "Starlight." The sentences are heavily punctuated, and the tension between long sentences and short ones further emphasizes a kind of tug-of-war of effects. There are puns and wordplay throughout, but this isn't a lighthearted poem, by any means. Sometimes I need to express difficulty, struggle, social concern, as much as private passion or enlightenment.

So, to the new poems. "Benton's Clouds" and "Forced Bloom" were composed, at about the same time, a couple of years ago, and both employ a new fascination of mine, the syllabic line. I'm interested in tension again. I want to use a regular line length (ten syllables, in these cases) to see how much variety of pace or effect I can create.

Thomas Hart Benton is another of my heroes, a painter from my home state of Missouri. I love his sweeping, heavily populated paintings and murals; I love the sinuous connection in his paintings between the movements of the body and the movements of land, or clouds, or water. Many of his paintings feature clouds—usually very brooding, black clouds—that serve as warning of bad weather, or warfare, or sometimes as announcements of progress, the smoke of a train, the exhaust of a factory. I wanted to write a poem that in some detail captures the complexity of a Benton painting: He can be intellectual, allusive, speculative, and he can be rowdy, dangerous, and blunt. I further wanted to double-expose some things, blending my own personal narrative onto a Benton canvas, and making use of his images with my own story of a lakeside storm and a near-tragedy. I wanted a complete history, but one captured in the lightning strike of an instant. It took me two months to write the first three stanzas, then a week to finish the poem.

"I wanted a complete history, but one captured in the lightning strike of an instant. It took me two months to write the first three stanzas, then a week to finish the poem."

"Forced Bloom" derives from a challenge I issued my students a couple of years ago. I wanted them to take more risks, to go in a poem to a place they didn't want to go, or to say something they wouldn't normally say out loud. Shame, again, is the subject. And sex. And delight.

For more than a year my wife suffered from a bizarre condition in her hands and arms, eventually spreading. She suffered bouts of great pain, freezing skin, burning nerves. After months of misdiagnoses and useless treatments, her doctors determined she was genetically deficient in the tendons of her hands, which resulted in nerve as well as bone damage. They fairly successfully remedied the trouble with an operation and lots of therapy. But for months she couldn't use her hands—couldn't write, or comb her hair, or tie her shoes, or drive.

How does one find pleasure? How can a lover not touch? I wanted to explore the ways by which we please ourselves—spiritually, sexually, in our decorations and houses, in our choice of mates. I see now that I wanted to probe the irony of lovers: When we make love to our lover, whom are we really pleasing? My students, of course, were scandalized. Then they looked at each other as if to say, *You too?* Now remember Whitman: What binds us is often what shames us, what we want to disguise or hide, what we want never to say. I wanted a poem about hands.

Finally, "Snow Figure" is a poem I wrote seven or eight years ago, midway between the two other pairs of poems. It has been anthologized only one other time. It's a love poem, too; maybe there is something erotic or intimate about a couplet stanza. In fact, "Snow Figure" is the first poem in my book *After the Reunion*, which is comprised entirely of love poems and elegies. As with the four previous poems, I aspired to construct tension out of opposites or out of unlike impulses. I wanted, on one hand, to write a pretty, hushed love poem; on the other, I wanted to investigate a rather discursive or theoretical notion. The sensual meets the professorial, perhaps. Perhaps these two elements are the real lovers of the poem.

A figure is a body, a shape, a torso. It is also, in ice skating, a compulsory part of a competitor's program. Thus the lovers here recall their lovemaking during the previous night, as now they walk together over a winter landscape and, gingerly, over the ice of a frozen creek. Their presence, and more importantly their passing, are marked by the tracks they leave behind. Their steps are their trace, the evidence they leave. I wanted to make the tone here as silent as walking on snow, as deliberate as treading on ice. The two figures holding hands—one seems reluctant while the other seems insistent. Why, the speaker wonders, do lovers tempt the fates? Why do they want to walk over the deepest part of the frozen waters? What if the ice were to crack? Lovers know that time never holds still for them, that passion is fleeting. Perhaps that is why love is the most recurrent subject of lyric poetry: Language can sustain passion longer than lovers can.

In important ways, therefore, "Snow Figure" is about language. Remember, a figure is also a metaphor, a trope, a figure of speech. So there are three significant elements to this poem—and three sections. A third entity (time? death? the awareness of self?) accompanies the lovers. The critic Anne Carson agrees when she asserts that there are three structural components to an erotic poem: "lover, beloved, and what comes between them." Perhaps that's why I felt compelled to match the sensual language of the lovers with the discourse of a professor, to make a highly self-conscious analysis of the poem within the poem.

The desire of this poem is the same, it seems to me, as the four other poems: to express love or need for something that is vacant, erased, or lacking. These poems may or may not be my best. But they do represent my best efforts. Each exemplifies my obsession to double-expose or overlap our loves and fears. Or, in Whitman's words, to cross our "meagre" realities with our "great thoughts."

Writing Suggestions

1. As Baker suggests, write a poem that takes risks. Write a poem and let it go to a place you don't want to go, or let it say something you wouldn't normally say out loud. Write about shame, delight, insecurity, fear.

2. Reread Baker's comments on the idea of the poetic double exposure. Write your own multiple-part poem (number the sections 1, 2, 3, etc), where each section superimposes a new idea/image atop the one before it such that the sum of the whole is much greater than its parts. This same concept works well for using details within a single poem, allowing multiple (possibly conflicting) details to add up to surprising meanings.

3. Write your own erotic poem entitled "Snow Figure." Keep in mind Anne Carson's idea about erotic poems having three structural components: lover, beloved, and what comes between them. After you've written your poem, compare it to Baker's. What are the differences? Similarities? Retitle yours, if you want, and revise it when you feel you're ready.

4. Go to Poetry Daily (http://www.poems.com) and look through an entire week's worth of poems in the Archives Section. What similarities can be said about the poems that appear in Poetry Daily? Are they all (more or less) a certain length? A specific style? A similar voice? Listen to Baker's selections on the audio CD. What claims might this lead you to make about trends in contemporary American poetry? Is Baker the only poet who's working with the idea of the double exposure?

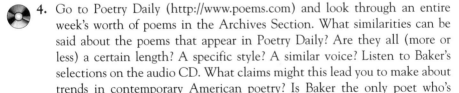

"*Form is never more than a* revelation *of content.*"
—Denise Levertov

Robert Bly

Snowbanks North of the House

Those great sweeps of snow that stop suddenly six feet from the house . . .
Thoughts that go so far.
The boy gets out of high school and reads no more books;
The son stops calling home.
The mother puts down her rolling pin and makes no more bread.
And the wife looks at her husband one night at a party, and loves him no more.
The energy leaves the wine, and the minister falls leaving the church.
It will not come closer—
The one inside moves back, and the hands touch nothing, and are safe.

The father grieves for his son, and will not leave the room where the coffin stands.
He turns away from his wife, and she sleeps alone.

And the sea lifts and falls all night, the moon goes on through the unattached heavens alone.
The toe of the shoe pivots
In the dust . . .
And the man in the black coat turns, and goes back down the hill.
No one knows why he came, or why he turned away, and did not climb the hill.

Bly on Assertions and Associations

William Stafford has spoken so beautifully about what an assertion means in a poem, and how early you can make one. In one of his books, maybe *Writing the Australian Crawl,* he says if you make strong assertions too early in the poem, you can lose the reader. The reader needs to receive a couple of assertions first that he or she can agree with, such as "It's summer," or "Animals own a fur world," or "Those lines on your palm, they can be read," or "There was a river under First and Main." The reader needs to experience rather mild assertions so that he or she can begin to trust your mind; then when you make a wilder assertion later, the reader is more likely to climb up with you into that intense place from which the assertion came. My first assertion in "Snowbanks North of the House" is

Those great sweeps of snow that stop suddenly six
feet from the house . . .

Some snow blows all the way down from Canada and then stops six feet from the house. For people who've never lived on the prairie and have experienced only gently falling snow or snow interrupted by woods, my first line may seem a risky assertion. So my second line is mild.

> *"The reader needs to receive a couple of assertions first that he or she can agree with, such as 'It's summer,' or 'Animals own a fur world,' or 'Those lines on your palm, they can be read,' or 'There was a river under First and Main.'"*

Thoughts that go so far.

I want my poem to continue, but not to ascend, so I need an ordinary event, something we've all noticed:

The boy gets out of high school and reads no more books.

I can stay with that ordinariness for a little while:

The son stops calling home.

I experienced that refusal to call home when I lived in New York during my late twenties. Certain ways of living come to an end:

The mother puts down her rolling pin and makes no more bread.

I was thinking of my grandmother making Norwegian flat bread; readers correctly told me that ordinary bread these days is not made with rolling pins. But the child in me wrote that line. The adult in me wrote the next:

And the wife looks at her husband one night at a party, and loves him no
more.

I'm not conscious that that line happened to me, but it's possible. I do recall seeing both halves of the line at one instant in the wife's glance. It's another sadness. It's just an ordinary sadness. It doesn't happen only to special people.

The energy leaves the wine, and the minister falls leaving the church.

My father always had a particular tenderness for the old Lutheran minister in our town, and made sure that he received game such as pheasants in the fall, and geese at Christmas; I had some sympathy for the way a minister has to hold himself up and perform his role no matter what is happening in his private life. He has to keep giving the Communion.

A month or two after I wrote the poem, I read it to a friend who was an Episcopal priest of great spirit; he told me that I had described exactly what had happened to him a month before. He couldn't say the Communion words wholeheartedly on that particular Sunday, and he fell on the steps outside. One could say that for many ordinary people—and I am one of those—a fine energy sometimes refuses to become friends with us, or perhaps we refuse to make the courtly gesture that would welcome that energy. When we fall, it's an ordinary sadness.

It will not come closer—
The one inside moves back, and the hands touch nothing, and are safe.

I think a lot of my childhood is alive in that last half-sentence. In my mid-twenties I spent two years alone in New York, talking to people barely once a month. It was all right. I felt safe: "The hands touch nothing, and are safe."

The poem is moving away from sadness now and toward grief. I must have felt that grief during the poem.

I recalled a scene from Abraham Lincoln's life. He loved his son Tad very much, and when the boy was eight, he died of tuberculosis or some such thing. They placed the coffin in a room by itself in the kind of home visitation that people did at that time. Lincoln went into the room and didn't come out. He stayed there all afternoon, and then he stayed there all night, and then he stayed there the next day. Around noon people started pounding on the door and telling him to come out, but he paid no attention. There was something a little extraordinary in that, but the general situation is not unusual, it's something we've all noticed or heard about many times. Sometimes after the death of a child, the husband and wife never do come back to each other.

The father grieves for his son, and will not leave the room where the coffin stands.
He turns away from his wife, and she sleeps alone.

Now what to do? Now we've arrived at a really ordinary place, in which life and its motions go on, but the shocked man or woman doesn't pay much informed attention to those motions anymore. Donald Hall has written about this place in his poem called "Mr. Wakeville on Interstate 90":

I will work forty hours a week clerking at the paintstore . . .
I will watch my neighbors' daughters grow up, marry,
raise children. The joints of my fingers will stiffen.

The way such a life moves mechanically is a form of depression. At the beginning of *A Farewell to Arms*, Hemingway says, "That fall the war was still there, but we didn't go to it anymore."

And the sea lifts and falls all night, the moon goes on through the unattached
heavens alone.

I loved that word "unattached" when I saw it on the page. It brought together the son who stops calling home and the man who lives alone in New York for two years.

Then I saw the toe of a black shoe. It seemed like an ordinary shoe, not standing on marble or red carpet, but on ordinary dust. Some elegant movement as of a hinge suddenly arrived, breaking all these long forward motions:

The toe of the shoe pivots
In the dust . . .
And the man in the black coat turns, and goes back down the hill.

The first time I read the poem to an audience, there was some silence afterwards, and a woman asked, "Who is the man in the black coat?" I said, "I don't know." She said, "That's outrageous; you wrote the poem." I didn't answer. It was only when I got back to the farm that I thought of the proper answer: "If I had known who the man in the black coat was, I could have written an essay." I don't mean to demean essays with such a sentence, but it's good to think clearly in an essay, which can be a series of really clear and interlocking thoughts that are luminous. But sometimes a poem amounts to the creation of some sort of nourishing mud pond in which partly developed tadpoles can live for a while, and certain images can receive enough sustenance from the darkness around them to keep breathing without being forced into some early adulthood or job or retirement. It's possible the man in the black coat is Lincoln. He did turn and go back down the hill, and his face got sadder every year that the war went on. The other day I noticed in a family album a photograph of my father about 25 years old, standing by a windmill holding a baby rather awkwardly crouched in his right arm; it's possible the baby was myself. He was wearing a large black coat.

No one knows why he came, or why he turned
away and did not climb the
hill.

"Sometimes a poem amounts to the creation of some sort of nourishing mud pond in which partly developed tadpoles can live for a while, and certain images can receive enough sustenance from the darkness around them to keep breathing without being forced into some early adulthood or job or retirement."

I don't know exactly why the last line closes the poem. I didn't intend it. It just came along. Perhaps it's the most ordinary thing of all. Our mother, or our grandmother, or our grandfather, or our father, goes through incredible labors, keeping—despite turbulent winds and strong blows—the chosen direction forward, following some route. But why? What was the aim of Lincoln's life? What was the aim of my father's life? Or my life? We know a little bit of the story—what's the rest of the story? Why don't we know that?

Writing Suggestions

1. Write a poem that begins with two firm assertions that readers can agree with. Then challenge yourself to see how far you can take the reader. Break down barriers, let your imagination roam free. (Variation: Begin your poem with assertions, and continue making them all the way through, an entire poem based on assertions. Is this poem more successful than other first poem drafts you've written? What are its strengths? Weaknesses?)

2. Write a narrative poem that begins with a wild assertion, then build off that in any way you choose. Remember that the trick with narrative poetry is to do something other (and more) than a story can do. Otherwise, just write the short story! Let language take the place of plot, and allow readers to make their own discoveries and associative leaps.

3. Take a draft of a poem you've worked on that's still problematic. Replace the first line with an assertion that any reader can agree with. Add another assertion in the middle of the poem. Do these additions help you envision a way to ground the reader throughout? If you think of a poem as a kite, remember to tie its string to the ground or it'll blow right off into the clouds.

4. Bly has written extensively on his views of poetry. Find two or three of his articles, essays, or interviews and see what else he has to say (use the websites listed in Appendix D to get you going). Read one from years ago and another that's recent. Have his views changed? Do you believe many of the things that you once did about poetry? What is the future of poetry?

"Poetry is not an expression of the party line. It's that time of night, lying in bed, thinking what you really think, making the private world public, that's what the poet does."

—Allen Ginsberg

Michael J. Bugeja

Ars Poetica: The Influence of Lady Mary Wroth

A crown of sonnets
In this strange labyrinth how shall I turn?

I.
Epigram: To the Earl of Pembroke

Will not thy rage be satisfied with this?

My sonnet is more lethal than your sword.
My feather has a sharper point. You dip it
In a vial of poison ink and sip it
Up as ears do gossip. You say you heard
Talk of my treason among the many lords
At court who fear a confessional poet,
Discovered my scribbles in the closet,
Exposing the king to ridicule. One word,
You warn, and you shall inform James the First
Who also loves a sonnet. In the tower
I can immortalize Scots on the throne,
Or abdicate to you in bed. Lips pursed,
Tapping my heel to the pentameter,
I'm memorizing sestets till you're done.

II.
Warning: To the Earl, Her Cousin

If lust be counted love t'is falsely nam'd

I'm memorizing sestets till you're done,
Completing what you started in the bed.
The latest sonnet echoes in my head

As you profess your love. I let it drown
Your sorry proclamations—you'll atone—
And now betray the libel you have said
In my presence about the late beheaded
Catholic queen whose son converts a throne.
In time the king will lead us to the same
Bloody stump as half our heirs. I am kin!
You do not talk of love but lust and took
What noblemen protect, a widow's name.
You took far more than that, unkind cousin.
Recite me now, and you recite your book.

III.
Apology: To Uncle Philip

> *There came to my remembrance a vanity*
> *wherein I had taken delight*
> —Sidney's final confession

Recite me now, and you recite your book,
Dear Brave Bulleted Uncle Philip. Misled
By your *Defence of Poesie*, I read
Your arguments with girlhood glee, mistook
Your talk of Eros as to me and undertook
To base my poetry on the purebred
Theme of beknighted love. Such love is dead.
You see it in the eyes of earl and duke
When noblemen invoke your name at court.
They cannot rouse the king or rob his purse
As you did vain Elizabeth. They cannot
Appease him with apologies or thwart
Their enemies with elevated verse.
They march to meter, rhyme to counterplot.

IV.
Masque of Blackness

> *Better are they who thus to blackness run*

They march to meter, rhyme to counterplot,
The knights who saw us masque, to mask the night.
We shadowed ladies danced to candlelight,

Delighting in the deeper shades. We forgot,
For a little while on stage, our clotted
Bloodlines of spouse, paramour, parasite.
We moved freely as Moors or nomads might,
Our bodies and faces blackened with soot.
The king enjoyed himself, watching women
Painted and still panting in their costumes,
Bow down to him. He talked about that theme.
Later, when we soaped and scrubbed our skin,
More rosy than white, his men would consume
Cups of ale and wine, continue to blaspheme.

V.

Song: To Ben

> *Drink to me only with thine eyes,*
> *And I will pledge with mine*
> —from Jonson's "Song: To Celia"

Cups of ale and wine continue to blaspheme
My role at court. When drunken bouts begin
To undermine me, I can discipline
Crueler than a man. I'm not what I seem,
A widow in the Earl of Pembroke's home.
He talks of us at masques. The guise is thin,
Insiders say. You solicit him as patron,
But he suspects that "Celia" is my name.
Do not reveal my real one and sober up.
Cease using similes of drink and death
To symbolize the love you claim for me.
Stop looking for my kisses in a cup
And likening red roses to my breath.
I wouldn't get that close, Ben. Take pity.

VI.

Warning: To the Drunken Playwright

> *What pleasure can a banish'd creature have?*

I wouldn't get that close. Ben, take pity
On yourself instead of me. You invite
My rage, not my patronage, when you write

Poems and dedicate your plays to me.
You talk of me as *woman* or as *lady*.
Such titles don't entitle but affright,
And I must lose them to attain the height
That I have set within my coterie.
Compare your influence to mine. I'll sing
So loud of your abuse, the king shall ban
Your comedies and cage you like a dove.
The truth is that I know you're suffering
As you deserve. But you'll suffer again
To pen more verse, indicting me of love.

VII.
Another Warning

> *I that have been a lover, and could show it,*
> *Though not in these, in rhymes not wholly dumb,*
> *Since I exscribe your sonnets, am become*
> *A better lover, and much better poet*
> —from Jonson's "A Sonnet, to the Noble Lady, the Lady Mary Wroth"

To pen more verse indicting me of love!
Then to pun my sonnets as your teacher
And my title twice in yours! You butcher
Poetry to make it. Your slow rhymes rove
Like lurid eyes over the corpus of
My passion and your thumpety meter
Bores my ears like talk. You're but a fixture
Now before me, a sty I must remove.
Fact is, when you close your eyes you see me.
When you stopper your ears, you hear my song
Tapping the inner drums of your muses.
You write a masque of blackness or of beauty
And cast a role for me to woo the king.
The woman you would use also uses.

VIII.
Yet Another

> *Good now be still, and do not me torment*

The woman you would use also uses
Weapons at her disposal to expel

Men who hem her at the Pembroke table.
She has forked deer hearts here and kicked bruises
With the toe horn of a boot. She confuses
Repartee for back talk, knives for scalpels,
And won't play Stella to your Astrophel
Nor listen to your iambs of excuses.
She has abandoned the arts of apology
And embraced the sciences of torment.
She'll play you as Cupid plays the lute.
Be still, or you shall hear your elegy
At court. The sonnet is her instrument.
This lady aims her quill and executes.

IX.
Elegy: To Her Late Husband

Think then your will, and left, leave me yet more

This lady aims her quill and executes
Your testament. The sum that you bequeath
King James is more of your abuse. Even death
Alas in England cannot stop a brute
Who leaves a widow, bruised and destitute,
To the whims of court. You consumed my youth.
My father hanged me on you like a wreath
Upon a grave. I will resurrect, uproot
The romance of an unromantic age.
The earls will analyze my lines anew
And liberate my swallows like a hawk.
I will spill rivulets of verse on the page
As men spill blood on snow, and malign you,
My dead indecent master. *Lord, I will talk.*

X.
Epistle: To the King

Implore not heaven, nor deities
They know too well his forgeries

My Dear and Decent Master: Lord, I will talk
About my estate and bid your help today.
Debts mount, I dwell with kin. To my dismay
I cannot come to court when men provoke

My wrath and women sneer behind my back.
I plead my case with pen and ink, convey
Apologies, and ask that you defray
Loans my husband left to me. Out of wedlock,
I cannot pay my creditors and risk
My widowed coat of arms. I feel defiled.
The only labor I anticipate
Employs a bed and afterward my desk
To write my masterwork. I am with child
Whose father is the broker of my fate.

XI.
Lament: To the King

Let not his falsehood be esteemed
Least your self be disesteemed

Whose father is the broker of my fate?
What man becomes the agent of demise?
What dashing uncle dashes dreams with lies?
Which eager cousin comes to procreate
The next in line? Which poet laureate
Convinces me that I should compromise?
What king awards a woman like a prize
And asks her to submit to his mandate?
So I will keep his house, but not his name.
So I will raise his heirs, but not his hopes.
So I will cede my body, but not my worth.
So I will forfeit love, but not acclaim.
So I will cease my talk, but not my tropes.
So I will lose my head, but not my truth.

XII.
Letter: To the Libeled Lord Denny

I never thought of you in my writing

So I will lose my head. But not my truth:
The facts differ, my doubtful Lord Denny.
First, the simple matter of names: Do I
Disclose your own, or in-law son's, or both?
The reason for your beaten daughter's death,

Dearest honest Honora? Or identify
Those who'd indict her of adultery?
The evidence is neither above nor beneath
Your checked and checkered life. It's parallel:
I never thought of you in my writing
But Honora whose pain pained me to such extent,
I had to talk for her. If there's libel,
It's what I have withheld. So tell the king
The facts are wrong. Produce your documents.

XIII.
Penance: To the King

> *Let not them fear . . . what my blood calls me*
> *to be and what my words have said me to be*

The facts are wrong. Produce your documents
Indicting me. I'm banished anyway.
Invite me back to hear what others say
About my book. In any case I sent
My servants here and on the continent
To confiscate all copies and repay
Nobels who have bought them. Without delay,
You may assail or silence me. I repent,
A candid woman, who talks and ridicules
Your men so awesome in their iron coats.
They serve as soldier, knight, or diplomat,
Protect your castles, legislate your rules,
Command your armies, commandeer your boats.
I thought a man was mightier than that.

XIV.
Promise: To the Earl of Pembroke

> *Gods do princes hands direct,*
> *Then to these have some respect*

I thought a man was mightier than that,
My sullen earl. Did you dissolve your will
To learn I was bequeathed to you but still
Not yours to tether like a common cat?
I purr to bear your heirs. My habitat

Becomes a bed within your domicile.
I will go down loving you, not the aisle;
I will never talk of marriage nor combat
Your appetites. So have your way with me.
I promise to conceal your impotence
Before the king. I will give you my word,
My body, my babies, and my pedigree,
But not my poetry. Make no pretense:
My sonnet is more lethal than your sword.

Bugeja on the Sonnet Crown

I had no idea what a sonnet crown was until I read one in a marvelous book—*The Poems of Lady Mary Wroth* (Louisiana State, 1983)—edited by Josephine Roberts. I was fascinated by the form. Soon I became fascinated with Lady Mary Wroth (1586–1640), niece of another great poet, Sir Philip Sidney. Wroth began her literary career when Ben Jonson was at the pinnacle of Elizabethan fame. Today Jonson is still remembered for his plays, the best of which remains *The Alchemist*, and for his immortal lyric, "Song to Celia," which begins: "Drink to me only with thine eyes/ And I will pledge with mine;/ Or leave a kiss but in the cup,/ And I'll not look for wine."

Among other things, Jonson dedicated his play *The Alchemist* to Wroth (along with three of his most tender poems). Odds are she is "Celia."

No one can say why Wroth has been ignored for so long. In later life Wroth was shunned at the court of King James I after one Lord Denny accused her of libeling him. (Roberts's book reprints the fiery exchange of letters between Denny and Wroth, who informed him: "I never thought of you in my writing.")

Fact was, however, that Lady Mary Wroth had a controversial love life and bore two children from her first cousin, the Earl of Pembroke (William Herbert). She lived and loved the way she saw fit with little regard to social conventions. You see such strength of will in her work. As a poet, Wroth is a master craftswoman who rivals Shakespeare when it comes to technique (in the sonnet) and certainly surpasses Jonson.

Here is a sample sonnet (with modern spelling) from Roberts's book so that you can hear Wroth's poetry without being distracted by Elizabethan variations:

Good now be still, and do not me torment
With multitudes of questions, be at rest,
And only let me quarrel with my breast
Which still lets in new storms my soul to rent;

Fie, will you still my mischiefs more augment?
You say I answer cross, I that confessed
Long since, yet must I ever be oppressed
With your tongue-torture which will ne'er be spent?

Well, then, I see no way but this will fright
That devil-speech; alas, I am possessed,
And mad folks senseless are of wisdom's right,

The hellish spirit-absence doth arest
All my poor senses to his cruel might,
Spare me then till I am my self, and blessed.

The sonnet above features a natural voice empowered by well-crafted lines. Consider how the first line of her sonnet sets the mood and theme in one complete declarative phrase. You might want to read it as if you were wagging your finger at a persistent lover who accosts you in public so that you have to whisper in hard, staccato tones: GOOD NOW BE STILL, AND DO NOT ME TOR-MENT. As for her lines, consider how that first one works in tandem with the second and enhances meaning: *do not me torment* as in "leave me alone" and then *do not me torment with questions* as in "leave me alone to make up my own mind."

You see this type of layered meaning throughout her lyric (especially in the second stanza). Indeed, her lines are so polished as units of speech that you can lift them like building blocks and place them elsewhere in the poem, and have the piece make sense.

Go ahead and read it backward:

Spare me then till I am my self, and blessed.
  All my poor senses to his cruel might,
  The hellish spirit-absence doth arest

And mad folks senseless are of wisdom's right.
  That devil-speech; alas I am possessed.
  Well, then, I see no way but this will fright

and so on. By the way, you can't do this with the typical Shakespeare sonnet:

So long lives this, and this gives life to thee.
So long as men can breathe, or eyes can see,
When in eternal lines to time thou grow'st:
Nor shall death brag thou wander'st in his shade

and so on.

One can argue that Shakespeare is more universal and appealing than Lady Mary Wroth, but one can also argue that the lady's lines (occasionally, at least) are better crafted. Her sense of craft inspired me to compose what I consider one of my best poems, appropriately titled, "Ars Poetica: The Influence of Lady Mary Wroth."

To create a sonnet crown, I had to become familiar with the form. A crown is a sequence between 3 and 14 sonnets (in any style—Shakespearean, Petrarchan, Spenserian, etc.). The beauty of a crown is in the stitching. You can weave sonnets into a fine poetic cloth so that the last line of the first sonnet becomes the first line of the second. The last line of the second sonnet becomes the first line of the third, and so on, until the final sonnet, which ends with the *first* line of the *first* sonnet. Thus, the crown is as repetitive and circular as a fixed form.

Crafting such a poem is a complex undertaking, as you can well imagine. The keys are to conceive a circular topic and a powerful first line. The two work in tandem. So in contemplating my sonnet crown, I asked myself:

- What is the repetitive nature of my topic?
- What aspect of my idea is present from start to finish?
- How many segments does my idea require from start to finish?

In my dramatic crown, written in what I imagined her voice to be, from reading her poems, I analyzed high-, low-, and turning points of her life. I came to believe that Wroth had a guiding principle, one that *you* might share: a belief that the word was mightier than the sword. Thus, the first line of my crown: "My sonnet is more lethal than your sword." Wroth composed 14-sonnet crowns so in tribute to her, I also chose 14 segments, based on facts and speculations about her life.

"My crown took five months to complete, with my writing every day. But I knew when I attempted the form that I was going to learn much about the poetic process, so I was willing to devote the effort."

Before composing my crown, I sketched out a "storyboard," noting the content of individual poems in the sequence. This gave me a sense of direction. My storyboard reads thusly:

Sonnet I:	Seduction of Earl of Pembroke
Sonnet II:	Assault of the Earl of Pembroke
Sonnet III:	Anger Over Uncle Philip Sidney
Sonnet IV:	Participation in the "Masque of Blackness"
Sonnet V:	Encountering a Drunk Ben Jonson
Sonnet VI:	Warning Jonson
Sonnet VII:	Confronting Jonson
Sonnet VIII:	Humiliating Jonson
Sonnet IX:	Despising Her Dead Husband
Sonnet X:	Bearing Illegitimate Children
Sonnet XI:	Complaining to the King
Sonnet XII:	Libeling Lord Denny
Sonnet XIII:	Censorship
Sonnet XIV:	Submitting Again to Pembroke

As you can see, this is a lot of work. You have to commit to a crown, or you will commit costly errors. My crown took five months to complete, with my writing every day. But I knew when I attempted the form that I was going to learn much about the poetic process, so I was willing to devote the effort. That kind of discipline, as well as love of verse, represents "the influence" that Lady Mary Wroth has had on me.

Writing Suggestions

1. Use the Internet to find some of Shakespeare's sonnets (they're easily accessible from any search engine). Read a half dozen or so, then write your own single Shakespearean sonnet. It can be a response to any of Shakespeare's or on a topic/idea entirely of your own making. Try to remain faithful to meter, rhyme, and structure. Does form restrict you or offer possibilities you might

otherwise not have thought of? (Variation: Use the Internet to find some of Petrarch's sonnets, which are easily accessible from any search engine. Read a half dozen or so, then write your own Petrarchan sonnet. Try to remain faithful to meter, rhyme, and structure. Is this sonnet type easier to write in than the Shakespearean sonnet? Which do you find more limiting?)

2. Select one of the poets from this book whose work interests you. Ask yourself some simple but hard questions. What three specific things do I like about this poet's work? What three specific things am I not as pleased with about his or her work? Now write your own poem on a topic or in a style that mirrors your chosen poet's, or go completely on your own. How much has the poet's work influenced your own? Poets have been influencing other poets for hundreds of years and by learning what you can from other poets, you'll speed up the learning curve and find your voice sooner.

3. Take a poem you've already written and draw a flowchart/schematic that shows exactly what the poem does, then draw another flowchart/schematic showing exactly what you'd like the poem to do. Does the reality of the poem meet your expectations? If not, why doesn't it? Be flexible in letting a poem find its own way, but also know when to nudge it back onto a path that looks more appealing to you.

4. Use an Internet search engine and type in "sonnet crown." How many hits do you get? Are there contemporary as well as classic examples of this form? How relevant is this form today? What are some ways you might "modernize" the form?

"Oh to be delivered from the rational into the realm of pure song."

—Theodore Roethke

Wanda Coleman

In Search of the Mythology of Do Wah Wah

the melodrama continues
we personifications of classic Greek-Roman tragedy/history
play a continuous bill
nightly show in hell/Hades featuring spades of every
co-mingling/variation:
sound trumph of defeat as the laboring armies of Egypt retreat
before the thundering chariots of corporate roma
and Medea, fleeced by her common law husband
loads the Saturday night special—turns it on her children
then herself—free at last from poverty's grasp
meanwhile Echo overdoses on seconal
while pimp Narcissus cruises avenues in search
of fresh meat and bigger mirrors
how many falls from success's skyscraper must Icarus take
before he learns that all the wax and feathers of a high school
mis-education
will net him is a spot on the sidewalk
Pandora's box is a festering place for venereal disease, tricks
and a boon to abortion clinics
and Apollo's sun was permanently eclipsed by the television
network
hatchet boys who are "tired of that niggah's antics"
mourning does indeed become Electra whose brother's heroin habit
was
paid for by ripping off their parent's home and sistuh Antigone
pickets Creon the police commissioner vainly charging brutal
tactics
against her brothers and sisters of skin and economic plight while

Oedipus, spawned on the breeding plantations of civil war America
slays his white father and covets his black mother
and Sisyphus, worshipper of blue-eyed Jesus perpetually
rolls his burdensome boulder of faith up the precipice of white
humanity
while Vulcan—in the sweltering pit of his ghetto discovers
department stores are flammable
alas Ulysses set sail/revolutionary ex-patriot journeying round the
world
to escape oppression returns years later
to declare "America ain't so bad after all" and
black Orpheus the painter/poet/musician/dreamer
turns back to find fame and immortality a vanished Eurydice
as our Caesars die prematurely
under the daggers of suspicious, envious, traitorous toms
lead by a sincere but deluded Brutus

the fault dear fellow blacks
is not in our astrology charts
but in our society
that we are run under

The California Crack

she didn't know he was so shook

it started in his system/an erratic prance
some mechanism gone wet
codeine induced cellulitis, acid trails and flashes

he had nightmares about his mother pinching him in his sleep
his youth authority internment
the scar up his ass where they removed some thing
the lesbian he loved in Yucaipa
the black bird smashed against the window
of the stolen car

he began to sweat out his nights
when he woke his long dark brown hair was plastered
to his head. he was always dripping

it got so she couldn't stand laying next to him
the stench nauseated her, caused her to vomit
sometimes she made him sleep outside on the porch
so she could get an occasional night's rest
but most times she took breath by mouth

he went to the hospital
they took tests and found nothing
he went to the police
profuse sweating was not a crime
he took daily showers
the water bill went up
the seams in his clothes began
to mold and erode
the sheets and comforter would not
wash clean

his septic sweat permeated everything
seeped down through the mattress into
the earth beneath their bed

one summer's midnight as they slept in his dampness
there was an earthquake
it measured 8.2 on the Richter scale
the bed split open the soft moist mouth of a scream
and she watched with mixed emotions
as he fell through

You Judge a Man By the Silence He Keeps

1.
he calls to tell me something. the something
gets caught and can't make it out
he struggles with it over the wire
my eyes straining to sniff the slightest touch

2.
biting snarling snapping words come out dum-dum bullets
into my chest and blood jumps out on me

and a little gets on him
he goes into the bathroom for a towel
hands it to me, mutely

3.
dialing the phone number
click—he's there on the receiving end
i hear him waiting for my voice
hang up hastily, flushing
he knows it's me

4.
my eyes are trapped in his fists
his mouth shapes the syllables that translate bitch
the scream hides between cold sheets
it snuggles against my thigh

5.
his smile enters the room cautiously
finds its way to my face
stays until i wash

Mr. Lopez

in German class they used to laugh behind his back
even his best pupils
but i liked to think i was his best pupil
and i didn't laugh

"why do you laugh at him" i once asked
and got no answer

perhaps it was his glasses. they were thick lensed
what we kids called "coke bottles"
or his black hair cut in a quarter-inch butch making
each shiny strand stand at absolute attention
or his crackling white shirts and severe neatness
or his manner. he was tough, daring us to
act up in his presence
like a sergeant "in the Gestapo" they smirked

but i saw a sincere man
who loved the German tongue as i was learning
to love it. so what
if his manner was militant, his walk a goose-step
"you've got a crush on him" they said
but that was not so. i respected him as an
excellent teacher
"but how can you" they laughed at me
"it's all so funny! what do you think this is?"

one day late in the semester
i asked the boy next to me, "what's so funny?
why do they laugh at him all the time?"

"because he's a Mexican."
i looked at him blankly. "don't you get it?
we're all blacks and here we are in German class
with a Mexican for a teacher"

but at that time i was too dense
to get the joke

Prove It Why Don't You
FOX IN THE HEN HOUSE SHOO FOX SHOO

who say who suffer most? colored folk say
there's little cultural guilt & less national empathy
(one is always used to one's own stink)
about so-called misery, present the irrefutable
evidence. take it skip-to-my-loo. all have crosses to bear
except some have great big wooden ones with splinters
and termites and some got little 24K gold diamond studded
crosses and some are born nailed to theirs and others
got to make 'em themselves and still others
buy theirs at the finest roodmakers. show the wound
let's touch to see if it hollers
squeeze it and let the pus owl-eye to the surface

now, darlin', who co-opted your form and
coyoted your content?

but seriously—birds do sing
and telephones ring-a-ling

as for slavery
don't come crying about what's been stolen
from you. Besides

acts of oppression are sexy and
good hard thangs grow in tight wet places

All of That
—after Aaron Shurin

she woke to find the pillow strapped between her
legs and no memory of how it got there.
was it Hegel or Heidegger? Kafka or Malraux?

she found the closet door difficult to open and
steadily jerked the knob. in seconds she was
teen-aged, popping the fingers of her left hand
and getting down those bop steps

(do the spirit-walk do the spirit-walk
wiggle and squiggle and jiggle when you talk)

smoothly skillfully exhaustively researched
his huge purpose entered into her reluctance
it was savage. he split her sensibility in two
later she would discuss the ramifications
with a girlfriend over espresso

head in hands she dwelt on the details of
her resume. she was making too much sense. it
was time for a semi-drastic change. tragedy lay
in her preoccupation with the soprano staccato
of her own breathing

when the door finally opened
she was assaulted by the odor of toe jam
stinky sneakers and socks standing at attention
without the benefit of feet

Neruda

few quiet hours
i spend them soaking in the tub with my Neruda

in a dream a bearded moreno stranger
approaches me along a dark street in the plaza
as we pass he whispers hoarsely, "Neruda"

on Sunset Boulevard a beggar accosts me
for spare change. i hand him my collected Neruda

while my lover takes siesta i walk down to
the neighborhood bar for a game of pool solo. i order
dos besos. i put a quarter in the juke and notice
all selections read Neruda

while standing at the supermarket checkout stand
i read tabloid headlines. one screams
"man force-feeds wife Neruda"

(he tells me he is worried Neruda is coming between us)

note found in Cantonese fortune cookie:
Neruda slept here

Hand Dance

this is the ritual of the hand becoming
the whole. a body of itself
the gesture that allows
possession

if i am not all, who am i
if i am i how am i all?

at the tip of each finger a separate universe

if i am you
then why aren't you me
and if you are me
then why the deep silence

this is the ritual of the whole becoming the hand
shaping a certainty

to complete the cycle. to share my life
with my man. to feed my children. my hands

(they dance this anger. they sing it, paint it
make it pay. it is bigger than mere hands can hold)

born in slavery died enslaved
yet not a slave

born in misery died miserably
yet not miserable

hand story: once upon a time i laid hands in love
the sinister and the dexter
in the hope of a man. to give him

light by which to see me. once
upon a time i laid hands in love
to cure his flesh in the fire of
mine. burning together. once upon
a prayer

these hands

i am rooted in a tree of hands where i nest
give birth. stretch my arms to take the wind

here. a forest of hands where the only fauna
are my eyes

Muse and Mastery: Coleman on the Poet-in-Progress

(oh Humpty was it like this?)

I've selected these diverse poems from three of my books based on the criteria of "like" rather than "best"; I *enjoy* having written these and *enjoy* rereading them, and in presenting them aloud in public forums. I qualify the word enjoy with italics, though, because it inadequately expresses how I feel about my work which, for thirty-odd years, I've been compelled to produce. "Hand Dance" is a summary of the scope of my voyage into the poetic, I think. That content/material, which is deeply autobiographical, is usually difficult for me to reencounter, and often painfully evocative, as in "The California Crack." I prefer the narrative when attempting to fix those moments when cultures come into clash, as in "Mr. Lopez." I get a thrill out of linguistic play when making something daring work, as much as I get a kick out of transforming and transcending the mundane (in "Neruda"). I dig tapping into that rhetorical fierceness that characterizes much of what's identified/misidentified as Black poetry/blackness whenever it suits my disposition at the moment of creation, as in "Prove It Why Don't You." In so doing, I'm acutely aware of the influences and social circumstances that set me apart from many of my post–WWII boom generation literary peers. Coincidence and confluence are one thing, conscription quite another. I insist on being an individual—as much as that is possible in this world—and resent being forced into the posture of parroting going agendas—literary or otherwise—from any quarter.

> *"I get a thrill out of linguistic play when making something daring work . . . as much as I get a kick out of transforming and transcending the mundane. . . . Yet, I remain deadly rigorous in my pursuit of literary excellence and self-discovery, pushing myself to new challenges/directions, oft times going back and retrieving failures."*

My sense of humor has been described as offbeat; as I've matured, my taste for the absurd, surreal, and the elusive has increased geometrically and much of my work—particularly that in which I'm having fun ("In Search of the Mythology of Do Wah Wah" and "All of That"), reflects the change. Yet, I remain deadly rigorous in my pursuit of literary excellence and self-discovery, pushing myself to new challenges/directions, oft times going back and retrieving poems and poem parts that seemed failures. Then, there are those aspects of myself that remain wistful and tender—as the introvert, beneath the functional extrovert, reasserts herself—and brings forth a searing sentiment or two, gropes for the essences of a relationship as in "You Judge a Man By the Silence He Keeps."

> *"My line breaks are apt to be theatrical pauses or musical rests as well as enjambments. I like it when form tickles content."*

I have selected these poems, too, because I have lived them psychologically the longest. They repeatedly take me to the heights and depths I prefer. I love pathos, poetic leaps, wordplay (when time permits), complex and broken rhythms (and love seduction by the rhythms and/or forms of certain other poets). My line breaks are apt to be theatrical pauses or musical rests as well as enjambments. I like it when form tickles content. I enjoy the kind of masculine discord found in Satie, the Sex Pistols, or Shepp. In poems I confront phobias and defeat enemies. Place is important to me, and I seek to define it as it circumscribes me—a Southwesterner, urban yet rural yet suburban . . . daughter, Mom, wife, worker. Life lived outside of the proper context is no life at all.

Poetry is my greatest pain-pleasure source. I have tried to abandon them, but the poems find me. I thrive on the strong poetic line. Levels of intensity matter. I didn't quite understand imagery until 1972 (an insightful critic with tempered biases gives great pedagogy).

As primary among my many mentors, Henri Coulette provided me with my first and finest illumination, setting me further on the difficult path he himself was staggering at that time, in fall of 1964 (he was the winner of The James Laughlin Award, 1965). I never graduated college, nevertheless I have Coulette to thank for a degree beyond measure—to thank for a truth, sensitivity, and bold critique untainted by the racism that ruled the day. He revealed himself by treating me as an intelligent being, and giving me a honest and insightful critique, and while I once attempted to thank him, it was just months before his death. Some twenty-odd years later, and while I'm not sure, I believe I did so inadequately.

On the trail to good writing, which, for me, began with hours spent reading good books plucked from library shelves, the craft of writing, found in numerous how-to books and guides, have kept me going. Periodically I teach from my favorites of these texts—two of which are *Structure, Language and Style: A Rhetoric Handbook* by W. Ross Winterowd, one of the finest minds on the subject I've ever encountered; and, *A Glossary of Literary Terms* by M. H. Abrams. I believe that, after a point, one absorbs these lessons if not flat-out memorizes them; therefore, revision becomes professional in nature. I usually allow a work to "stew" or sit a few days—if there's no deadline—to give myself some distance from the content and allow my biases toward that content to cool. Then I go back and trim as much dead and/or extraneous language as I can detect under the givens, uproot or morph clichés, and so on.

Like beauty, what's "hokey" in poetry is often in the eye of the reader. One reader's hokey may be another reader's meaty verse. There are instances when the "hokey" is poetically preferable to juvenile crassness, easy *orality* (lame self-scripting), or the intellectually sterile and/or dishonest. However, I largely attempt to avoid it by imbuing my text with the particulars that define my microcosm, my characteristic choice of words, which demands considerable self-scrutiny and criticism. Words and street jargon that I've plucked from the African-American subculture of south-central Los Angeles, and a few I've coined, have, over the decades, worked their ways into the larger lexicons of American slang. Recently, I roared when the word "pimpmobile" was awkwardly spat from the lips of actor Harrison Ford, a word I put into vogue with the publication of my book *Mad Dog Black Lady* in 1979, although the actual poem in which the word appears was published years earlier. Fusing the words mother and father to make "muthafatha"—a word I got a kick out of recently hearing on the lips of a single mother three thousand miles away and twenty years my junior—during a TV interview. I have presented a number of original expressions, words, and ideas, and told many original stories unique to my experience—and I take great pride in having done so.

Anything I'm interested in is worth writing about. The more stymied I feel, the more I write about writing. I am interested in the uglinesses that comprise human interaction, particularly since they seem the norm and not the other way around. However, as I have become more accomplished as a writer, my sense that the poem comes looking for me, and that I am simply the means to its independent end has become hauntingly stronger—that it's writing me.

*

Dear Lord George, my truths-made-fictions are stranger than strange. Too many defy telling regardless of form.

Writing Suggestions

1. Pay attention to neologisms (newly coined words or expressions) when you read a poet's work. Wanda Coleman has coined a few expressions, and plenty of earlier writers (Lewis Carroll and many others) have come up with their share of new words. How many of your own neologisms have you used in your work? Think up ten and jot them down in your notebook. Try to use at least one in the next poem you write.

2. Coleman's poems often have a sexual, very physical level to them, although she often handles sexual content in an unusual and creative way. Write your own poem about something decidedly unsexual (a junkyard, shopping mall, or perhaps a garage) and eroticize its landscape and features. Be suggestive, elusive, imaginative. Let language and structure add to the enticement. In the hands of a skilled writer, anything can be sexy.

3. Coleman's titles ("Hand Dance," "The California Crack," and "In Search of the Mythology of Do Wah Wah," to name just a few) are often real eye-catchers that demand readers read at least a bit more of the poem. Take five

poem drafts of your own that you've worked on and come up with five alternate, exciting titles for each. What makes one poem title better than another? What promises do your titles make? Is your first poem title still the best? Why?

4. Listen to Coleman read "Prove It Why Don't You" on the audio CD. Most people would never think of using an epigraph such as "fox in the hen house shoo fox shoo" or putting a line such as "take it skip-to-my-loo" in a poem, but Coleman manages to turn these childish phrases into the basis for a deep, meaningful poem. Challenge yourself to write the hokiest poem you can. Pick a hokey topic, use a hokey voice, and put the poem in a hokey form. Is there anything about this poem that you find yourself liking? As Coleman says, "Like beauty, what's 'hokey' in poetry is often in the eye of the reader." Don't be afraid to be hokey. At least sometimes.

"There are people who would say, 'Well, how can I relate to your poetry? I am a white male.' But I write about being human. If you have ever been human, I invite you to that place that we share, and I think you can then share it."

—Lucille Clifton

Billy Collins

A History of Weather

It is the kind of spring morning—candid sunlight
elucidating the air, a flower-ruffling breeze—
that makes me want to begin a history of weather,
a ten-volume elegy for the atmospheres of the past,
the envelopes that have moved around the moving globe.

It will open by examining the cirrus clouds
that are now sweeping over this house into the next state,
and every chapter will step backwards in time
to illustrate the rain that fell on battlefields
and the winds that attended beheadings, coronations.

The snow flurries of Victorian London will be surveyed
along with the gales that blew off Renaissance caps.
The tornadoes of the Middle Ages will be explicated
and the long, overcast days of the Dark Ages.
There will be a section on the frozen nights of antiquity
and on the heat that shimmered in the deserts of the Bible.

The study will be hailed as ambitious and definitive,
for it will cover even the climate before the Flood
when showers moistened Eden and will conclude
with the mysteries of the weather before history
when unseen clouds drifted over an unpeopled world,
when not a soul lay in any of earth's meadows gazing up
at the passing of enormous faces and animal shapes,
his jacket bunched into a pillow, an open book on his chest.

Questions About Angels

Of all the questions you might want to ask
about angels, the only one you ever hear
is how many can dance on the head of a pin.

No curiosity about how they pass the eternal time
besides circling the Throne chanting in Latin
or delivering a crust of bread to a hermit on earth
or guiding a boy and girl across a rickety wooden bridge.

Do they fly through God's body and come out singing?
Do they swing like children from the hinges
of the spirit world saying their names backwards and
forwards?
Do they sit alone in little gardens changing colors?

What about their sleeping habits, the fabric of their robes,
their diet of unfiltered divine light?
What goes on inside their luminous heads? Is there a wall
these tall presences can look over and see hell?

If an angel fell off a cloud, would he leave a hole
in a river and would the hole float along endlessly
filled with the silent letters of every angelic word?

If an angel delivered the mail, would he arrive
in a blinding rush of wings or would he just assume
the appearance of the regular mailman and
whistle up the driveway reading the postcards?

No, the medieval theologians control the court.
The only question you ever hear is about
the little dance floor on the head of a pin
where halos are meant to converge and drift invisibly.

It is designed to make us think in millions,
billions, to make us run out of numbers and collapse
into infinity, but perhaps the answer is simply one:
one female angel dancing alone in her stocking feet,
a small jazz combo working in the background.

She sways like a branch in the wind, her beautiful
eyes closed, and the tall thin bassist leans over
to glance at his watch because she has been dancing
forever, and now it is very late, even for musicians.

Osso Buco

I love the sound of the bone against the plate
and the fortress-like look of it
lying before me in a moat of risotto,
the meat soft as the leg of an angel
who has lived a purely airborne existence.
And best of all, the secret marrow,
the invaded privacy of the animal
prized out with a knife and swallowed down
with cold, exhilarating wine.

I am swaying now in the hour after dinner,
a citizen tilted back on his chair,
a creature with a full stomach—
something you don't hear much about in poetry,
that sanctuary of hunger and deprivation.
You know: the driving rain, the boots by the door,
small birds searching for berries in winter.

But tonight, the lion of contentment
has placed a warm, heavy paw on my chest,
and I can only close my eyes and listen
to the drums of woe throbbing in the distance
and the sound of my wife's laughter
on the telephone in the next room,
the woman who cooked the savory osso buco,
who pointed to show the butcher the ones she wanted.
She who talks to her faraway friend
while I linger here at the table
with a hot, companionable cup of tea,
feeling like one of the friendly natives,
a reliable guide, maybe even the chief's favorite son.

Somewhere, a man is crawling up a rocky hillside
on bleeding knees and palms, an Irish penitent

carrying the stone of the world in his stomach;
and elsewhere people of all nations stare
at one another across a long, empty table.

But here, the candles give off their warm glow,
the same light that Shakespeare and Izaak Walton wrote by,
the light that lit and shadowed the faces of history.
Only now it plays on the blue plates,
the crumpled napkins, the crossed knife and fork.

In a while, one of us will go up to bed
and the other one will follow.
Then we will slip below the surface of the night
into miles of water, drifting down and down
to the dark, soundless bottom
until the weight of dreams pulls us lower still,
below the shale and layered rock,
beneath the strata of hunger and pleasure,
into the broken bones of the earth itself,
into the marrow of the only place we know.

Nightclub

You are so beautiful and I am a fool
to be in love with you
is a theme that keeps coming up
in songs and poems.
There seems to be no room for variation.
I have never heard anyone sing
I am so beautiful
and you are a fool to be in love with me,
even though this notion has surely
crossed the minds of women and men alike.
You are so beautiful, too bad you are a fool
is another one you don't hear.
Or, you are a fool to consider me beautiful.
That one you will never hear, guaranteed.

For no particular reason this afternoon
I am listening to Johnny Hartman
whose dark voice can curl around

the concepts of love, beauty, and foolishness
like no one else's can.
It feels like smoke curling up from a cigarette
someone left burning on a baby grand piano
around three o'clock in the morning;
smoke that billows up into the bright lights
while out there in the darkness
some of the beautiful fools have gathered
around little tables to listen,
some with their eyes closed,
others leaning forward into the music
as if it were holding them up,
or twirling the loose ice in a glass,
slipping by degrees into a rhythmic dream.
Yes, there is all this foolish beauty,
borne beyond midnight,
that has no desire to go home,
especially now when everyone in the room
is watching the large man with the tenor sax
that hangs from his neck like a golden fish.
He moves forward to the edge of the stage
and hands the instrument down to me
and nods that I should play.
So I put the mouthpiece to my lips
and blow into it with all my living breath.
We are all so foolish,
my long bebop solo begins by saying,
so damn foolish
we have become beautiful without even knowing it.

The Ride of Poetry: Collins on Metaphor and Movement

Of the many pleasures that poetry offers, one of the keenest for me is the possibility of imaginative travel, a sudden slip down the rabbit hole. No other form can spirit its reader away to a new conceptual zone so quickly, often in the mere handful of lines that a lyric poem takes to express itself. Whenever I begin to read a new poem, I feel packed and ready to go, eager to be lifted into new territory. Of course, such hopefulness is regularly quashed. And I am not just talking about the poetry of others. Too often, a poem never gets off the ground—sometimes never leaves the hangar. But in the best cases it clears the trees at the end of the runway and carries me off into a fresh imaginative space.

"Of the many pleasures that poetry offers, one of the keenest for me is the possibility of imaginative travel, a sudden slip down the rabbit hole. . . . For me, the most reliable indication that a poem is a good one is my desire to reread it, to get right back on the ride and take it again."

If we view poetry as an affordable—cheap, really—means of transportation, we can see the development of a poem as a series of phases in the journey, each of which has a distinct function. The opening of the poem is the point of departure; the interior of the poem is the ground that will be simultaneously invented and covered through a series of navigational maneuvers; and the ending of the poem is the unforeseen destination—international arrivals, if you will. As the poems finds its way through itself while being composed, the course of the reader's journey is being laid out. I am hardly alone in saying that the poem can act as an imaginative vehicle, a form of transportation to a place unknown. But I expect my company would thin out if I admitted that I usually fail to experience the deeper, more widely celebrated rewards of poetry, such as spiritual nourishment and empathetic identification, unless the poem has provided me with some kind of ride. For me, the most reliable indication that a poem is a good one is my desire to reread it, to get right back on the ride and take it again.

I do not mean to suggest that poetry is a verbal amusement park (or do I?) but I do hold up as a standard for assessing a poem its ability to carry me to a place that is dramatically different from the place I was in when I began to read it.

To view a poem as a trip means taking into account the methods that give a poem vehicular capability. It means looking into the way a poet manages to become the poem's first driver and thus the first to know its secret destination.

In teaching or reading poetry, a question I habitually ask my students or myself is how does the poem get from its alpha to its omega. Obviously, the question does not apply to the many poems that exhaust themselves crawling in the general direction of beta. How, for example, in "Dover Beach" does Arnold leave the quiet simplicity of "The sea is calm tonight" and arrive at the climactic vision of the world as a frightfully disorienting battlefield, "a darkling plain . . . where ignorant armies clash by night?" The question is easily answered because the steps of the poem's development are so visible. He steps from the initial calmness of a seascape to the hollow sound of retreating waves, to ancient Greece, to an allegory involving the Sea of Faith, to an impassioned plea for constancy in love, hence to the pessimistic spectacle of a world of enmity and hopelessness. And he steps stanza by stanza in easily discernible increments.

In other cases, the stages in a poem's journey are less conspicuous, more mysteriously executed. The poem intuits its passage as one would find one's way by feel in the dark. Take this poem by Paul Durcan:

THE MAYO ACCENT

Have you ever tuned into the voice of a Mayan?
In his mouth the English language is sphagnum moss
Under the bare braceleted feet of a pirate queen:
Syllables are blooms of tentativeness in bog cotton;
Words are bog oak sunk in understatement;
Phrases are bog water in which syllables float
Or in which speakers themselves are found floating face upwards
Or downwards;
Conversations are smudges of bogland under cloudy skies.
Speech in Mayo is a turbary function
To be exercised as a turbary right
With turbary responsibilities
And turbary irresponsibilities.
Peat smoke of silence unfurls over turf fires of language.

A man with a Mayo accent is a stag at bay
Upon a bog rock with rabbits round its hooves.
Why then, Daddy, did you shed
The pricey antlers of your Mayo accent
For the tree-felling voice of a harsh judiciary
Whose secret headquarters were in the Home Counties
    or High Germany?
Your son has gone back to Mayo to sleep with the island woman

Who talks so much she does not talk at all.
If he does not sleep with her, she will kill him—the pirate queen.

[from A *Snail in My Prime*, first published by the Harvill Press in 1993]

The seemingly innocent question of the first line is followed by a pileup of bog-obsessed metaphors that conjure up the landscape of the west of Ireland on which a man—we find out later—has turned his back in an attempt to de-Hibernicize himself. The second stanza introduces the striking metaphor of the stag which provides the poem with its opening into quite a different room, in this case a familial one in which a child appears out of nowhere to question its father. Even more unexpected is the appearance of the son who has returned to the family's Mayo roots and is now sleeping with a dangerous woman, the "pirate queen," surely an allusion to the real historical pirate Grace O'Malley (1530–1603). The poem advances by moving sideways, sliding rather than stepping from one place to another. We begin with a comical question about a regional accent, and we end—23 lines later—facing the specter of a murderous wild woman from Elizabethan Ireland (if you'll pardon the oxymoron).

In writing my own poems, I try to remain on the lookout for a way to kick the poem into another dimension, some parallel linguistic universe. Every poem offers (or conceals) its own possibilities. The four poems of mine to be briefly touched on here may serve as modest examples.

"In writing my own poems, I try to remain on the lookout for a way to kick the poem into another dimension, some parallel linguistic universe. Every poem offers (or conceals) its own possibilities."

There is no secret to "A History of Weather." The poem travels backwards through time until it runs out of history. Having arrived at prehistory, the poem wants to turn its reader into the sole witness of the weather that occurred on earth before humans took their first evolutionary steps onto the scene. The poem finds a reassuring place to settle by placing (by his absence) in this fantasy scene the figure of the dreamy vagabond, the familiar image of the Romantic wool-gatherer.

In "Questions About Angels" a set of speculative, essaylike questions is followed by a radical hypothesis: that the head of a pin may accommodate only one angel. We then enter the interior of the hypothesis (as one might walk into a hologram) where we find one jazzy angel—an angelic "chick"—and, why not?, a quartet of musicians. The poem begins as a satire on the hair-splitting abstruseness of medieval scholasticism and finds its destination by landing on the wristwatch of a bass player. That's a bit of travel for you.

Seen as a vehicle, "Osso Buco" might be said to start out at the dinner table and wind up at the center of the earth. The poem moves from the domestic to the strangely geological through a set of expanding views—one of world hunger, another of the history of the candle. The final movement involves a shift into dreamland where, as we know, anything can happen.

And finally, "Nightclub." This one started out as a simple rumination on a romantic cliché. In the second stanza, the circumstances of the poem's composition are admitted—always good as a last resort—and from the stereo room of the narrator we move to an imagined nightclub scene, again penetrating the scene as one would walk "inside" a hologram. The radical shift occurs when the tenor man "hands the instrument down to me." At that moment, the ego of the speaker commandeers the poem by taking center stage and playing a saxophone solo on an air-saxophone in a nightclub also made of air. A little secret is that this shift was the result of a mental lapse. In the last handwritten draft, the line appears as "hands the instrument down to you," an obvious attempt to drag the reader into the poem by means of the second-person pronoun. But when I typed up the poem, I inadvertently wrote "hands the instrument down to *me*." I suppose my inner narcissist must be blamed for what, I think, turned out to be a happy accident. Afterward, I felt honored to have been given such a prominent role in the poem's dramatic conclusion and to join the company of that other notoriously terrible typist, Robert Burns.

Writing Suggestions

1. Take a copy of your local newspaper and read through the headlines until one catches your eye. Use it as the title of your poem. If the poem doesn't seem to emerge, go back and select a new headline. (Variation: Use a tabloid newspaper like *The National Enquirer* or *Weekly World News*.)

2. Think of three unrelated nouns (ex: a forklift, a skipping stone, a lifesaver), and write a poem that includes all three. Let your mind do a little free association to figure out what each element brings to the poem. Try to utilize a bit of creative frisson in the juxtaposition of these three nouns.

3. Take one of your own poems and identify its alpha and omega. Then pay particular attention to the movement and travel the poem takes in getting from one point to the other. Does your poem meander? Does it meander enough? Drive forward relentlessly? Be aware of the possibilities that your poem does (and doesn't) conceal. Don't be afraid to explore shortcuts, side avenues, or even dead ends as you're en route to the best poem your poem can be.

4. Go to Billy Collins's Web site (http://www.bigsnap.com) and listen to a few of his poems in the audio archives. Do the poems "sound" the way you

expected them to? See if you can find audio files of the poems included here via his links. Do they "read" differently than they sound? Can you hear the "ride" in the audio versions of the poems? What is the relationship between a poem's audio components and a poem's visual components on a page?

"For me poems usually begin with 'true feelings'—people, experiences, quotes—but quickly ride off into that other territory of imagination which lives alongside us as much as we will allow in a world that likes to pay too much attention to 'facts' sometimes."

—Naomi Shihab Nye

Denise Duhamel

Ego

I just didn't get it—
even with the teacher holding an orange (the earth) in one hand
and a lemon (the moon) in the other,
her favorite student (the sun) standing behind her with a flashlight,
I just couldn't grasp it—
this whole citrus universe, these bumpy planets revolving so slowly
no one could even see themselves moving.
I used to think if I could only concentrate hard enough
I could be the one person to feel what no one else could,
sense a small tug from the ground, a sky shift, the earth changing gears.
Even though I was only one mini-speck on a speck,
even though I was merely a pinprick in one goosebump on the orange,
I was sure then I was the most specially perceptive, perceptively sensitive.
I was sure then my mother was the only mother to snap—
"The world doesn't revolve around you!"
The earth was fragile and mostly water
just the way the orange was mostly water if you peeled it
just the way I was mostly water if you peeled me.
Looking back on that third-grade science demonstration,
I can understand why some people gave up on fame or religion or cures—
especially people who have an understanding
of the excruciating crawl of the world,
who have a well-developed sense of spatial reasoning
and the tininess that it is to be one of us.
But not me—even now I wouldn't mind being God, the force
who spins the planets the way I spin a globe, a basketball, a yo-yo.
I wouldn't mind being the teacher who chooses the fruit,
or that favorite kid who gives the moon its glow.

Superego

A few days ago I wrote this poem "Ego,"
and when I showed it to my husband, he said,
"Satan went to hell for wanting to be God, you know . . .
Remember Lucifer?" He laughed, half
sort of believing in hell and half not.
I tried to look smart, paraphrasing John Gardner
who wrote about how for a while the third person omniscient
went out of fashion because no writers wanted to be God
and/or no one believed in Him anymore anyway.
By Him with a capital "H," I mean God.
Not many writers believe in God,
but they still believe in Gardner.

A while ago my friend Maureen Seaton and I
made this prose poem "Hemisphere" in which I wrote:

> I am trying to be an omniscient narrator like God who supposedly can be inside your mind and outside at the same time. That's why most humans write in the first person—because they are not God although most humans don't write at all except for grocery lists and postcards.

Then Maureen wrote:

> Since I read what I wrote about God, I have experienced a tinker of my brain or a tinker in my brain—and that tinker, the noun, is you, the omniscient narrator in the second person.

I was the one to bring up God in the poem, but Maureen and I try to find
this third voice when we collaborate so we're sort of mushed into one,
sort of, I suppose, a chorus. Sort of the opposite of God.

We wrote the poem "Hemisphere" before I read John Gardner's book,
before I read what John Gardner said about how imperative
it is for writers to read everything so that we don't repeat great ideas
in a lesser way. I suppose that's what happened with "Hemisphere."
John Gardner already had the idea about the writer being God
at least two decades earlier. But I'm glad at least Maureen
took the idea further. She's probably never read Gardner,
because she's not interested in writing prose. I'm still thinking about "Ego,"

that whole thing about the moon being a lemon—does it even work?
It's really sort of hard to write about the moon
unless you're Michael Burkard. He has this great line—
one gets more used to the moon when one knows one is a piece of it.
Or what about Lorca—
. . . *an incomprehensible moon illuminating dried lemon rinds* . . .
My husband Nick says Lorca's moon is even better in Spanish.
In one of his own poems, Nick tries
to figure out which language does the moon the most justice—
. . . *la luna, la lua, la lune, ang buwan* . . .

Now I'm embarrassed that three of my favorite moon references
are by male poets. Part of me wants to hop up
and scour my books to find three female poets
with something equally enchanting to say about the moon.
But another part of me thinks that's cheating,
like when people add epigraphs *after* they've finished a poem.
I'd be too scared to do it, embarrassed that someone
would find out. I get embarrassed a lot lately. I blushed
all through Ellen Hinsey's essay, "The Rise of Modern Doggerel,"
in which she claims, more or less
that most contemporary personal poems,
the ones with the "therapeutic I," are pathetic.
I felt sick when I read that essay, sure she was talking about me
and all my therapeutic poems.
(See poem written a few days ago, "Ego.")

Later I was embarrassed when I saw the woman
who suggested I read the essay in the first place.
I mean, I felt that same sort of shame that I had
reading Gardner's *The Art of Fiction* on the subway.
A student/writer-type sitting on the orange seat next to me
asked me if I was reading Gardner because I was trying to write a novel.
The truth was I'd already finished the novel
and was reading the book to see where I'd gone wrong.
I felt like everything was going backwards, like the subway itself
was backing up and I was getting younger instead of older,
like every poem I'd ever written was unraveling into meaningless syllables.
I started taking advice from this undergraduate from NYU
who was sure he was sitting on a best seller.

I started telling him about the moon, how I have about twenty-five drafts
of the same poem, trying to write about the time
when my sister and her husband were out of town
and my niece and I slept in the same bed,
her breathing a small wind-up toy,
her curls crunched between her face and pillow
carving curlicue sleep lines on her cheek.
The poem was like "The Rise of Modern Doggerel" itself
when she woke me up at three in the morning
because she couldn't see the moon through the window.
"It's out there," I promised, but my niece explained
she really *needed* to see it. More than anything in the world,
she needed something to drink and needed
the moon. She drank tap water from her favorite cup,
then I lifted her onto my hip so her feet wouldn't be cold.
I stood in the driveway in a small town in Rhode Island
where the moon was a communion wafer poker chip
and as white as my niece's milk teeth,
as white as the whites of her eyes.

I wasn't afraid then of hell or God. My niece was sure
Jesus was a girl because His pajamas looked like girl pajamas.
Whenever I held her, I didn't even care about poems.
I wanted her to believe that Jesus was a girl.
I hadn't yet met that NYU student who I let intimidate me.
I hadn't even heard of John Gardner.
The driveway, the moon, my niece's Care Bear pajamas.
I didn't know then Care Bear cartoons came *after* the Care Bears,
that Care Bear cartoons were really sinister
commercials to sell the pajamas et al.
It was just the alabaster moon, a little girl, and a young woman.
It was definitely one of those "therapeutic I" moments.
A moment that would have reminded Gardner
of a much better literary moment, maybe something
that Shakespeare wrote about with more flare.
A moment that would have made Ellen Hinsey shudder.
A moment the NYU student would have been too busy to notice,
what with his big novel to revise.
My niece was so little then, with a little ego.
She said, "I love you moon!"
then the moon said, "I love you, too."

Id
for Lexia

I'm having coffee at the Last Stop with Amy
who tells me about her teaching—
she teaches adjunct composition even though she has a Ph.D.
just like my friend Page. Amy says her students at FIT
really love Sylvia Plath—
The moon sees nothing of this. She is bald and wild.
The line falls off her tongue like rain or salt,
something easy and helpful.
It's the day after *Prairie Schooner* has accepted "Superego"
(even though when I originally wrote it, it had the title
"The Other Day I Wrote This Poem Ego"). It was Amy's idea
to change the title—and I think she was right,
especially because it is a companion poem
to this other poem "Ego" and now to this poem "Id."

In the poem "Superego," I presented this moral,
or rather, this to-revise-or-not-to-revise dilemma:
should I go back to change the lines in which I can
only think of men who write about the moon?
Should I plug in Sylvia Plath's lines as if I really knew them
without looking them up? As a poet, I just want my reader
to trust me. Would they believe I actually knew all those lines by heart?
I'd just been reading an article about memoir writing
which cautioned memoirists against using dialogue—
if you really want your reader to believe you,
you shouldn't use artifice, you shouldn't write,
Then Mommy said and launch into a paragraph of her exact words
since no one has a memory like that. Rather, the author
of the article advised, you should paraphrase.

I used to try to teach my composition students to paraphrase
when I taught at Baruch College, the same place where Page teaches now—
I'd give them a paragraph, but they'd basically copy the whole thing
changing one or two words like "carry" to "lift up." Anyway, the truth is
I should have known those Plath lines, and as soon as Amy said them,
I did. I even remembered some other lines—
The moon is no door. It is a face in its own right.
White as a knuckle and terribly upset.

There was a time when I was obsessed by Plath, so when Amy tells me
Meg Ryan has just bought the movie rights to tell Plath's story,
we both agree—"Bleck! What next? Ted Hughes played by Tom Hanks?"
But who knows, maybe Meg is obsessed with Plath like I was
when I visited Smith College and looked through Sylvia's papers
and the little hairs on my arms bristled with electricity
the same way they did when I saw my first dead body.
My eyes grew all moist and blurry when I saw her juvenalia,
her "Angel with Guitar" drawn in colored pencil, so sappy
a picture I knew she must have been happy when she drew it.
Maybe Meg Ryan will do a good job.

The picture was before any of Sylvia's poems.
My trip to Smith was before Sylvia's lines settled like dust bunnies
under the couch in my brain, before I'd lost Plath's moon that
drags the sea after it like a dark crime. I'm always forgetting
not only lines of poems, but names and phone numbers
and where I put my keys. I forget the facts of stories
I thought I knew. For example, the other night,
after I read another one of my poems
"The Difference between Pepsi and Pope" at a reading,
my friend Page came up to me and said,
"Hey, don't you remember? I was that cookie!"
(I'd referred to a poet whose job it was to dress up like a cookie in a mall.)
"Why did you turn me into a man?" she asked. The thing was
I was sure the person in the cookie costume was Michael Burkard
when I wrote the poem, so I made the cookie a he.
I didn't want to use Michael's real name
because I hadn't been in touch with him
in a long time and I thought maybe he wouldn't want
anyone to know about his cookie-dressing days.
Besides, it was such good material I thought
he might want to use it for a poem of his own.

But the real story, Page reminded me,
is that while she dressed up as a cookie in a mall in Maryland
to pass out free samples to shopping customers,
Michael would come by to visit her since he lived in the neighborhood.
All those years I had Michael's head on top
of a chocolate-chip-speckled body, but now I've corrected it
in my mind, now Page's head is there instead.

More than ever, I think it's about time Page got a really good job,
one with tenure and sabbaticals and even an expense account.
Maybe Amy could teach in the sister school and only have to go in
twice a week. I wish this poem could serve as a recommendation letter
for Page and Amy, or introductory letter for myself
since I adjunct as well. I wish the three of us had big jobs
with pension and dental plans. I first became aware
of Page when I read one of her poems
in *Prairie Schooner* in the mid-eighties. It was a great poem,
I read it over and over again, and it finally dawned on me
that she was the same Page whose mailbox "Delano" at Baruch
was right above mine. I wrote her a fan letter and we became friends.

At the reception for the reading,
Stephanie and Kathy (or Stephanie <u>or</u> Kathy) said Page
should change her name to Lexia, the name for a page in hypertext.
My friend Amy (with whom I'm sipping coffee
at the Last Stop, remember?) is explaining why she didn't make the reading.
I tell her her friend Shira was there. Shira's blonde hair
hung like a shiny shawl over her arm as she looked at the cookies
and wondered if she should have one. I opted for Chex Mix
and apple juice because I knew if I had sugar
my head would start racing even faster than it already was
talking to my friends who I hadn't seen since before Christmas.
Marcia's mother had Alzheimer's, just like Nick's.
I was trying to set up Scott to run this reading series.
I'd just missed Mark's reading which made me feel bad.
I'd just met Kate Light and Johanna Keller. I'd just heard Pat Mangan
read for the first time. Stephanie asked him if he was related
to a famous Mangan and he was. I looked again at Shira's long hair
since I was getting my hair cut short the next week
and was starting to have serious doubts.

Someone turned the lights on and off, meaning the reception was over.
Someone came and took away the Chex Mix and picked up
the empty paper cups. Stephanie and I got our coats.
Since we were both reading with Pat,
we were supposed to have traveled together to the West Village,
but we had missed each other
at the Lexington station where the N (my line) meets the 6
(the train Stephanie takes). We were supposed to meet at the escalator,

but there are at least three escalators at that stop so I ran back and forth
between the ones I saw while Stephanie waited
at the only one she knew of (which was the one I couldn't find).
Anyway, we both gave up after half an hour
and took the N then the 1 and met instead on Christopher Street.
We'd given up exactly at the same time, we'd talked to the same set
of policemen at Lexington Station. We just began walking
towards Barrow Street as though it were unremarkable.
But it was pretty remarkable, the way the timing went,
the way we were probably on the same trains.

On the way home, we got off at Lexington again and found the escalator
where Stephanie had waited—there was actually a set,
one going up and one going down with a flight of stairs
in the middle. It was on the opposite side of one of the platforms
where I'd waited. I realize now, as this poem comes to a close,
that it's sort of New York School
the way I put in the names of my friends. When I told David
I was working on a poem called "Id," he said that I should
only use words that contain the letters "id," maybe even
put his name in the title, "(Dav)ID." Even though
he was only kidding, I considered
his idea for a minute—then this sentence
would have instead read "Kidding considered idea."
I like language techniques and surrealist games, but the truth is
I'm always trying to say something, I'm always that earnest kid
with her hand up, with an idea the teacher
has to help her sputter out. I'm really sorry
I mixed Page up with Michael, even though Page
says she doesn't care. Amy's really sorry
she didn't make the reading because she's never heard Stephanie before.
Did I mention Stephanie is a wiz at hypertext?
If I were one, too, there'd be these links to help you
get through "Id." For example, you'd click on the word "Page"
and it would take you back to the dedication.

Duhamel on the Serial Poem

I wrote all three poems, "Ego," "Superego," and "Id," in September of 1998, following a rather strange and nonproductive summer. I'd been to two residencies, which should have made me happy and prolific, but there were complications. I stayed a month at Villa Montalvo in California—the residency, however, also involved teaching which, along with my severe allergies to whatever was growing there, really drained me. Then I had a two-week stint in La Château de Lavigny, Maison d'ecrivains in Switzerland. I thought I'd be smart and spend a few days in Paris prior to the residency. Well, so much for my glamorous plan. My husband and I were robbed on the RER, the train from Paris to the airport. This incident really clouded the rest of our trip and I wrote very little in Switzerland. Ever since the early 1990s, I'd become accustomed to getting much of my writing done in the summer, since, being an educator, I am usually able to finagle almost two months off. But this summer, I felt robbed of more than my camera and traveler's checks. It was the first summer since I began writing in earnest that I'd experienced something of a writer's block.

I was back to school—adjuncting—and trying to keep afloat financially. Then one morning before I left for school I wrote "Ego." I was just so happy to have written anything that I rushed to show it to my husband, Nick Carbó, also a poet. He really did give me the line "Satan went to hell for wanting to be God . . ." and I thought about that all day and wrote "Superego" a few days later.

In writing "Superego," I felt like I was breaking through something—what my assumptions were about what a poem looked like. "Superego" isn't "neat," the stanzas aren't of a uniform size. I quote other poems (including my own collaborative poems with Maureen Seaton) and at some point, as I was writing, I remember thinking, "I'm writing an essay, not a poem." But I pressed on—I was just happy to be writing anything at all. At the time I was reading David Lehman's book about the New York School of Poets, *The Last Avant-Garde*, and I know that book had a strong influence on me. The self-referential anecdotes and the naming of poet friends was definitely New York School–inspired.

> *"Now, when I read these poems again, I think of them as poems being written as life goes on around me, poems that I wrote even though I didn't have time, poems that I attended to instead of doing the laundry, poems that were about life as I was living it."*

I thought that "Ego" and "Superego," though, would be the end of it. I thought the poems were companion poems, like Kenneth Koch's two poems both called "Circus." I sent them off to Hilda Raz, the editor at *Prairie Schooner*, but then about a week later wrote "Id." The occasion of this poem really was having coffee with my friend Amy Lemmon, with whom I'd shared "Ego" and "Superego." I told her that I was trying to also work on a poem called "Id," just as a joke, and then I came home and just began writing notes to myself. My plan was to go back and revise "Ego" and "Superego" later, based on Amy's suggestions—but instead of just jotting down her ideas, I began writing a whole new poem. Even as I ended the first stanza, I knew that this poem would be even longer than "Superego." I began to patch in passages from my journal and freewriting (which I do on the computer), such as my entry from a reading I'd given a few nights before. I don't think the poem is actually a collage in that I worked hard to smooth the patches it was made from into a cohesive narrative. But I do think the poem's origins were of a montage nature. I worked on revising the poem for weeks, knowing that it would always be dependent on "Ego" and "Superego."

I wrote to *Prairie Schooner* the day they accepted "Ego" and "Superego," enclosing "Id" and basically begged them to publish it too. I knew if the three poems weren't published together, that "Id" wouldn't be published at all. "Ego" has since been anthologized solo, but the other two would really have problems standing on their own.

Now, when I read these poems again, I think of them as poems being written as life goes on around me, poems that I wrote even though I didn't have time, poems that I attended to instead of doing the laundry, poems that were about life as I was living it. In that way, I suppose I was helped along not only by Kenneth Koch, but by the whole New York School, especially Frank O'Hara who made gossip from his lunch dates great poetry. I was also influenced by the New York School's willingness to name names, to put real names of their friends into poems. I think "Id" was sort of a magic poem for me in that shortly after I wrote it complaining about not having a full-time job, I got one! My friends mentioned in the poem also began to have good luck—Amy was hired full time and my friend Page had her first book accepted. So this poem seems like a talisman to me.

"I have always strived to have a very plainspoken, poet-to-reader voice in my work, but I felt here (especially in "Superego" and "Id") that I went further than I'd previously been able. I'm not talking about subject matter—I'd written "riskier" poems, that's for sure, but I guess I was just letting everything in. I wasn't afraid of my leaps . . ."

I have always strived to have a very plainspoken, poet-to-reader voice in my work, but I felt here (especially in "Superego" and "Id") that I went further than I'd previously been able. I'm not talking about subject matter—I'd written "riskier" poems, that's for sure, but I guess I was just letting everything in. I wasn't afraid of my leaps—I just included them, for better or worse. I revised as I went along, meaning that I revised what I said in the poem(s) beforehand in the poems I wrote after. This was really freeing to me. And it also captured the way I thought more closely than in other poems. These poems took a great deal of energy—I wrote "Ego" and "Superego" each in one sitting and tinkered later. I wrote "Id" in two very long sittings. The poems came to me in such an urgency that I couldn't ignore them.

The poems got bigger as I went along, like sections of a snowman. "Ego" is the head, "Superego" is the torso, and "Id" is the bottom mound. I published them in this order in my book *Queen for a Day: Selected and New Poems*, whereas *Prairie Schooner* published them in the order the snowman would have been made, with "Id" first, which made for a really interesting reading—to me, anyway. So even though I'd broken a poetry rule (don't beg editors to publish a poem) with my overeagerness, *Prairie Schooner* was kind enough to take all three—and this trio went on to win their annual Strousse Award.

Although they seem so obvious to me now, the titles stumped me for a while. It's true, as I write in "Id," that Amy Lemmon gave me the title for "Superego." Once I had that, I knew that the last poem had to be called "Id"—what else? I wanted to actually call my last book *Id* instead of *Queen for a Day*. I thought the word "Id" would also suggest I.D. (identity) besides the Freudian stuff. But my husband and Stephanie talked me out of it—and I took their advice since they've given me so much in terms of my poems.

Writing Suggestions

1. Rainer Maria Rilke claims that there are two inexhaustible sources for poetry: childhood and dreams. Write a poem about your childhood, about the deep past. Dredge up what you can remember and reimagine the rest. Decide whether your poem will be all in the past, partially in the past, entirely in the present, or leap back and forth through time. Think about what triggers memories.

2. Go to Wal-Mart (Target, Kmart) and buy a package of glue sticks, some cheap kiddie scissors, and most importantly, a cheesy romance novel. Fabio need not be on the cover, but some sort of country girl milking a cow or Viking hunk is a plus. Rip the romance novel down the spine (a dramatic gesture showing the dismantling of the text). Extract from either half of the book a maximum of two pages, and then cut out strange and interesting words and/or phrases from these two pages only. Use the glue stick to connect the words and phrases into a coherent poem on a sheet of paper. Don't use any words except those that you find on these two pages. If they need a "the" or an "a," they have to find it or a suitable replacement on the page. Does using a limited word/phrase bank force you into using language more creatively? You have many pages left in the two book halves, so feel free to do this cheap-o magnetic poetry assignment again and again.

3. Take a poem you've already written and cut out every other line. What does this do for flow? Unity? Meaning? Put those lines back, but take out all the other ones. Does this forced attention to line make you reevaluate the strength of each? Do any lines not seem as strong as they did before?

4. Compare Elizabethan poem sequences (Samuel Daniel's "Delia," Sir Philip Sidney's "Astrophil and Stella," Michael Drayton's "Idea," or Edmund Spenser's "Amoretti") with modern ones (Marilyn Hacker's "Love, Death, and the Changing of the Seasons," A. R. Ammons' book-length poem *Garbage*, David Wojahn's *Mystery Train*, Rita Dove's *Tomas and Beulah*, Quan Barry's tightly linked collection *Asylum*, John Berryman's "The Dream Songs," Duhamel's series included here). Have the "rules" for poem sequences changed? What is the value of a poem sequence? Watch how poets use recurring ideas, images, styles, structures, and voices to pass the narrative torch, as it were, linking the poems into a unified, cohesive whole. What can a poem sequence or book-length poem do that single poems cannot? In your notebook, jot down three ideas that interest you enough to begin a poem sequence about. You don't need to start writing these poems today, but write down any ideas about how you might handle writing these poems. Let the idea of the poem sequence simmer in the back of your head for a few weeks, a few months, perhaps a few years. When you're ready to begin writing it, you'll know. Listen to Duhamel's interview on the audio CD for more of her thoughts on the serial poem. Pay particular attention to what she says about the line length in relation to poem length and how one affects the other.

"We trouble the waters, we tend to pose questions. Perhaps poets are really the active philosophers in this time and age."

—Yusef Komunyakaa

Stephen Dunn

DESIRE

I remember how it used to be
at noon, springtime, the city streets
full of office workers like myself
let loose from the cold
glass buildings on Park and Lex,
the dull swaddling of winter cast off,
almost everyone wanting
everyone else. It was amazing
how most of us contained ourselves,
bringing desire back up
to the office where it existed anyway,
quiet, like a good engine.
I'd linger a bit
with the receptionist,
knock on someone else's open door,
ease myself, by increments,
into the seriousness they paid me for.
Desire was everywhere those years,
so enormous it couldn't be reduced
one person at a time.
I don't remember when it was,
though closer to now than then,
I walked the streets desireless,
my eyes fixed on destination alone.
The beautiful person across from me
on the bus or train
looked like effort, work.
I translated her into pain.
For months I had the clarity
the cynical survive with,

their world so safely small.
Today, walking 57th toward 3rd,
it's all come back,
the interesting, the various,
the conjured life suggested by a glance.
I praise how the body heals itself.
I praise how, finally, it never learns.

Tenderness

Back then when so much was clear
    and I hadn't learned
young men learn from women

what it feels like to feel just right,
    I was twenty-three,
she thirty-four, two children, a husband

in prison for breaking someone's head.
    Yelled at, slapped
around, all she knew of tenderness

was how much she wanted it, and all
    I knew
were backseats and a night or two

in a sleeping bag in the furtive dark.
    We worked
in the same office, banter and loneliness

leading to the shared secret
    that to help
National Biscuit sell biscuits

was wildly comic, which led to my body
    existing with hers
like rain that's found its way underground

to water it naturally joins.
    I can't remember
ever saying the exact word, tenderness,

though she did. It's a word I see now
    you must be older to use,
you must have experienced the absence of it

often enough to know what silk and deep balm
    it is
when at last it comes. I think it was terror

at first that drove me to touch her
    so softly,
then selfishness, the clear benefit

of doing something that would come back
    to me twofold,
and finally, sometime later, it became

reflexive and motiveless in the high
    ignorance of love.
Oh abstractions are just abstract

until they have an ache in them. I met
    a woman never touched
gently, and when it ended between us

I had new hands and new sorrow,
    everything it meant
to be a man changed, unheroic, floating.

Ars Poetica

I'd come to understand restraint
is worthless unless
something's about to spill or burst,

and that the Commandments
understand us perfectly, a large No
for the desirability of everything

vengeful, delicious, out of reach.
I wanted to write ten things
that contained as much.

Maybe from the beginning
the issue was how to live
in a world so extravagant

it had a sky,
in bodies so breakable
we had to pray.

I welcomed, though,
our celestial freedom, our promiscuous flights
all returning to earth.

Yet what could awe us now?
The feeling dies
and then the word.

Restraint. Extravagance. I liked
how one could unshackle the other,
that they might become indivisible.

Astaire's restraint was a kind of extravagance,
while Ginger Rogers danced backwards
in high heels and continued to smile!

She had such grace it was unfair
we couldn't take our eyes off him,
but the beautiful is always unfair.

I found myself imagining him
gone wild, gyrating, leaping,
his life suddenly uncontainable.

Oh, even as he thrashed,
I could tell he was feeling
for limits, and what he could bear.

Something Like Happiness

Last night Joan Sutherland was nuancing
the stratosphere on my fine-tuned tape deck,
and there was my dog Buster with a flea rash,

his head in his privates. Even for Buster
this was something like happiness. Elsewhere
I knew what people were doing to other people,
the terrible hurts, the pleasures of hurting.
I repudiated Zen because it doesn't provide
for forgiveness, repudiated my friend X
who had gotten "in touch with his feelings,"
which were spiteful and aggressive. *Repudiate*
felt good in my mouth, like someone else's tongue
during the sweet combat of love.
I said out loud, *I repudiate,* adding words
like *sincerity, correctness, common sense.*
I remembered how tired I'd grown of mountaintops
and their thin, unheavenly air,
had grown tired, really, of how I spoke of them,
the exaggerated glamor, the false equation between
ascent and importance. I looked at the vase
and its one red flower, then the table
which Zennists would say existed
in its *thisness*, and realized how wrong it was
to reject appearances. How much more difficult
to accept them! I repudiated myself, citing my name.
The phone rang. It was my overly serious friend
from Syracuse saying *Foucault, Foucault,*
like some lost prayer of the tenured.
Advocates of revolution, I agreed with him, poor,
screwed for years, angry—who can begrudge them
weapons and victory? But people like us,
Joan Sutherland on our tapes and enough fine time
to enjoy her, I said, let's be careful
how we link thought and action,
careful about deaths we won't experience.
I repudiated him and Foucault, told him
that if Descartes were alive and wildly in love
he himself would repudiate his famous dictum.
I felt something like happiness when he hung up,
and Buster put his head on my lap,
and without admiration stared at me.
I would not repudiate Buster, not even his fleas.
How could I? Once a day, the flea travels
to the eye of the dog for a sip of water.
Imagine! The journey, the delicacy of the arrival.

IMAGINING MYSELF MY FATHER

I drove slowly, the windows open,
letting the emptiness within meet
the brotherly emptiness without.
Deer grazed by the Parkway's edge,
solemnly enjoying their ridiculous,
gentle lives. There were early signs
of serious fog.

Salesman with a product
I had to pump myself up to sell,
merchant of my own hope,
friend to every tollbooth man,
I named the trees I passed.
I knew the dwarf pines,
and why in such soil
they could grow only so tall.

A groundhog wobbled from the woods.
It, too, seemed ridiculous,
and I conjured for it a wild heart,
at least a wild heart.
My dashboard was agleam with numbers
and time.

It was the kind of morning
the dark never left.
The truly wild were curled up, asleep,
or in some high nest looking down.
There was no way they'd let us love them
just right.

I said "fine" to those who asked.
I told them about my sons, athletes both.
All day I moved among men
who claimed they needed nothing,
nothing, at least, that I had.
Maybe another time, they said,
or, Sorry, things are slow.

On the drive back
I drove fast, and met the regulars

at the Inn for a drink.
It seemed to me a man needed a heart
for the road, and a heart for home,
and one more for his friends.

And so many different, agile tongues.

A Postmortem Guide
for my eulogist, in advance

Do not praise me for exceptional serenity.
Can't you see I've turned away
from the large excitements,
and have accepted all the troubles?

Go down to the old cemetery; you'll see
there's nothing definitive to be said.
The dead once were all kinds—
boundary breakers and scalawags,
martyrs of the flesh, and so many
dumb bunnies of duty, unbearably nice.

I've been a little of each.

And, please, resist the temptation
of speaking about virtue.
The seldom-tempted are too fond
of that word, the small-
spirited, the unburdened.
Know that I've admired in others
only the fraught straining
to be good.

Adam's my man and Eve's not to blame.
He bit in; it made no sense to stop.

Still, for accuracy's sake you might say
I often stopped,
that I rarely went as far as I dreamed.

And since you know my hardships,
understand they're mere bump and setback

against history's horror.
Remind those seated, perhaps weeping,
how obscene it is
for some of us to complain.

Tell them I had second chances.
I knew joy.
I was burned by books early
and kept sidling up to the flame.

Tell them at the end I had no need
for God, who'd become just a story
I once loved, one of many
with concealments and late-night rescues,
high sentence and pomp. The truth is
I learned to live without hope
as well as I could, almost happily,
in the despoiled and radiant now.

You who are one of them, say that I loved
my companions most of all.
In all sincerity, say that they provided
a better way to be alone.

The Guardian Angel

Afloat between lives and stale truths, 1
   he realizes
he's never truly protected one soul,

they all die anyway, and what good
   is solace,
solace is cheap. The signs are clear:

the drooping wings, the shameless thinking
   about utility
and self. It's time to stop.

The guardian angel lives for a month
   with other angels,
sings the angelic songs, is reminded

that he doesn't have a human choice.
   The angel of love
lies down with him, and loving

restores to him his pure heart.
   Yet how hard it is
to descend into sadness once more.

When the poor are evicted, he stands
   between them
and the bank, but the bank sees nothing

in its way. When the meek are overpowered
   he's there, the thin air
through which they fall. Without effect

he keeps getting in the way of insults.
   He keeps wrapping
his wings around those in the cold.

Even his lamentations are unheard,
   though now,
in for the long haul, trying to live

beyond despair, he believes, he needs
   to believe
everything he does takes root, hums

beneath the surfaces of the world.

John & Mary

> *John & Mary had never met. They were like*
> *two hummingbirds who also had never met.*
> —from a freshman's short story

They were like gazelles who occupied different
grassy plains, running in opposite directions
from different lions. They were like postal clerks
in different zip codes, with different vacation time,
their bosses adamant and clock-driven.
How could they get together?

They were like two people who couldn't get together.
John was a Sufi with a love of the dervish,
Mary of course a Christian with a curfew.
They were like two dolphins in the immensity
of the Atlantic, one playful,
the other stuck in a tuna net—
two absolutely different childhoods!
There was simply no hope for them.
They would never speak in person.
When they ran across that windswept field
toward each other, they were like two freight trains,
one having left Seattle at 6:36 P.M.
at an unknown speed, the other delayed
in Topeka for repairs.
The math indicated that they'd embrace
in another world, if at all, like parallel lines.
Or merely appear kindred and close, like stars.

MIDWEST
AFTER THE PAINTINGS OF DAVID AHLSTED

We have lived in this town,
have disappeared
on this prairie. The church

always was smaller
than the grain elevator,
though we pretended otherwise.
The houses were similar

because few of us wanted
to be different
or estranged. And the sky

would never forgive us,
no matter how many times
we guessed upwards
in the dark.

The sky was the prairie's
double, immense,
kaleidoscopic, cold.

The town was where
and how we huddled
against such forces,
and the old abandoned

pickup on the edge
of town was how we knew
we had gone too far,
or had returned.

People? Now we can see them,
invisible in their houses
or in their stores.

Except for one man
lounging on his porch,
they are part of the buildings,

they have determined
every stubborn shape, the size
of each room. The trailer home
with the broken window

is somebody's life.
One thing always is
more important than another,

this empty street, this vanishing
point. The good eye knows
no democracy. Shadows follow

sunlight as they should,
as none of us can prevent.
Everything is conspicuous
and is not.

Knowledge

Some things like stones yield
only their opacity,
remain inscrutably themselves.

To the trained eye they offer their age,
some small planetary news.

Which suggests the world
becomes more mysterious, not less,
the more we know.

God knows is how we begin a sentence
when we refuse to acknowledge what we know.

Gravitas is what Newton must have felt
when gravity became clear to him.

Presto, said the clown as he pulled
a quarter from behind my ear
when I was five. The very same ear in fact
that pressed itself to a snail's vacant house
and found an ocean.

The problem is how to look intelligent
with our mouths agape,
how to be delighted, not stupefied
when the caterpillar shrugs
and becomes a butterfly.

It takes a clear surface
to properly lead us into mystery.

God knows nothing we don't know.
We gave him every word he ever said.

"Artful Talk": Dunn on Drift and Counterdrift

Ever since I've been inclined toward what Dave Smith calls "artful talk" in my poems (maybe from my fourth book on), I've known the delicate balance between what's said and the orchestration of it. While I'm overtly talking out loud I'm of course making behind-the-scenes arrangements. I'm constantly aware of the necessary compromises between original intent and the poem's found language. I'm not sure that these selections are my best poems, but each in its own way found a language and a shape as it evolved and ended in what Frost called "a small clarification." That clarification at first may have been just for me, by which I mean it constituted both a personal discovery and a solving, if you will, of the poem's own exigencies, but I write my poems with a sense that they are being overheard. Finally, they are constructed for the alert reader.

> *"While I'm overtly talking out loud [in my poems] I'm of course making behind-the-scenes arrangements. I'm constantly aware of the necessary compromises between original intent and the poem's found language."*

Drift and counterdrift seem central to the way many of my poems behave. It's also the way my mind works. I can hardly make a statement without immediately thinking of its opposite. At their best, my poems enact and orchestrate mixed feelings and contrary ideas. So when "Desire," for example, found its counterdrift ("I walked the streets desireless"), it was on its way to discovering its ending, which of course was not available to me before the poem began. That small clarification ("the body . . . never learns") was, when I wrote it, the happiest of compositional moments: when we arrive at what we didn't know we knew, and it seems inevitable.

It took approximately eight years for me to find out how to orchestrate "Tenderness." It is an example of the difficulty of writing the experiential poem in which we might include details because they actually happened. I selected badly before I selected well. As I remember, the poem started to take on its present life with the writing of its first discovery ("a word I see now/you must be older to use,/you must have experienced the absence of it"). In essence, the poem got going the first time I was able to abstract what I was saying. This led to the lament and insight, "Oh abstractions are just abstract/until they have an ache in them," which I trust is what the poem in its entirety is an enactment of.

"Ars Poetica" began as a complaint against another poet's mode of working, and as a quarrel with myself. Someone had praised a particular poet's restraint when it seemed to me from the outset that the poet had just a small investment in his poem. It struck me that restraint in service of what was tepid to begin with was a paltry thing indeed. Then I began to worry about my own work in that regard, and I was on my way. Restraint, of course, suggested extravagance, and I had my drift and counterdrift, which enabled me to refine and exemplify my thinking. By poem's end, the poem itself had made an argument to be so titled.

I chose "Something Like Happiness" because it has several drifts and counterdrifts, and a few different tones as well. I'm always pleased when I can blend tones, and here the comic and the meditative seemed to conspire to be equal to/with the deliberate qualifier in the title. (The title came *after* I wrote the poem, and I think it was the major discovery that helped me revise and pace what I had written.) This is a poem in which early on I gave myself permission to meander. Some of the pleasures for me, therefore, were how I was able to keep and defy the poem's promises as I played and mused. I've no idea if the ending is true; it came and startled me, so I decided to keep it.

"Drift and counterdrift seem central to the way many of my poems behave . . . I can hardly make a statement without immediately thinking of its opposite."

I don't know how to talk about "Imagining Myself My Father," except to say that by adopting the persona of my father and placing him in my present environment, I found myself writing with a new empathy for him and his difficult life. With the help of his mask, I also managed to discover some things about the vagaries of my own life and, I hope, the lives of men in general. I'd like to think that the poem is evidence of how the imagination finds truths that the straight biographical impulse cannot.

Sometimes you write a poem that feels like a crystallization of your other poems, if not also a distillation of a lifetime's preoccupations and concerns. "A Postmortem Guide" is such a poem for me. I leave it at that.

In trying to be true to the imaginative imperatives in "The Guardian Angel," I learned (many years later) that I had written another ars poetica. At the time of its writing I was only conscious of trying persuasively to imagine what a life of a disaffected Guardian Angel might be like. Perhaps fifteen years later, when asked to discuss it, I found myself saying that the poem was a metaphor for how an American poet lives with neglect, how he or she continues in spite of being ineffectual and not taken seriously. That was what unconsciously drove the poem, I realized, and enabled me to find its next moments as much as the conceit did.

"John & Mary" seems the best of a certain kind of poem I've written over the years. It's a rip-off of the epigraph, it immediately found its energy, rhythm, and playfulness, took about twenty minutes to write, and was never revised—a gift.

My painter friend David Ahlsted did a series of realist, yet highly stylized paintings of small Midwestern towns, which I was especially drawn to, I'm sure, because of my three years of small-town living in Minnesota during the early seventies. I think his paintings gave me permission to do my own stylized take on the Midwest. What pleases me most in "Midwest" is how I was able to orchestrate and pace the poem's effects. The pacing, most particularly the variations in syntax and sentence, seem intimately part of the content. It's a poem, I think, in which I was able to make image and rhythm fully cooperate.

"Knowledge" is a very recent poem, so it may be hubristic of me to include it in a "best of" grouping. As much as we've all been cautioned about the abstract, probably it's the poem that wishes to survive on statement that has, in my experience, raised the most red flags. I've been drawn to the poem of statement, and how one might get away with it, ever since I read Carlos Drummond de Andrade's poem, "Your Shoulders Hold Up the World" about twenty years ago. "Knowledge" is a poem that attempts to survive on statement, which flirts with the didactic, and had many different arrangements of detail before its present incarnation. For example, the stanza with *Presto* in it was, in most drafts, the penultimate stanza. The now penultimate stanza was a late addition to the poem. Such rearrangements, of course, are normal compositional behavior; it's often desirable to break up a too-linear flow. I should mention there are at least eight lines that the poem shed once it found its true order. So this poem does not represent a natural flow of mind; few poems do. It's the illusion of such that I strive for. Perhaps "Knowledge" is indicative of an evolution in the way I handle drift and counterdrift in a poem, most of the "turning" words suppressed.

> *"Sometimes you write a poem that feels like a crystallization of your other poems, if not also a distillation of a lifetime's preoccupations and concerns."*

Writing Suggestions

1. An exercise Dunn particularly likes is for you to take any failed poem of yours and extract the single line that interests you most. Use it as the first line of a new poem, and strive to make that new poem live up to the high standard of thought and language that the first line has. (Variation: Borrow a line from a poem you admire, use it as your first line, then after you've written your poem, cut that first line. Replace it with one of your own or leave your second line as [now] the first.)

2. Write a philosophical poem. Select a premise that is obvious (the sun is hot or things fall because of gravity) and in your poem, claim the opposite is true. Remember that in the world of your poem, the opposite *can* be true. How does this relate to Bly's comments on assertions?

3. In your notebook, list what you know to be true about poetry. Now list what you think might be true about poetry. Now list what you know isn't true about poetry. Now that you've cleared your mind, write down sentences

that begin "Poetry is _________" and see if your answers surprise yourself. Continue this "Poetry is _________" endeavor for a number of weeks (months?) and when you feel you have enough material, try writing your own ars poetica, a poem about poetry. The best of these are often rooted in concrete images and language, but are also philosophically and linguistically evocative. Remember that even a poem about ideas should use the five senses.

4. Part of being a writer is realizing that you're part of a community. The next time you run across a poem that really strikes you as wonderful (from this book or elsewhere), write a letter to the poet c/o his or her book publisher or journal the poem appeared in or through the university where they teach. Don't just write a fan letter, but talk specifically about the elements of the poem that really captured your interest. Send it to them. Try doing this once a month to remind yourself you're part of a community, but also do this because the poet you're writing to might find in you a kindred spirit and suddenly you've got a writing friend for life, a wonderful thing. If a poet doesn't respond, down the road when you receive your first (or twentieth) letter in response to one of your poems, remember what it felt like for your letter to go unanswered. Remember that as a writer you're always part of a community.

"Poetry began when somebody wandered off a savanna or out of a cave and looked up at the sky with wonder and said, 'Ahhh!' That was the first poem."

—Lucille Clifton

Stuart Dybek

Sirens

Tonight, they seem to be calling
from afar, conversing
like chained dogs carrying on an argument
from blocks away,

open windows still gasping from the night before,
and yet a firetruck screams more flame,
while the domelight on an ambulance ricochets
across the carats of dark panes.

A network of stained crazing
like the backside of the moon
spreads beneath tea leaves, through a china cup
in which the future is contained,

but would the Black Maria be allowed
if its soprano struck the perfect pitch of glass,
if its aria was graphed
by a crack traveling the luminous city

reflected along the cliffs of the Gold Coast?
As any dreamer knows, it's possible
to rush in silence toward disaster
the way one rushes toward desire.

Windy City

The garments worn in flying dreams
were fashioned there—
overcoats that swooped like kites,

scarves streaming like vapor trails,
gowns ballooning into spinnakers.

In a city like that one might sail
through life led by a runaway hat.
The young scattered in whatever directions
their wild hair pointed, and gusting
into one another, they fell in love.

At night, wind rippled the saxophones
that hung like windchimes
in pawnshop windows, hooting through
each horn so that the streets seemed haunted
not by nighthawks, but by doves.

Pinwheels whirred from steeples
in place of crosses. At the pinnacles
of public buildings, snagged underclothes—
the only flag—flapped majestically.
And when it came time to disappear

one simply chose a thoroughfare
devoid of memories, raised a collar,
and turned one's back on the wind.
I remember closing my eyes as I stepped
into a swirl of scuttling leaves.

Three Nocturnes

#1
Imperfect dreams,
each sleeper hung

on the meathook
of a question mark,

clocks stuck
on an hour

when loneliness
seems just another

way of loving
only yourself.

What's the plural of dark?
Nighthawks

reciting a thousand names
for night,

a moon
you'd have to sort

through thousands of streetlights
to find.

#2

An impression of her body
left tangled in sheets

patterned with moonlit craters
by the lace curtain

that had printed her back
with sprays of wildflowers

native, perhaps, to a field
in southern Bohemia.

And, beyond the field,
through an open window,

a moonlit river
that, despite its pessimism,
mirrors swans.

Or so the bed, abandoned,
was dreaming on its own.

I wouldn't sleep there,

I wouldn't kneel and pray
beside it.

for John Woods, 1926–1995
#3

Pizzicato of nightwings
against screens . . . Listen to the roar

of weedlots, or the wilds
behind illuminated billboards

where shadows of nighthawks soar
across blank, enormous faces.

You'll hear hunger that can't be
satisfied in an all-night diner.

Nightflyers don't want night to stall.
Their wingbeats fan darkness

as if it were a flame
able to flare up darker still.

By disappearing green taillights
of fireflies, moths in which the moon

is visible, unfold
from cocoons of oblivion, while

time metamorphoses into a perfume
of black marigolds.

TODAY, TONIGHT

Today, wild parakeets awoke
confused to find themselves chattering
in a strange patois.

Today, even the ants are tourists,
and the iguana, camouflaged as a mirror,
has forgotten his true reflection.

The goats must be sorry
they've eaten their passports
because today, like us, they're no longer

sure of who they are or what they're
doing here, otherwise, why else
would goats be swimming out to sea?

*

Even the ants are tourists:

they scurry among their ruined pyramids,
toting seeds as if wearing
tiny, white sombreros
a thousand times their weight,

but that's nothing beside the golden weight
of noon—

the heft of light on shoulders,
the enormous shadow
each body tugs along—

so it seems impossible that a red umbrella
opened beside a chrome blue sea
supports the tonnage of a star
descending now too close for comfort

or that an eyelid
can eclipse such radiance.

*

As rising squid knew it would,
a moon that's been hanging around
all day, finally makes its move

and from groves of mango trees
fruit bats unfold their black
umbrellas and hurry to its pull

while a tide ripples through a choir
of mutts on French Town Hill.
Tonight, parakeets retire mimicking

the sputter of sunspots, of dying
frequencies, and citronella candles.
The iguana has assumed

the shape of moonlight.
Are the ants asleep?
Do they dream in unison?

They climb into the starry sky;
by dawn, they've carried off
the Milky Way.

Overhead Fan

Beneath an overhead fan, a man and a woman,
slatted with light leaking through green shutters,
are unaware that they, too, are turning.
The shadow of the blades imparts a slow rotation
to each still object in this hazy room,
and the wobbling fan chirps at its mounting
as if the gecko doing pushups on the mirror
is counting time. Otherwise, it's quiet
but for the whir above the sweaty friction
of their skin. Her mouth gapes
as if emptied of speech, her closed eyes
can't see the shadow that plays
across her eyelids and breasts, and that later
will play across the man's memory.
And though their bodies now press
as if pinned together by centrifugal force,
they feel the spin as if they're hovering—
not like the souls of the newly dead
are said to hover above their abandoned bodies,
but like the hummingbird above the red lips
of the hibiscus just beyond the shutters,
or, high overhead, the black blades
of a frigate bird, circling on extended wings,
above the Gulf Stream's azure gyres.

Inspiration

Finally, down an askew side street
of gingerbread houses held up by paint,
where bony kids crowded around the body

of a cripple who'd been trampled
when the shots rang out,
I spotted a taxi with a raised hood.
The driver was adding motor oil
which was leaking into the gutter
nearly as fast as he was pouring.
I threw in my suitcase and we started
down the mobbed streets,
him laying on the horn, yelling in Creole,
driving, by necessity, with his head
craned out the window. Cracks
ran the length of the windshield
from where the old wound of a bullet
had left a crater that vaguely resembled
the shape of a pineapple. A cabbie
could never afford to replace the glass,
so he'd painted the crater instead—
pineapple yellow with the bullet hole
gleaming at its center like a worm hole
emitting another dimension.
And once he'd painted the pineapple,
wasn't it not only logical, but inspired
to see the cracks that ran from it
as vines? He'd painted them
a tangled green that transformed driving
through the streets of Port-au-Prince
into racing blindly through a jungle.
But he wasn't finished yet—
the vines grew flowers: rose red, orchid,
morning-glory blue, and to the flowers
came all manner of butterflies
and newly invented species of small,
colorful birds, twining serpents,
and deep in the shadows,
the mascaraed black-slit, golden eyes
of what may have been a jaguar.

Dybek on Pleasure and Mystery

I hope the first impression of these poems is sensual; that they're vivid in the mind's eye, and strike the ear as musical. When poems give sensual pleasure as paintings and music do, then I trust that, like the visual arts and music, the poems also will convey emotion. Even though the medium of poetry is language, I hope that the emotion in the poem proves elusive to verbal articulations other than that of the poem itself. It's a paradox—and one of the beautiful mysteries at the heart of the literary arts—that a poem can be clearly experienced on the level of feeling, and yet remain elusive to be reduced to the kind of paraphrase that makes it seem as if poems are merely ideas done up in fashionable dress.

"It's a paradox—and one of the beautiful mysteries at the heart of the literary arts—that a poem can be clearly experienced on the level of feeling, and yet remain elusive to be reduced to the kind of paraphrase that makes it seem as if poems are merely ideas done up in fashionable dress."

Both pleasure and mystery—and sometimes the pleasure of mystery—prompt a reader to reread a poem. Upon the scrutiny of rereading, I want the poem to cohere, to have solidity like an object, a solidity that comes, at least in part, from compression. And I want the poem, like an object, to throw a shadow, a shadow that makes the poem larger than itself.

I've chosen poems from two different books that I've been at work on. "Sirens," "Windy City," and "Three Nocturnes" are poems that explore an urban landscape; whereas "Today, Tonight," "Overhead Fan," and "Inspiration" are set in the Caribbean.

Place isn't discussed as often in regard to poetry as it is to fiction, which I also write. In fiction, it's a given that a sense of place can be a significant element in the makeup of a writer's voice, and, to my taste, a recognizable voice, whether in poetry or prose, is important. It's impossible to imagine the unique voices of, say, Eudora Welty or James Joyce without summoning up the places that each writer made on the page—worlds made from voice, yet from which voice in turn seems to spring. In such writers place informs style as well as content. The same relation between place and individual voice is no less true of poets like Yeats and Frost. Poets—Homer and Dante, being two rather sturdy examples—have always been world makers.

Place is a term for an obsessive return by an artist (whether the medium be the visual or the literary arts) to images that convey both an outer and inner geography. The visible world the artist details for the eye expresses the invisible topology of the psyche. A sense of place can lend to a series of poems—and to a poet's entire oeuvre—a dimension of context, and an overarching unity we experience as a voice. To my mind, a poet's voice is an invention, a grand fiction—be it the public, rhetorical voice of Walt Whitman or the private voice of Emily Dickinson. But should the reader rather perceive the poet's voice in the way that one experiences voice in a memoir—as some intimate communication with the person rather than the poem—then that's the reader's right. It seems academic to deny it.

I grew up in a city and images that I internalized from as far back as childhood appear in the three urban poems. Sometimes the images arise from experiences that aren't part of the poem. I know in "Sirens" there's a connection between a city screaming with the sounds of constant crisis and the years I spent as a caseworker for the Cook County Department of Public Aid. But the poem itself has nothing to do with being a caseworker. My energy in writing it went into evoking sirens—a word that, of course, has a double meaning. I believe if I can make the impression of sirens tactile and emotionally resonant, then the reader will collaborate with the poem to find meaning in it. That is, after all, the process we use in understanding our dreams.

"I want the poem, like an object, to throw a shadow, a shadow that makes the poem larger than itself."

There was a specific catalyst for writing "Windy City." One afternoon in the pitch of a Chicago winter, I took a photo for two Japanese tourists who, because of the gusts, were having trouble focusing a camera while keeping their hats from blowing away. They didn't speak much English, and when I handed back their camera, they bowed their thanks, gleefully repeating, "Windy City! Windy City!" The poem obviously isn't about Japanese tourists, but it does try to convey something of the wonder with which they imbued those words. I tried to make from language a little wind machine.

Poems are sometimes collections of disparate lines and images that accumulate in notebooks until some synergy teases out connections between them and suggests the unity of a design. That's the case with "Three Nocturnes."

The desire to write nocturnes came to me while I was writing a story titled *Chopin in Winter*. I listened over months to Chopin's nocturnes as if to a sound track for my story. I knew there was a tradition of the nocturne in painting, as well, that includes such painters as Aleksander Gierymski, James Whistler, and Ruth Bohan, so I thought I'd like to try to write a literary equivalent of the nocturne. In music, the word nocturne isn't defined by a particular formal arrangement, but by mood—a dreamy night piece—a notion that translates easily into other mediums. Besides Chopin, I thought of Bartók, a composer whose music has been tremendously important to me. Bartók never wrote nocturnes, but he referred to certain haunting passages in his music as "night music." He is not alluding to Mozart's *Eine Kleine Nachtmusik* in which night is playful and decorous. There's aloneness and tension in Bartók's soundscape of night, threat, loss, and yet a dissonant shimmer of strings that summons up an alien beauty. It's a mood that reminds me of a phrase of F. Scott Fitzgerald's from *The Crack Up*, about "the 3 A.M. of the soul," a phrase that seems to me a perfect epigraph for Edward Hopper's masterpiece of a nocturne, "Nighthawks." Thus can an emotion travel between mediums.

My intention for these urban pieces is that they summon up a night music of words rather than notes. The conventional sources for music in poetry are not just viable, but crucial to me. My primary response to poets such as Emily Dickinson, William Butler Yeats, Wallace Stevens, T. S. Eliot, Theodore Roethke, Seamus Heaney—poets whose work I've memorized—is on the level of sound. (Artists copy drawings so as to appreciate them through the intelligence of the hand; memorizing a poem can be akin to engaging that kind of physical intelligence.) A prominent feature of modernism has been to blur the distinction between genres. Forms such as the prose poem and the short short, for example, blur the border between poetry and fiction. Because I write fiction as well as poetry, at some point I found the question: what can I do in poetry that I can't do in fiction, to be inescapable. The answer, for me—and I mean it here only as a personal response, not a generalization—is that poetry with its interplay of line and sentence rhythm, plus the surrounding white space of silence, affords different possibilities for harnessing sound. Not surprisingly, sound—sirens, wind, nocturnes—becomes not just something for language to mimic, but a subject in these poems.

> *"Poems are sometimes collections of disparate lines and images that accumulate in notebooks until some synergy teases out connections between them and suggests the unity of a design."*

The urban poems also share darkness as a subject.

William Carlos Williams coined a famous axiom: *no ideas but in things*, a position echoed in "Ars Poetica," a poem by Archibald MacLeish—once a staple in anthologies—that concludes: *a poem should not mean/but be*. A basic aim for me in these urban poems is to make darkness *be* on the page; to make of darkness a theme and variations, to create not an idea, but aspects of a city of night whose streets a reader can walk.

Conversely, in the three poems that are set in the Caribbean, the intention is to make light. I'm afraid that sounds more biblical than I mean it to be. One doesn't have to look to Genesis or Thomas Edison or Impressionist painters, there are numerous examples of light makers among poets. The greatest modern Italian poet, Eugenio Montale, comes immediately to my mind, and Derek Walcott, and among Americans, Elizabeth Bishop—has any writer captured the clarity of light in language better?

I was a butterfly collector as a kid, exploring the patches of wild surviving along railroad tracks, the Sanitary Canal, in the abandoned back lots of factories. The little hideaways of nature in cities have always fascinated me, as in "Three Nocturnes." As I grew older, I wanted to live somewhere where the natural world was still a powerful presence—so, in my twenties, I moved from Chicago to the Virgin Islands. The difference was so profound that there remains a split in my consciousness between the urban self and the self that inhabited those islands.

Moving to the Caribbean created a life long love affair with tropical places and the surrounding reefs. I taught at the local junior high, the only junior high on the island. It was built on landfill, and short on resources, including textbooks appropriate to the local culture. Sometimes my students and I would make up our own texts, such as a calypso dictionary, on the single mimeograph machine. The students were a delight and my relationship with them transformed living in a foreign place from the experience of a tourist to that of someone who had some purpose in the community. But I knew I was only a visitor, a traveler at rest, that no matter how much I loved those islands, they could never be my place in the way they belong to writers such as Derek Walcott or Jamaica Kincaid.

I hope that doesn't sound forlorn. Such a situation is an invitation to make of the experience a subject. I've always had an interest in the subgenre of such writing—I hesitate to call it travel writing, as often the real subject is not travel but the sense of being foreign, though sometimes travel is necessary to arrive at that sense. One feels it profoundly in writers like Franz Kafka and Rainer Maria Rilke. Whatever it's called, I have a special fondness for writers working in this mode, whether it be prose writers like Bruce Chatwin, Paul Bowles, and Graham Greene, or poets such as Elizabeth Bishop, and Wallace Stevens, and Hart Crane before her, and Richard Hugo, W. S. Merwin, James Wright, James Merrill, and so on. One could assemble quite an interesting anthology on the subject.

"Today, Tonight" addresses that sense unique to human beings of feeling foreign in the world. Though another way to read "Today, Tonight" is as an account of how the optic nerve can, in such preserves of light, be stimulated to a point of the ecstatic. The liberating experience of travel can result in peaks of the ecstatic, too. The first notion of the poem came when one day I saw a herd of goats swimming out to sea. The poem is essentially a celebration of the natural world, as is "Overhead Fan," which juxtaposes the intimate shadows in a hotel room with the blaze of light just outside.

Despite its resource of great natural beauty, the Caribbean is a Third World region; behind the facade of resorts, there is grinding poverty. In the late '70s the brutal Haitian dictator "Papa Doc" Duvalier was succeeded by his son, "Baby Doc," who reportedly wanted to turn Haiti into a tourist destination. I accepted a magazine assignment at the time to visit Haiti and write an article as to how the change in government was affecting tourism. It's an article I was never able to write. Haiti was then, and remains, one of the poorest nations on earth. The Ton Ton Macoute, the lethal goon squad that kept the population oppressed under Papa Doc, was still conducting drills in broad daylight on the Champ Mars in Port-au-Prince, while white men from the United States and Europe inspected impoverished Haitian women who stood in lines to sell their bodies. Once in Haiti, in the face of such suffering, the very premise of an article on tourism seemed obscene. "Inspiration," the most narrative of these six poems, recounts an incident that occurred during that aborted assignment.

Writing Suggestions

1. Write a poem that's entirely about place. Don't populate it with people, just let the landscape be the focus of the poem. Use "pleasure and mystery" as Dybek suggests. Make the place, the landscape, live on the page with images that utilize all five senses. For some good examples of poems about place, read Mary Oliver (nature), Pablo Neruda (nature), Steve Fay (rural America), and Tony Saunders (urban America).

2. Reread what Dybek writes about the nocturne, and then write your own nocturne poem. Let language evoke a mood. As with fiction, try to do more showing than telling—involve the reader intimately.

3. As Dybek did with many of his favorites, memorize a single poem. Just one. It can be one of Dybek's, or a poem from one of your favorite collections. But learn this poem such that you can recite it clearly, carefully, and without pause. Practice "performing" it. Try reciting it powerfully as you imagine a great orator (think Martin Luther King Jr.) might perform it. Then try reciting it as if you're reading mechanically off a page. Find somewhere in the middle that feels comfortable for you, then perform the poem for a friend. Remember that poetry was originally an oral art form and that a quality performance can greatly add to a poem's effect. A good poem read wonderfully can be great, whereas a great poem read in a so-so fashion is just so-so, and any poem read badly comes off badly, even if the poem was great to begin with.

4. Research is an important component of many poems. Poems that have specific, significant details (historical or otherwise) are compelling. Find some background information on a world event within the last forty years or so that you know only a little about (Vietnam war, space shuttle *Challenger* explosion, Desert Storm, assassination attempt on President Reagan, Cuban Missile Crisis, etc.) and see if informing yourself evokes a reaction. Turn the energy of this reaction into a poem. See how others have responded to world events and political issues—read Martín Espada, Carolyn Forché, Miguel

Hernández, or Pablo Neruda. Read Ai, Maya Angelou, Rita Dove, or Sapphire. Read Yusef Komunyakaa, Norman Dubie, Charles Wright, or A. R. Ammons.

> *"I don't consider my poems masks for myself. To me, they're characters. In that way, I am more like a playwright. They are not me to me. Sometimes they surprise me."*
>
> —Ai

Ray Gonzalez

Kiva Floor at Abo

What do I know in my confusion?
How does it shape my legs and arms
as they sink deeper into the earth,
ancient red walls smothering something
I was taught long ago, forgotten words
written in a place I will never look?
If I hear the drum, I am mistaken.
To ask for directions is to pretend
I can identify three or four worlds
where no pumas were trapped
to strengthen this room.
It is the whispering that taught me
how the white dot in the window
is larger than itself—
its dimensions injuring several families
before healing them of ambition?
What if I can't climb out and dirt
warnings explode over my arms?
Skin inside second skin where
the afternoon reveals how far
the wooden ladder goes down.
To descend is to listen.
Climbing back up kills necessity,
shards littering the floor in patterns
I saw when my troubles began.
Though I speak softly, the galaxy
embedded in these old bricks

will not emerge, the search
for the other room a wish
from a god who wants one
full circle of sweating men.
Do I know where to kneel and dig?
Will this desecration last a lifetime,
or will the weight of the blue fly
etched on this stone mean a theft,
a way of bowing down, tasting
the dirt as if water is not water
and greed is fed by shadows moving
to the other side of the eclipse?

Federico Garcia Lorca's Desk

It was tied with guitar strings
into a sack that held pigeon feathers,
the hair of lost dogs—cardboard
from a box of trinkets
he received from North Africa.
Garcia Lorca's desk was a bundle
of things bearing down like an easy shot,
words recalled when discontent
was a shade of black,
coffee beans stolen in silence—
a clock over the hills waiting
for the next moon.
Garcia Lorca's desk was a head
of lettuce, a bowl of goat soup,
the place where tiny hands
were named for their fingers,
ink spotting the pages to buy time
before three doors were slammed.
Garcia Lorca's desk was his vow
to stir the rain with rootless awe,
then hide for years, come out
singing, reciting poems
from the warmth of laps,

paper flattened on the desk
so the sun could read.
Garcia Lorca's desk was found
decaying in an empty field
where they lined him up,
the feathers falling out,
guitar strings rounding the sky
with wired light that sank
into the soft paper he used
to wipe his hands
before he was shot.

I Am Afraid of the Moon

I am afraid of the moon when it comes down
to touch my throat, its light weaving
the white vein into my heart,
its brief cycle shimmering with evidence
that I have been wrong.
I am afraid of the moon when the toads
have become extinct, their legs deformed
into red spiders that drown their voices,
moonlight exploding in the water
to warn me I am still wrong.
I fear the full moon above the mountains,
its yellow wash the gold left behind by
men who loved night skies with stars,
their ancestors mistaken when they believed
there was no earth to flee to without
the light of their shadows falling into
their tombs to wash their toes.
That time the moon was wrong.
I do not trust the moon when
everything is gone, my companions from
the translucent land fleeing the cycles
of madness long ago, their terrible cries
beyond the seasons bringing them back
by the quarter moon where they try
to catch one dimension, but can't

separate it from the bloodless sky.
I am afraid of the moon because
it changes my home each time it arrives,
its dangling power ignored for a few nights
before the desert floor becomes a storm where
those of us blinded at birth by moonlight
don't know what it is like to be wrong.

Kick the Heart

Kick the heart.
Kick the starting lance.
Throw the ground a word and stand back.
The color of terror is the envy
on body rags, the dragonfly war
scraped off a painting inside the door.
Kick the shame.
Kick the falling dawn as fortunate.
Throw the corrupted guest out the door.
A sequence of rhythms bound for
the light on your bed.
On the eggplant cooked for the husband
working late: an ant, a hair—
the only thing said to race the mind.
Take someone else's voice and touch their ears.
Make sure they hear you cry
in their own whispers, their harangue.
Kick the soil.
Kick the sweet drowning as if you know
the round jubilance of pear is afraid
of a darkening spoon, a honey of flavor,
the tender one who never touches your plate.
The tired one who rations food
to thank God eternity is here and there.
Slip the eye the blue-black stranger,
his instrument of scars and neglect,
its tune of every wish besides
the grave of a careless, quiet man.
Shape his sound into the thumb asking

for a ride in the years of not going anywhere.
Kick the alphabet.
Kick the hungry thigh and try again.
Reduce yourself to a moving mouth, a solemn happiness
that smells of the past, takes hold of the throat
and teaches you to despise omens—
ignore Apache mirrors on rock arches
as if you knew what their scratchings meant.
Kick the heart.
Kick the starting lance.
It moves deeper into the mouth of blinking neon
where vertigo is perfume, desire foaming
on your bare feet killed by frost,
taken by the animal waking inside your holy cross—
a figure of green gowns and things
that follows you until you dance.
Kick the truth.
Kick the belly until it confesses.
Admit you were fed by a woman
flapping in the wind, told to sit there by a father
who made her give birth to a shimmering head,
your brain of flowers blossoming upon
the body always first to confess.
What snow is left is tired water unmoved by your
seasonal words, your circle healing by slowing down,
swelling to the size of God,
yellow leaves in the blood nothing dangerous—
this impulse, this kick to the brittle lake
where the snow goes away.

Under the Freeway in El Paso

I hear streets light up
with secret weeping,
wish I could really hear it,
be given the owl,
the route of his veins
pulsing under the freeway

where the house of my birth
stands and decays.
Strangers have lived there
for the last forty years.
I have wanted to knock on the door
and breathe inside the house.
Someone wants me
to disguise myself as a street,
a traffic signal, a dark alley,
the imploded house across
from the last residence of
the ghost who follows me inside.
Someone wants me to thrive,
surpass the disappearance
of my father, my dead grandfathers,
my missing uncle, my cousins
who won't speak to me because
I came from that house of candles,
that room of saints, the walls of glowing
crucifixes that broke the arms
of those who didn't believe,
who cursed the smoke
and blew it toward me,
the blankets I found inside
shattered rooms under
the freshly built freeway.
I went crazy with hope there,
restless as the prisoner
who fell down the concrete hill,
impaled himself on yucca,
the turnpike of America,
the pointed staff of the priest.
I am the man who ate catacombs
of honey out of the walls,
raised my lips to the wiping hands
that took care of me inside the house,
giving me sweetness of prayer,
a stranger waiting there for my return,
so he could light the candles that never
melted in all the years of the passenger.

WHITE

Written after several treks through White Sands National Monument, New Mexico, site of Trinity, the first atomic Bomb explosion, 1945. My parents were in high school at The time and told me El Pasoans, that morning, saw a White flash in the sky one hundred miles to the north.

The White Silence

The white silence is absolved.
It murmurs in the body and heaves.
It sees me and arms itself with warmth.
The white silence is a reward
worth the wet hair and angry eye.
It shifts into a love for windows.
The white silence is feeding,
thinks of me coming back talking,
but to talk would be a white noise from
white flowers I stepped on long ago.

The White Iguana

The white iguana sits on my wife's head.
Its tail covers its eyes.
She can't know I am coming back.
The white iguana prays on the head
of the woman I have loved for years.
When I open my eyes, the iguana hisses,
combs the hair of my wife with its claws.
When my wife opens her eyes,
the white iguana loves the light,
leaps off her head and flies.

The White Tarantula

The white tarantula crawled out of my heart,
moved down my chest and brushed my nipples.
The white tarantula visited me in my sleep.
When I woke, it waited, hidden somewhere in the room.
When I woke, I had crossed to the other side,

was no longer afraid.
The white tarantula denies it came out of my heart.
When I reach for it in my room,
its absence tells me it is back in my blood.

The White Tree

The white tree grew at my window.
One night, I heard someone climb its branches.
When I went to look, a white shadow crossed
itself, then disappeared.
In two days, the white tree died.
The first night of its decay, I could not sleep.
The white tree shed its light.
When I sat up in bed, its leaves were singing
and changing color in the air.

The White Hair

I found the white hair sticking to my shirt.
When I plucked it between two fingers,
I saw it was the hair that grew on my head.
I found the white hair was twisted, tiny knots
bending its fiber like a line on a map.
I found the white hair and thought she was gone.
When I looked in the mirror, my entire head was white.
I dropped the white hair in surprise.
It disappeared as it hit the floor.
When I looked in the mirror, my entire head was black.

The White Guitar

The white guitar was stolen from my closet.
When I found it was gone, music came through the walls.
The white guitar had twelve strings,
given to me by my father before he died.
I played it only once, the day before he left,
but I hid the guitar in the closet for years.
Then, it was stolen from my house.
When I open the doors, I hear the strumming
and there is a song.

The White Fountain

The white fountain sprays a mist over the streets.
Shoots higher, and all is cold.
The white fountain collects coins and wets the dog,
soaks me when I walk.
The white fountain blinds me when I pause,
water rising from the thirst for love.
The white fountain is a cloud that cleans me,
freezes in midair when I have a name.

The White Room

I found it in my forty-sixth year.
The white room opened and shared its furniture.
When I entered, I found a huge bed
the size of desire.
The white room was empty, but kept me.
When I sat in the white chair, I thought of plants.
When I lay on the cold bed, I had no words.
The white room kept me forty-six years.
When I rose to leave, I had no ideas.
When I touched the doorknob, the windows opened.

The White Sirens

The white sirens called when the city burned.
They shattered my ears and gave me hope.
I walked the streets and saw black buildings.
The white sirens shrieked with hope.
I hid in the alleys and waited for smoke.
The white sirens showed me the way.
When they rose in a deafening sword,
I found the shoe in the trash can.
The white sirens drove me out of town.
When I listened, all I heard was the wailing,
the cry to look up at the radiating sky.

The White Cars

The white cars followed me into September.
They were everywhere like crickets.

When I hid in the barrio, headlights danced.
When I crossed the street, I was the traffic.
The white cars were full of gasoline.
They waited at intersections, engines thriving.
When I thought of waving one down, I cried.
The white cars followed me into the world.
When I recognized one driver, he was my father,
age twenty, returning from the U.S. Navy.

The White Streets

The white streets have no home.
I walk them in search of fame,
find nothing but white dirt in my socks.
Signs on street corners spell God in Spanish.
The white streets have no lanes,
lead to the desert,
but the desert is no longer there.
I watch boys fight on asphalt and let them pass.
I cross and cross and never get lost.
The white streets have no seasons.
I return from white dunes and am touched.
I return on them and no one knows
I am greeted by a glowing, white cross.

Lifted White

They told me to lift my head and watch
the sun kiss the radiating century goodbye.
I lifted my soul instead and was blinded
by the flash my spirit released.
They told me to let go of my past
so I could see how many miracles
I could find in the fever of loneliness.
I gave them my history instead,
was blessed with knowing how many years
it would take to say, "I am no longer afraid."
They told me to embrace the child
On either side of my path, listen
to their weeping as if it was my own.
I told them to sing, instead,

gave them years to finish their songs.
When they let go of my hands,
I was too old to understand.
Thinking the century was over,
I lay down to die.
When I opened my eyes,
I was still there and saw
The white light was one god
with one hand, pulsing his defiant veins.

The Composition of Landscape: Gonzalez on Place and Imagination

When a poet looks back at old poems, recurring words and images remind him that he has taken a great journey. Deserts, mountains, and rivers surround the poems, but it is the composition of landscapes that reveals how far the poet has truly gone. A poet of the desert can never leave the harsh terrain behind, yet each new poem set in the Southwest is an exploration of familiar territory in search of previously unexplored terrain. Over several decades of writing, poetic desire and revelation offer the poet a chance to move away from his origins. Attempts at fresh poems or different approaches to common subjects may give the poet breathing room to experiment with imagery, tone, and syntax, but the makeup of ancestral landscape, deeply rooted in the biographical origins of the poet, will draw him back to write about things closest to him.

"Kiva Floor at Abo" is a poem about the magnet of history and the phantoms of lost time. When the speaker enters the ruins and risks spiritual annihilation by going down into the ceremonial cave, previous attempts to write about ancestry are finally successful in drawing him into the earth. His discoveries underground, and the visions of ancient life intact on the walls, force the process of poetic union to get underway. But, history also stands as a barrier because a poet can't romanticize a visit to ancient ruins. As a native of the area, he knows he must acknowledge the sacred spaces of the desert, while he is there to take from the past.

"Writing a poem like 'Kiva Floor at Abo' involved compiling a list of words that allowed the mystery and the stillness of the place to emerge. . . . [This] list was longer than the poem itself, but had to be used because the strangeness of the place and the weight of the desert demanded these kinds of entries toward a new poem."

Writing a poem like "Kiva Floor at Abo" involved compiling a list of words that allowed the mystery and the stillness of the place to emerge. Images like "red walls," "wooden ladder," and "blue fly" resonate with the challenge of ancient time and ceremony as they serve to implant the speaker right into the ground. The list was longer than the poem itself, but had to be used because the strangeness of the place and the weight of the desert demanded these kinds of entries toward a new poem. One way to encounter or weave a poem out of such images is to ask questions—the asking itself becoming an entrance into dark, confined spaces. "What do I know in my confusion?" and "Do I know where to kneel and dig" become reminders to the speaker that his quest is a lone one while, at the same time, it is poetic involvement toward the communal past of ancestry.

These questions can only be answered by the poet describing the visit to the kiva as a very physical process that yields answers once the poet works with his list of images and his subterranean examination. As the poem proceeds, it follows the speaker into tight quarters where the breathing presence of the body must realign itself with centuries of lost time. To describe the individual descending into the darkness is to take lists of words and images and reconstruct what happened. This may be a common approach in many poems, but the environment of sacrificial and ceremonial acts insists upon a different kind of poetic building. The composition of landscape means the poet gives in to the physical earth and to invisible forces that weave the poem for him. The speaker remains in the poem and winds up in ultimate revelation at its end, but "Kiva Floor at Abo" is also an exercise in allowing environment to draw from the poet's notebook, instead of the subjective choices the poet might normally make in bringing his emotions, insights, and insecurities to the poem. The kiva itself, as a black hole of sacrifice and redemption, writes the poem. Not every poet attempting to reconstruct his or her past will have such powerful settings for poems, of course. Yet, the gathering of a poetic voice and the arrangement of work over decades has to involve a determined search for sites of composition beyond the normal. Once a poet is willing to look into geographical, familial, or personal dramas in a variety of ways, a body of triumphant writing will emerge because the poetic character of what the poet writes about will no longer be taken for granted. Rebuilding, rewording, and reconstructing where the writer came from is a manner of honoring the landscape of origins by yielding to its composition. The lesson here centers around any poet, regardless of background or experience, challenging the possibilities of poetry by writing about home and going beyond mere description to create a poem where the dilemma of familiar landscapes is made new.

Reenactment is a challenge because the writer must use memory, visual recollection, and intense tone and setting to write the poem. What do I know in my confusion? I know "ancient red walls smothering something I was taught long ago." The poet has to describe what it is like to violate sacred spaces because of the need to go back to his origins and give thanks. He has to ask questions in the poem, in order to buy time to think, to examine, and to be in the earth. Most important of all, the poet can never leave this kind of poem. Even at the end, when everything is revealed and the round room of centuries remains, the poet as creator must stay there beyond the eclipse. This is another way of saying that to write this kind of poem is to be aware of how the composition of landscape is a magnetic force that dictates subject, tone, diction, and sense of time. "Kiva Floor at Abo" suggests to any poet that personal immersion and deep concentration on the self is necessary to write about those things that were learned in ancient times.

It is also a poem that challenges the writer to combine this real space of time with the trapped surrealism of the past. This means finding "the galaxy embedded in these old bricks," along with surrendering to the "shadows moving to the other side of the eclipse?" By describing what it is like to explore old ruins and imagining their dark secrets revealing themselves during the visit, the poet has fused everyday language and perception with mystical and spiritual awareness of his past.

Looking back on decades of poetry about the Southwest desert means taking a long view at the erosion of landscape and its replacement with poetic involvement. To stay in the kiva means to stay in the desert, though the writer left it years ago. Regathering poems from the past is also a reminder that any composition of landscape, resulting in a poem, is a mature signal the poet has approached a lifetime of writing poems in manners that rely on the natural curiosities of the writer, while they surrender to the nature of his past and his need to honor that history through poetry.

Writing Suggestions

1. Write your own "Kiva Floor at Abo" poem, which describes what it's like to explore a specific place/environment and imagine its dark secrets revealing themselves during your exploration. As Gonzalez does, try to fuse everyday language and perception with a mystical and spiritual awareness of his past. Feel free to let the poem become surreal, dreamlike.

2. Write an occasional poem for a holiday, a relative's birthday, or any upcoming occasion of celebration. Dylan Thomas wrote poems for his own birthdays. Maya Angelou and Miller Williams were each commissioned to write a poem for the inaugurations of President Bill Clinton. Many Romantic and Victorian writers wrote coronation poems. Ancient Chinese poetry (the work of Li Po, Tu Fu, and many others) is full of occasional verse. Though sometimes spoken of derogatively, the occasional poem has a rich tradition—try your hand at a poem that celebrates some happening, large, or small. Is it difficult writing a poem "occasioned" by something external?

3. Take a poem draft of yours that you'd like to improve upon, and try this: take every substantive noun and replace it with the seventh noun after it in the dictionary. The results depend upon the dictionary and the accuracy of noun-counting and are sometimes quite surprising. Does an unexpected word give new (more?) meaning to the line? To the stanza or entire poem? Discard those new words that don't fit your vision of the poem, but keep those that challenge you or work against your expectations. Revise accordingly.

4. Since Plato threw out the poets in his utopian Republic, it's been the aim of many poets and poetry fans throughout time to write defenses on why poetry matters. Using the Internet, find the original texts to one or more of the four major defenses of poetry: Wordsworth's "Preface to *Lyrical Ballads,*" Coleridge's *Biographia Literaria,* Shelley's *The Defence of Poetry,* and Keats's

letters. What sort of arguments are these writers making? Try your hand at a defense of poetry, an explanation of its meaning and relevance in your life, as well as in the lives of others. Another way of asking this question might be: Why write poetry at all?

"It pleases me always to endanger whatever form I'm working in. I've written very few sonnets, but when I work in the sonnet, I try to threaten the form, expressively."

—Richard Wilbur

Bob Hicok

Other Lives and Dimensions and Finally a Love Poem

My left hand will live longer than my right. The rivers
of my palms tell me so.
Never argue with rivers. Never expect your lives to finish
at the same time. I think

praying, I think clapping is how hands mourn. I think
staying up and waiting
for paintings to sigh is science. In another dimension this
is exactly what's happening,

it's what they write grants about: the chromodynamics
of mournful Whistlers,
the audible sorrow and beta decay of *Old Battersea Bridge*.
I like the idea of different

theres and elsewheres, an Idaho known for bluegrass,
a Bronx where people talk
like violets smell. Perhaps I am somewhere patient, somehow
kind, perhaps in the nook

of a cousin universe I've never defiled or betrayed
anyone. Here I have
two hands and they are vanishing, the hollow of your back
to rest my cheek against,

your voice and little else but my assiduous fear to cherish.
My hands are webbed
like the wind-torn work of a spider, like they squeezed
something in the womb

but couldn't hang on. One of those other worlds
or a life I felt
passing through mine, or the ocean inside my mother's belly
she had to scream out.

Here, when I say *I never want to be without you*,
somewhere else I am saying
I never want to be without you again. And when I touch you
in each of the places we meet,

in all of the lives we are, it's with hands that are dying
and resurrected,
When I don't touch you it's a mistake in any life,
in each place and forever.

Radical Neck

A match beaten by frail wind lights the cave
of his hands, lines that jump like the ibex
of Cosquer in the rippling glow of a torch,
the hunting-magic of vanished men. Smoke
weaves through his lungs into blood, ghost
of plants, of the earth returning to his body.
One Camel down, nineteen to go. Another image:
on the train to St. Louis when windows still
opened: when men wore hats like boys now aspire
to tattoos: one hand on his hip, the other
swinging a smoke back and forth, a small
rhythm falling inside the generous rhythm
of the train. He turned and smiled at my mother,
pointed to a red barn falling down, being
absorbed by the horizon. He stood almost
the whole way, giving his glance to the distance,
and returned to our seats larger, puffed
as if he'd become part of land's green wish.

"The skull had a tongue in it, and could sing
once."

Always the question of how to address the dead.
Dear sir. Beloved though rotted man. You

who dwell in the scented couch, fabric of walls.
Yet my father remains exact in what he says,

each communiqué encoded in action, something
he did, as if he returns through what I recall.

Visitations, translucent frames, his arms arcing
toward a block of wood, the ax bold in appetite:

the bow his hands made tying shoes, always left
then right, a celestial order: wrist-snap of Zippo

top, the crisp click into place like the settling
of doubt, his fingerprints on the metal case

proof he'd mastered the prophecy of fire. His
advantage: forever happy in these things:

or precisely morose: or bent toward a river's
"slow and mile-consuming clatter" with a face

washed of need or edge, the only moment I saw him
absolved of himself. A crystal will only form

around a speck, an imperfection: in a rush a world
arises, encloses, becomes. Like this he comforts,

intrudes, a twin voice in a restaurant invokes his face,
then slides his laugh and fetid breath into place,

and for a second nothing lives that isn't him:
I've no recourse but to pursue: yet he's done with me.

Radical
neck:
dissection and removal of jaw, lymph nodes, tongue.

At the VA they called them half-heads, chop-blocks.

I visited intending to stare like a child,
to covet his words, by then muted by phlegm,
the esophageal churnings of an aborted throat.

But I looked in bursts, seconds before I'd turn
to Williams Pond or the far copse of alders,
hoping wind was caught in the water, in the hair
of trees, that robin or rose would hover as excuse,
a glory requiring my eyes.

No one came close, even staff strayed until
it was time to wheel him in.

All the while he smoked, plumes escaping the tube,
all love given that pursuit, a reflex gone deeper
than life.

As a child I loved the smoke because it adored him, clung
to, stroked his face, filled the Valiant with an animal
made of endless shapes. And the packs themselves, smell
of tobacco new, unlit, the music Raleigh, Chesterfield,
Lark, ashtrays shaped as buddhas, crowns and spaceships.
The cough was always there, his second voice, and when
wasn't someone asking him to stop, my mother, then me,
then doctors holding his clubbed fingers, explaining
a man shouldn't pass out getting dressed. The smoke clung,
became his skin. When asked what I wanted done I said
burn him, make him ash: my revenge: his only wish.

To Err is Humid
for D.

Long ago we sat on a lake.
He said errata sounds erotic,
I get excited by mistakes.
Snow was falling in a lonely
way, many feet between flakes.

What if by accident two
fell the same, would the sky
be ashamed? This was another
thing one of us said or meant
to say. Maybe if I'd looked
with a lantern into his eyes
I'd have seen the little man
digging a grave. It's not
so hard to walk on water
he said as we left
the frozen lake. Actually
he shuffled, watching him
I knew how a deck of cards
would walk. In spring,
robins and daffodils bloomed.
I don't think he meant
to kill his ear, it just got
between the gun and his brain.

Process of Elimination

For 71 days I've tried to write about Eichmann
shitting. At no time did this preoccupation
threaten national defense. This is my first
excretory obsession, I wasn't one of those kids
who fish out their little creation,
their sunken boat, and hold it up for mamma
like a cat delivering the trophy of a mouse.
I blame a book. I blame Gutenberg because
moveable type made it possible for Eichmann's
captor to convey over time and distance
characteristics of the man more compelling
than rain and beta-carotene and the plaster
cracking beneath my living-room window,
leaving a hole that would otherwise
be an adorable fixation were it not
for pages 199 to 201 of "Eichmann In My Hands".
This is where Malkin says Eichmann was a very
bad boy who wouldn't eat or move or defecate
until ordered, until his body was returned
to its niche in the chain-of-command, a grid

that braces the stars and provided
all the hands needed to salute the vanishing
of the Jews. This is where the narrative
suddenly turns into a frat movie, Eichmann
in the stall with pajamas at his ankles, asking
May I begin?,
apologizing after each seismic fart, screaming
Entschuldigen Sie, Entschuldigen Sie, convinced
the mingled crimes of gas and constipation
require contrition, an apology for the stench
and frenzy he's introduced to the human sphere.
Over the course of 71 days I've deleted
thousands of words from this poem, some little
sentences but most long as freight trains,
most striving to list the terrible things
Eichmann did in a way that doesn't sound
like William Conrad or George Kennedy
narrating a PBS documentary, their heads
under water, their heads locked in a vault
to ensure the deep resonance required
when saying *Belsen, zyklon-B, bodies stacked*
like cord-wood. After decades this basso
profundo approach deafens like an all-drum
garage band, like a roof made of hubcaps
terrorized by rain. So I've decided to let Z
represent the quantity of suffering Eichmann
added to the world and admit the quality
of this suffering can't be understood,
an impossibility reminiscent of the koan
about the sound of one hand clapping
except the hand's been cut off and sleeps
in a pile with other hands. So I've decided
to tell a little joke: what happens
to an agent of the Mossad when an Ober-
sturmführer asks permission to wipe?
The short answer's tears of laughter
and his body doubled over into question mark.
But if you believe short answers, Pi stops
as 3.14 and Neanderthals had big brains
but were really dumb and Bill Thompson's
smile as he beat me with the banana seat
of his Stingray bike is only relevant

in another poem in a galaxy far, far away.
The longer answer ends with Malkin's revelation
some months later, when eating a fig
he realized Eichmann had asked forgiveness
for the sound and smell, for what his body
had to do, but that even with the zero
of the noose closing around his neck,
he'd only apologized for the shit,
for the need and nothing else.

Bottom of the Ocean

At least once you should live with someone
more medicated than yourself. A tall man,
he closed his eyes before he spoke,
stocked groceries at night and heard voices.
We were eating cereal the first time,
Cream of Wheat. He said that she said
we're all our of evers without explaining
who she was or how many evers we had
to begin with or where they were kept.
I slept with an extra blanket that night.
This was strange but that year
I had to read Plato for a grade,
each circle's the bastard child
of a perfect O I remember he said,
and Kierkegaard I thought was writing stand-up
with *the self is a relation which relates*
itself to its own self but my roommate
nodded as I read this aloud, he'd stood
so long before carnival mirrors
that the idea of a face being a reflection
of a reflection of itself was common sense.
On the calendar the strip tease of months,
dust quietly gathering on the shoulders
of older dust and because he'd not taken
the microwave apart and strapped its heart
to his head or talked to the 60 watt bulb
on the porch he thought he was better
and flushed his pills. Soon he was back
where windows are mesh and what's sharp

is banished and what can be thrown
is attached so unless you can lift
the whole building everyone is safe.
We had lunch a year later. Or
he spun the creamer and wore skin
made of glass while I ate a sandwich
and by that I mean I was hungry
and he was sealed in amber, a caul
of drugs meant to withstand ants and fire
nor did his mouth work but to hold words in.
I'd wanted to know all that time what happened
to our evers, to ask if he remembered
what he said and explain to him
he was an oracle that day, I wanted him
to tell me about the woman who whispered
or screamed that our chances were up
because the phrase had stayed in my life
as a command to survive myself.
That was the day I learned you can sit
with someone who's on the bottom
of the ocean and not get wet.
By the time he said things were good
he'd poured twelve sugars into a coffee
he never touched.

The Wish

On a Tuesday I learned I'd never sit
with my father on a curb and chuck
stones. Does it seem at times
the life you want runs to your left
and parallel to your own? I thought
we'd be planting a tree one day
and he'd stop, put down
his shovel and truculence
and ask some useless thing,
did I ever think of counting
the leaves on a maple or wonder
why it's easier to cry alone
in a car? We speak of parts
of ourselves and in some

unnamed place I'd decided
this was inevitable, that he
would soften into human form
as we watched a river
empty itself into its own mouth.
He'd not know what to say or do
and this would be fine, would be
what the sky wanted of him,
and we'd breathe, we'd move
our hands and feet and forget
we were father and son standing
at the hem of a river, until
one of us came back into our body
and said *I'm sorry, what*
were you saying? On a Tuesday
at his kitchen table I learned
from his eyes this would never
happen. There will always
be work, always fear and the need
to make the soul
small and impenetrable,
to be hard enough to get
the job done. Learned
that if I speak the truth
at his grave I'll be allowed
one phrase, that I have
no idea who this man was.

Hicok on Getting Out of Your Poem's Way

I chose these poems because they interest me now. Another day and I may well have selected other poems. This reminds me of the surprise of writing, how the context of any one session at my desk determines so much of what happens. Change by a day or hour and I'd write something different. If I saw a movie the night before I'll write a different poem than if I visited my family. When I'm writing well I believe I respond to the swim of impulses, the mix of memory and will and thought, that I make the things telling me they belong together fit. The debate between inspiration and work is yet another conversation we don't need to have. It's both. I think you sit down every chance you get and if you're living an active life, active personally, mentally, socially, if you're—and pardon me for saying this—if you're engaged, then there's no end of inspiration and if there's no end of inspiration there's no end of work.

"When I'm writing well I believe I respond to the swim of impulses, the mix of memory and will and thought, that I make the things telling me they belong together fit."

I like the poem "Other Lives and Dimensions and Finally a Love Poem" because love isn't verbal and the poem is sensible nonsense. "Radical Neck" is made up entirely. It came about when someone described to me what can happen to smokers. "To Err is Humid" occurred to me when someone on a frozen lake said we were walking on water. "Process of Elimination" is all about my surprise that a man capable of such evil could be governed by his bowel movements. "Bottom of the Ocean" is loosely about someone I shared an apartment with. Though he did go off his meds, the specifics are made up. It's one of those poems which has everything to do with wondering what happened to someone, in this case a very nice man who couldn't handle being alive. I've included "The Wish" because it's the poem I wrote today and because it's the closest I've come to expressing my disappointment that my father hasn't softened into a man capable of simple human interaction.

I've also included this poem because it's a good example of how I write. My habit is to move no further if I don't like everything that's come so far. Typically I write three to five lines, until I feel a sense of momentum and integrity, by which I mean that I have something which is compelling and holds together. By this point the poem does or doesn't have a motor. I read back and change what I must and only then move on to the next line or group of lines. When these are done, I read the entire poem and fix whatever needs to be fixed. In this manner I advance, perhaps altering line breaks, words, whole lines, sometimes changing the structure completely because of the rhythm the poem is developing or because a longer or shorter line will carry the poem's content or language better. By the last line, if I still believe in the poem, there's almost no editing to be done.

"The Wish" would be considered a first draft because it's the product of this morning's efforts. But the poem is done. I believe in it now and am quite certain that won't change. What I like about the method I've evolved is that it brings editing (work) and writing (inspiration) together and treats them equally. It also requires that, to the extent I'm able, I say what's on my mind now. In *Butch Cassidy and the Sundance Kid,* there's a point where the Kid/Redford asks if he can move when he shoots the little piece of wood he's been asked to peg to prove he's a good shot. Only when he moves can he hit the target. I've worked hard to get to the point where I can sit down, say what's on my mind, and move on. I enjoy the challenge, even enjoy that, as in each of these poems, I'll end up saying things I don't like, which make me uncomfortable, either stylistically or in terms of content, but they fit and have proven over successive readings that they belong, that they make sense to the poem. There's a line in "Other Lives and Dimensions and Finally a Love Poem" that makes me squirm. It offends my sense of where strange ends and silly begins. At a reading not long ago, a woman came up to tell me how much she liked the poem and to ask about that line. She hated it at first and tried to change it or take it out of the poem, as I had, but found the poem felt broken without it. I'm happiest when a poem feels like a conversation, like something that could happen only once. The greatest fun in writing is learning to accept on any given day what that conversation is, and how to lead it while not getting in its way.

> *"I'm happiest when a poem feels like a conversation, like something that could happen only once."*

Writing Suggestions

1. As Hicok does in "Bottom of the Ocean," take a person from your past (a fifth-grade teacher, an old childhood pal, the ex-cop next door, the neighbor who's militant about maintaining his lawn) and imagine the story of their life beyond what you know of it. Tell it from their own voice, or perhaps from a narrator who can expose that story for all its wonderful intricacies and ironies. Let specific, significant details mean more than the "story" itself. Let your imagination roam free.

2. As in "To Err is Humid," think about a simple everyday experience that you've observed and write a short poem in response. Use only simple words and images, and let the power of the poem come from nuance and suggestion. Remember that silence and blank spaces are important components of poetry.

3. The next poem you start to write, stop after three to five lines. Do you feel a sense of momentum and integrity? Is what you've already written compelling? Does it hold together? Does it have its own motor? If not, try a new three to five lines and see where you're at then. Try Hicok's technique a few times and see if it works for you. Not every idea or technique or style will work equally well for everyone, but make your decisions out of knowledge, not ignorance (i.e. try many ways before you decide which way is "best").

4. Take a moment and decide on a figure from Greek mythology that you know a little about, either Oedipus, Theseus, Apollo, or Medusa. For five minutes, jot down everything that comes to mind when you think about that figure. Don't worry about grammar or spelling—just get as much down as you can as quickly as you can. After five minutes, go back over your list and mark the phrases or words that leap out at you. Taking a bit more time, write out more elaborate, detailed responses to each word or phrase you marked. Next, pick one (or more) of these chunks of writing and start to craft that into a poem. Experiment with stanza and line structure. Add ideas, thoughts, images, and sensory details until you have a poem you like. Feel free at this point to leaf through a reference book or use the Internet for verisimilitude. (Variation: Select a historical figure and follow the same process to a poem.)

"Lucky accidents seldom happen to writers who don't work. You will find that you rewrite a poem and it never seems quite right. Then a much better poem may come rather fast and you wonder why you bothered with all that work on the earlier poem. Actually, the hard work you do on one poem is put in on all poems. The work on the first poem is responsible for the sudden ease of the second. If you just sit around waiting for the easy ones, nothing will come of it."

—Richard Hugo

Jane Hirshfield

For What Binds Us

There are names for what binds us:
strong forces, weak forces.
Look around, you can see them:
the skin that forms in a half-empty cup,
nails rusting into the places they join,
joints dovetailed on their own weight.
The way things stay so solidly
wherever they've been set down—
and gravity, scientists say, is weak.

And see how the flesh grows back
across a wound, with a great vehemence,
more strong
than the simple, untested surface before.
There's a name for it on horses,
when it comes back darker and raised: proud flesh,

as all flesh
is proud of its wounds, wears them
as honors given out after battle,
small triumphs pinned to the chest—

And when two people have loved each other
see how it is like a
scar between their bodies,
stronger, darker, and proud;
how the black cord makes of them a single fabric
that nothing can tear or mend.

The Love of Aged Horses

Because I know tomorrow
his faithful gelding heart will be broken
when the spotted mare is trailered and driven away,
I come today to take him for a gallop on Diaz ridge.

Returning, he will whinny for his love.
Ancient, spavined,
her white parts red with hill-dust,
her red parts whitened with the same, she never answers.

But today, when I turn him loose at the bent gate
with the taste of chewed oat on his tongue
and the saddle-sweat rinsed off with water,
I know he will canter, however tired,
whinnying wildly up the ridge's near side,
and I know he will find her.

He will be filled with the sureness of horses
whose bellies are grain-filled,
whose long-ribbed loneliness
can be scratched into no-longer-lonely.

His long teeth on her withers,
her rough-coated spots will grow damp and wild.
Her long teeth on his withers,
his oiled-teakwood smoothness will grow damp and wild.
Their shadows' chiasmus will fleck and fill with flies,
the eight marks of their fortune stamp and then cancel the earth.
From ear-flick to tail-switch, they stand in one body.
No luck is as boundless as theirs.

The Weighing

The heart's reasons
seen clearly,
even the hardest
will carry
its whip-marks and sadness
and must be forgiven.

As the drought-starved
eland forgives
the drought-starved lion
who finally takes her,
enters willingly then
the life she cannot refuse,
and is lion, is fed,
and does not remember the other.

So few grains of happiness
measured against all the dark
and still the scales balance.

The world asks of us
only the strength we have and we give it.
Then it asks more, and we give it.

Three Foxes by the Edge of the Field at Twilight

One ran,
her nose to the ground,
a rusty shadow
neither hunting nor playing.

One stood; sat; lay down; stood again.

One never moved,
except to turn her head a little as we walked.

Finally we drew too close,
and they vanished.
The woods took them back as if they had never been.

I wish I had thought to put my face to the grass.

But we kept walking,
speaking as strangers do when becoming friends.

There is more and more I tell no one,
strangers nor loves.

This slips into the heart
without hurry, as if it had never been.

And yet, among the trees, something has changed.

Something looks back from the trees,
and knows me for who I am.

The Poet

She is working now, in a room
not unlike this one,
the one where I write, or you read.
Her table is covered with paper.
The light of the lamp would be
tempered by a shade, where the bulb's
single harshness might dissolve,
but it is not, she has taken it off.
Her poems? I will never know them,
though they are the ones I most need.
Even the alphabet she writes in
I cannot decipher. Her chair—
Let us imagine whether it is leather
or canvas, vinyl or wicker. Let her
have a chair, her shadeless lamp,
the table. Let one or two she loves
be in the next room. Let the door
be closed, the sleeping ones healthy.
Let her have time, and silence,
enough paper to make mistakes and go on.

In Praise of Coldness

"If you wish to move your reader,"
Chekhov wrote, "you must write more coldly."

Herakleitos recommended, "A dry soul is best."

And so at the center of many great works
is found a preserving dispassion,

like the vanishing point of quattrocento perspective,
or the tiny packets of desiccant enclosed
in a box of new shoes or seeds.

But still the vanishing point
is not the painting,
the silica is not the blossoming plant.

Chekhov, dying, read the timetables of trains.
To what more earthly thing could he have been faithful?—
Scent of rocking distances,
smoke of blue trees out the window,
hampers of bread, pickled cabbage, boiled meat.

Scent of the knowable journey.

Neither a person entirely broken
nor one entirely whole can speak.

In sorrow, pretend to be fearless. In happiness, tremble.

Tree

It is foolish
to let a young redwood
grow next to a house.

Even in this
one lifetime,
you will have to choose.

That great calm being,
this clutter of soup pots and books—

Already the first branch-tips brush at the window.
Softly, calmly, immensity taps at your life.

The Envoy

One day in that room, a small rat.
Two days later, a snake.

Who, seeing me enter,
whipped the long stripe of his
body under the bed,
then curled like a docile house-pet.

I don't know how either came or left.
Later, the flashlight found nothing.

For a year I watched
as something—terror? happiness? grief?—
entered and then left my body.

Not knowing how it came in,
Not knowing how it went out.

It hung where words could not reach it.
It slept where light could not go.
Its scent was neither snake nor rat,
neither sensualist nor ascetic.

There are openings in our lives
of which we know nothing.

Through them
the belled herds travel at will,
long-legged and thirsty, covered with foreign dust.

Hirshfield on Mysterious Making, Revision as Instruction, and the Hunt for a Way to Go On

The earliest of these poems was written in 1982, the most recent in the year 2000. Selecting them was no simple process—how can a poet decide which few of her poems are the "best"? A poem is fitted to its circumstances and its moment as an iron shoe is fitted to the living hoof of a horse. The poem that speaks toward a time of darkness and bewilderment cannot be set for any useful comparison beside the poem that emerges when eros breaks into a life as fiercely and delicately as a seed's first leaves through spring ground. A glass shatters; a bow is drawn across the strings of a cello; neither sound is "best," each is only the music of what it is. Still, I was asked to choose. And so I have chosen a range of poems that have retained for me, and perhaps for others, the ability to reawaken and sustain some particular moment's complex meaning in a life.

"A poem is fitted to its circumstances and its moment as an iron shoe is fitted to the living hoof of a horse . . . A glass shatters; a bow is drawn across the strings of a cello; neither sound is 'best,' each is only the music of what it is."

"For What Binds Us" is the earliest of my poems that I still regularly give at public readings, the one with which I most often begin. It somehow steadies me and seats me in who I am; as poet, as person. Its themes of transience and loss; of interconnection and abidance; of how a person goes on, somehow, no matter what, have stayed in my work. Its images drawn from the earth, science, carpentry, horseflesh, the bodies and psyches of lovers, a cup—these seem also abiding terrain. The poem, like most of my work, is not narrative per se, but writes of the inner life by describing the outer. "Look," it requests of its reader, and makes a promise that if you do, you will see what it sees, feel what it feels. This is as good a description as any of the process by which certain kinds of lyric poems carry experience from one person into another.

"For What Binds Us" was written in one breath—it arrived at four in the morning and woke me while already speaking itself. A person cannot speak much of "craft" under those circumstances, except to the degree that craft is pressed into the psyche over a lifetime of reading and writing poems. An experiment: try writing a dozen or fourteen lines of iambic pentameter three times a day and see how quickly you will find yourself thinking iambic pentameter, sleeping iambic pentameter. Even in free verse, the same principle applies—practice of shapeliness and music and rhetoric enters the marrow. And then when the time comes that a poem awakens a writer during a lightless hour, they are there, holding the psyche, permitting the transformation between raw and overwhelming grief and the grief that becomes a poem by being caught in craft-amber, in the lasting sap of the heart-flood.

Even the line breaks came, as I recall it anyways, at first writing. This baffles. How, in the last stanza, does the pen know, before the mind knows, that when it writes "see how it is like a/scar between their bodies" that the noun following the article will be "scar," that the line break will mirror the same interruption of the seamless that a scar is, that the end of a relationship is? In general, I do not like the use of a line break following an "a" or a "the"—I find it tricky, overly visible, a gimmick to be avoided. Yet I have often found that whatever rules of writing one subscribes to, one finds oneself eventually breaking. The needs of a poem are more pressing than our ideas of what a poem should be.

"I have often found that whatever rules of writing one subscribes to, one finds oneself eventually breaking. The needs of a poem are more pressing than our ideas of what a poem should be."

Whether over a period of months or in one sitting, none of my poems escape the question of revision. In this poem I do remember changing one phrase, first one way, then another, innumerable times—the order of the final three words. When the poem was first published in *The American Poetry Review,* the order was not as it appears in its eventual book-published form, and here. Rather, the poem ended with the line, "that nothing can mend or tear." A far more optimistic statement, which in the end I decided against, in favor of the darker reverse: "tear or mend." In the end, I knew that the fracturing of my life the poem described was not a thing that could ever be patched or smoothed over. The poem ostensibly holds both terms in equal balance, either way. Yet the order—whether unmendability or untearability has the final say—makes an immense difference to the feeling one takes from the statement. Such a decision is not made by "craft" sense though; it is a matter of life.

This is the real matter of revision, and the deep instruction—as satisfying as the first writing—that revision can bring. During the process of "reseeing" a poem, the writer tests the words the initial writing has placed on the page against many things: intellectual knowledge, aesthetic attunement, the musics of ear and breath and heart, alertness to grammar, and also to his or her most deeply considered inward response to those words. Plato banned poets from his ideal Republic because he feared the powerful entrancement of beauty might overwhelm truth, and this can happen even to a poem's writer. When I was in my early twenties, I saw this happen one day in my own work: looking for an ending for a hard-to-end poem, I found one that brought a deeply satisfying closure—then realized that what the poem said was not in fact anything I believed. The moment shocked me, and also raised in me a vow to be alert in the future to a risk I had not until then even realized existed.

The second poem I have chosen, "The Love of Aged Horses," stands in this group as an example of a poem that looks entirely outward, at the imminent separation of a pair of old horses. For me, it holds two things. One is exactly what it appears to hold—the poem emerged from an actual event, an actual day—and that story, in itself, is sufficient. Yet there is also an under-meaning, not consciously in my thoughts as I wrote and yet unmistakably part of why I wrote, why this event and not some other made itself into a poem—the human correspondence and relationship to the event. How the inevitability of the horses' separation is the inevitability of our own, and also how different the experience of horses is in the face of that inevitability, as creatures neither graced nor cursed with the knowledge of time or future.

"The Weighing" is here for two reasons. The first is that it was for me a pivotal poem, the start of what would become a long series of works in which the words "the heart" would figure. Never "my" heart, always "the"—a difference that matters immensely, as small differences between articles and pronouns so often do. The second is that the poem's statement and meaning continue to affect how I move through the world. At the time this poem came to me, I needed its help, its reminder, to navigate a time of difficulty. I still draw from that well, and so the poem is here.

"Three Foxes by the Edge of the Field at Twilight" is another poem that began in the outer events it reports—a walk, a friend, actual foxes. In this case the poem moves from that locus into a parallel, overt account of the inner response it evoked. Unlike "The Love of Aged Horses," the poem knew its own resonances at least in part consciously. It also confesses a thing that still gives me pause, not because it is not the truth, but because it is a truth difficult to admit outright: "There is more and more I tell no one." The sentence is a self-contradiction, already revealing too much, and goes to the heart of the dilemma that exists for any writer who is by nature private rather than confessional. "It is a joy to be hidden, but a disaster not to be found," wrote the British psychologist D. W. Winnicott. Yet what of the hidden life in each of us that needs to stay hidden, protected by pelt or silence or interior darkness? For that, there is the witness of the onlooking foxes, who have themselves moved from the visible into the invisible realms.

"The Poet" is the poem in this group that includes, however subtly perhaps, the realm of the political, as well as addressing directly the making of art. The poem can be read two ways—as about a figure seemingly the Muse, or as about an imagined actual writer at work unknown and impoverished in a country so "minor" she is unlikely ever to be found by the world of literature at large. Either interpretation seems to me valid, appropriate, useful in different ways. I will also note here that even now, even for me, to title a poem "The Poet" and begin with the pronoun "she" was a noticeable act, whose consequences I considered for a long time. That grammar imposes the seeming exclusion of one half of humanity or the other grieves me; yet as a woman I found it impossible in the end to choose the supposedly neutral "he" for this poem.

"In Praise of Coldness," "Tree," and "The Envoy" are each taken from my most recent collection of poems at the time this commentary is being written, *Given Sugar, Given Salt*. They are poems less easy to speak of, because more freshly made. "In Praise of Coldness" began with Chekhov's advice to his brother that appears at its start. I have quoted the sentence for years, but suddenly something in me wanted to look more directly at his proposition, to discover for myself why I have come to find it not only useful but mysteriously moving. The "answer" I have arrived at is that the sentence accomplishes its own counsel: it holds its opposite so close to the surface that it is more present than if overtly said. Who would need to write more coldly who is not at risk of being utterly overtaken by heat? Without the shadow-twin of a barely suppressed heat, coldness would move us no more than does an algebraic formula. But when both sides are present in complex embrace, the sum of passion increases: the very need for restraint (in aesthetic tension, craft-form, widened perspective, sustained contemplation) shows the passion's power. Unchecked, feeling alone is flood and chaos; checked by "coldness," human awareness becomes possible, ethics becomes possible, art becomes possible.

"Tree" is the one example here of the brief poems to be found in each of my books. American culture, with its predilection for the heroic, the grand, and the long, tends to discount whatever is small as insignificant. Yet a single haiku by Issa can have as great a compassion and enormous a grief as any English elegy. As a practitioner and admirer of the very short poem, I did not want to pass over that approach to poetry in the selection given here. Plus, it pleased me to speak of the largeness of redwoods by the tiny, delicate tapping they make even today on my window.

"American culture, with its predilection for the heroic, the grand, and the long, tends to discount whatever is small as insignificant. Yet a single haiku by Issa can have as great a compassion and enormous a grief as any English elegy."

"The Envoy" I have included because (like each of these poems, in fact) it holds for me a constellation of feeling and meaning to which I return. Like the earliest of the poems in this group, it hunts some understanding that will permit going on—in this case, agreeing to be permeable to what comes, to live willingly in the hard knowledge that we do not know what will come to us in our lives, or how it comes or goes. And having arrived at that thought in writing these notes, I suddenly can see that each of these poems, in its own way, turns its face toward that one question—how to find a way to go on in the face of change and transience, how to increase rather than narrow a life in the face of what happens over its course.

Writing Suggestions

1. Take Hirshfield's advice and write at least a dozen lines of iambic pentameter twice a day. Call it a "loose" sonnet, if that helps, but don't use rhyme or any other elements of the sonnet—focus solely on iambic pen-

tameter. See if dedication and attention to the rhythms and sound of meter affects your work on other poems. Hirshfield suggests that once you've practiced "shapeliness and music and rhetoric," it becomes part of you, it "enters the marrow." After a week of this, the next time inspiration strikes, sit down and write a sonnet. Don't think of Shakespeare or Petrarch or Elizabeth Bishop, just write. Don't worry about rhyme schemes or which stanza should contain the "turn." Just focus on the iambic pentameter. Does meter free you or constrain you? How is this different from your experiences with meter before?

2. Write a very short poem concerning an emotion. Think of a strong feeling you have had or have witnessed in another. Imagine someone (or something?) to whom the speaker of the poem would share these feelings with. Think about attitude and nuance, metaphor and innuendo. Write it fast, then put it away. A few days later revisit the poem. How accurately have you captured the emotion? What are the challenges in writing a short poem about an expansive topic?

3. Take any of Hirshfield's poems and retype it, altering the line breaks so most end with articles, such as "the," or "a." Read the poem aloud. Then read the original aloud. Is there a difference in sound? In meaning? Pace? (Variation: Take this a step further by changing the line breaks so most end with verbs. How does this alter the poem?)

4. Perform a close reading of one of Hirshfield's poems. Examine grammar carefully for ambiguities and deviations from the norm. Approach the poem in a state of paranoid schizophrenia, suspecting that *every* word is somehow related to each other. Work inductively, meaning that you don't come to the text with preconceived notions but let the language of the work itself carry you along into making connections between its internal parts. Squeeze the text for every possible meaning. What does a close reading do for you that a casual reading doesn't? Can you perform a close reading on a poem of your own? Does a close reading of one of your own poem drafts reveal problems or possibilities that you might otherwise not have seen?

*"Talk with a little luck in it, that's what poetry is—
just let the words take you where they want to go.
You'll be invited; things will happen; your life will
have more in it than other people's lives have."*

—William Stafford

David Lehman

Sestina
for Jim Cummins

In Iowa, Jim dreamed that Della Street was Anne Sexton's
twin. Dave drew a comic strip called the "Adventures of Whitman,"
about a bearded beer-guzzler in Superman uniform. Donna dressed
like Wallace Stevens
in a seersucker summer suit. To town came Ted Berrigan,
saying, "My idea of a bad poet is Marvin Bell."
But no one has won as many prizes as Philip Levine.

At the restaurant, people were talking about Philip Levine's
latest: the Pulitzer. A toast was proposed by Anne Sexton.
No one saw the stranger, who said his name was Marvin Bell,
pour something into Donna's drink. "In the Walt Whitman
Shopping Center, there you feel free," said Ted Berrigan,
pulling on a Chesterfield. Everyone laughed, except T. S. Eliot.

I asked for directions. "You turn right on Gertrude Stein,
then bear left. Three streetlights down you hang a Phil Levine
and you're there," Jim said. When I arrived I saw Ted Berrigan
with cigarette ash in his beard. Graffiti about Anne Sexton
decorated the men's room walls. Beth had brought a quart of Walt
Whitman.
Donna looked blank. "Walt who?" The name didn't ring a Marvin Bell.

You laugh, yet there is nothing inherently funny about Marvin Bell.
You cry, yet there is nothing inherently scary about Robert Lowell.
You drink a bottle of Samuel Smith's Nut Brown Ale, as thirsty as
Walt Whitman.

You bring in your car for an oil change, thinking, this place has the aura of Philip Levine.
Then you go home and write: "He kissed her Anne Sexton, and she returned the favor, caressing his Ted Berrigan."

Donna was candid. "When the spirit of Ted Berrigan
comes over me, I can't resist," she told Marvin Bell,
while he stood dejected at the xerox machine. Anne Sexton
came by to circulate the rumor that Robert Duncan
had flung his drink on a student who had called him Philip Levine.
The cop read him the riot act. "I don't care," he said, "if you're Walt Whitman."

Donna told Beth about her affair with Walt Whitman.
"He was indefatigable, but he wasn't Ted Berrigan."
The Dow Jones industrials finished higher, led by Philip Levine,
up a point and a half on strong earnings. Marvin Bell
ended the day unchanged. Analyst Richard Howard
recommended buying May Swenson and selling Anne Sexton.

In the old days, you liked either Walt Whitman or Anne Sexton,
not both. Ted Berrigan changed that just by going to a ballgame with Marianne Moore.
And one day Philip Levine looked in the mirror and saw Marvin Bell.

CORRECTIONS

An article on Feb. 25 about President Kim Young Sam of South Korea erred in identifying him as an ex-playboy who was known as the Falstaff of Seoul because of his girth, his jollity, and his appetite for vast quantities of imported beer. The article should have described him as a well-respected man about town doing the best things so conservatively. Mr. Kim's speech, in which he apologized for his "youthful indiscretions," was not, as reported, preceded by the playing of the opening bars of Wagner's Walkyre. Mr. Kim has a preference for Rossini's "Thieving Magpie Overture" for state occasions. In addition, the article mistranslated one of Mr. Kim's remarks in some editions. The President said, "I guess all young men have oats to sow," not "I was a young buck with cojones."

A related article on Feb. 27 misstated the opinion of Sam Young Park, a professor of English at Martha Washington University, who specializes in Shakespeare's history plays. Mr. Sam was reported to say that Mr. Kim's remark, as originally mistranslated, alluded to "the macho ideal as Henry V practiced it and Hemingway codified it." He said no such thing. Mr. Sam, who, contrary to published reports, has seven nephews and is bald except for a shock of white hair, said Mr. Kim's speech did not propose concrete measures for dealing with Korea's problems; he did not say that it did propose such measures.

The Personal Health Column last Wednesday, about the hazards associated with the amino acid homocysteine, gave an imprecise figure for the amount of folic acid supplement prescribed for people with elevated levels of homocysteine in the blood. The correct amount is one milligram of folic acid daily, not one milligram.

A chart on Sunday listing people who had stayed overnight in the White House during the Clinton administration incorrectly described Sam Young Park as an illegitimate son of former baseball great Slammin' Sammy Young. According to the chart, the young man changed his name to Sam Young Park in order to trick his Korean in-laws into bestowing their parental consent when the lad was wooing their daughter, Sue, an exchange student studying the amino acid homocysteine at Martha Washington University in Bethesda, Maryland. There is no evidence at all for this hysterical flight of fancy.

Because of an editing error, an obituary for the playwright Kim Chadwick appeared in yesterday's paper. Ms. Chadwick did not die in her home last Thursday. The cause of death was not pneumonia resulting in cardiac arrest. Ms. Chadwick's daughter Esther did not discover the body. Ms. Chadwick had written eleven plays, not eight. She had dropped out of Bryn Mawr, not Smith, taken up with a musician named Pablo, not a shipping tycoon named Tom, and favored quiet meditation and sewing rather than boisterous games of Trivial Pursuit. Her first marriage, to the financier Maxwell Park, did not end in divorce. Mr. Park and the couple's three daughters are not properly to be considered survivors, since Ms. Chadwick (who retained her maiden name) is still alive, though we did not know this when we published her obituary, which had to be written in advance, like all our obituaries. Nevertheless, that is no excuse, and we know it.

In Stanley Kowalski's review of Kim Chadwick's new play Wild Oats, "Let us not hear that Ms. Chadwick has proved her critics wrong" should have read "Let us note here that Ms. Chadwick has proved her critics wrong." Mea culpa.

Wittgenstein's Ladder

> *"My propositions serve as elucidations in the following way: anyone who understands them eventually recognizes them as nonsensical, when he has used them—as steps—to climb up beyond them. (He must, so to speak, throw away the ladder after he has climbed up it.)"*
> —Ludwig Wittgenstein, *Tractatus*

1.
The first time I met Wittgenstein, I was
late. "The traffic was murder," I explained.
He spent the next forty-five minutes
analyzing this sentence. Then he was silent.
I wondered why he had chosen a water tower
for our meeting. I also wondered how
I would leave, since the ladder I had used
to climb up here had fallen to the ground.

2.
Wittgenstein served as a machine-gunner
in the Austrian Army in World War I.
Before the war he studied logic in Cambridge
with Bertrand Russell. Having inherited
his father's fortune (iron and steel), he
gave away his money, not to the poor, whom
it would corrupt, but to relations so rich
it would not thus affect them.

3.
On leave in Vienna in August 1918
he assembled his notebook entries
into the *Tractatus*. Since it provided
the definitive solution to all the problems
of philosophy, he decided to broaden
his interests. He became a schoolteacher,
then a gardener's assistant at a monastery
near Vienna. He dabbled in architecture.

4.
He returned to Cambridge in 1929,
receiving his doctorate for the *Tractatus*,
"a work of genius," in G. E. Moore's opinion.

Starting in 1930 he gave a weekly lecture
and led a weekly discussion group. He spoke
without notes amid long periods of silence.
Afterwards, exhausted, he went to the movies
and sat in the front row. He liked Carmen Miranda.

5.
He would visit Russell's rooms at midnight
and pace back and forth "like a caged tiger.
On arrival, he would announce that when
he left he would commit suicide. So, in spite
of getting sleepy, I did not like to turn him out." On
such a night, after hours of dead silence, Russell said
"Wittgenstein, are you thinking about logic or about
your sins?" "Both," he said, and resumed his silence.

6.
Philosophy was an activity, not a doctrine.
"Solipsism, when its implications are followed out
strictly, coincides with pure realism," he wrote.
Dozens of dons wondered what he meant. Asked
how he knew that "this color is red," he smiled
and said, "because I have learnt English." There
were no other questions. Wittgenstein let the
silence gather. Then he said, "this itself is the answer."

7.
Religion went beyond the boundaries of language,
yet the impulse to run against "the walls of our cage,"
though "perfectly, absolutely useless," was not to be
dismissed. A. J. Ayer, one of Oxford's ablest minds,
was puzzled. If logic cannot prove a nonsensical
conclusion, why didn't Wittgenstein abandon it,
"along with the rest of metaphysics, as not worth
serious attention, except perhaps for sociologists"?

8.
Because God does not reveal himself in this world, and
"the value of this work," Wittgenstein wrote, "is that
it shows how little is achieved when these problems
are solved." When I quoted Gertrude Stein's line

about Oakland, "there's no there there," he nodded.
Was there a there, I persisted. His answer: Yes and No.
It was as impossible to feel another person's pain
as to suffer another person's toothache.

9.
At Cambridge the dons quoted him reverently.
I asked them what they thought was his biggest
contribution to philosophy. "Whereof one cannot
speak, thereof one must be silent," one said.
Others spoke of his conception of important
nonsense. But I liked best the answer John
Wisdom gave: "His asking of the question
'Can one play chess without the queen?'"

10.
Wittgenstein preferred American detective
stories to British philosophy. He liked lunch
and didn't care what it was, "so long as it was
always the same," noted Professor Malcolm
of Cornell, a former student, in whose house
in Ithaca Wittgenstein spent hours doing
handyman chores. He was happy then.
There was no need to say a word.

The Gift

> *"He gave her class. She gave him sex."*
> —Katherine Hepburn on Fred Astaire and Ginger Rogers

He gave her money. She gave him head.
He gave her tips on "aggressive growth" mutual funds. She gave him a red rose
  and a little statue of eros.
He gave her Genesis 2 (21–23). She gave him Genesis 1 (26–28).
He gave her a square peg. She gave him a round hole.
He gave her Long Beach on a late Sunday in September. She gave him zinnias
  and cosmos in the plentitude of July.
He gave her a camisole and a brooch. She gave him a cover and a break.
He gave her Venice, Florida. She gave him Rome, New York.
He gave her a false sense of security. She gave him a true sense of uncertainty.
He gave her the finger. She gave him what for.

He gave her a black eye. She gave him a divorce.
He gave her a steak for the black eye. She gave him his money back.
He gave her what she had never had before. She gave him what he had had and lost.
He gave her nastiness in children. She gave him prudery in adults.
He gave her Panic Hill. She gave him Mirror Lake.
He gave her an anthology of drum solos. She gave him the rattle of leaves in the wind.

February 10

He was no altar boy
She was no chorus girl
He couldn't sit still
She couldn't drive
He couldn't sing
She couldn't stop
He wouldn't stop
She didn't say no
He hadn't planned to go
She wasn't born yesterday
He couldn't say
She wouldn't listen
He was no soldier
She was no nurse
It was no picnic

Lehman on the Writer's Life

Write any time, any place. Take a little notebook with you. Jot down possible titles, interesting phrases you overhear, your own mental association.

Write prose. All the writing you do helps all the other writing you do. Learn the prose virtues of economy, directness, and clarity. Good journalism or nonfiction writing or speech writing or technical writing can help your poetry. Writing to an editor's specifications, on deadline, with a tight word count, is a sort of discipline not unlike writing poems in rigorous forms. It teaches you brevity.

"Writing to an editor's specifications, on deadline, with a tight word count, is a sort of discipline not unlike writing poems in rigorous forms. It teaches you brevity."

I always liked writing captions and headlines, the haiku of journalism.

Write every day, or almost every day, even if only a few lines, not only to keep in fighting trim but because the results may be worth perpetuating. The quality of the writing may vary inversely with the amount of time expended.

Writing in forms, whether traditional or ad hoc, is a smart thing to do. The sestina form was once exotic. Now, after masterly examples by Auden, Bishop, Ashbery, Donald Justice, Harry Mathews, James Cummins, it sometimes seems as if the sestina is that restaurant Yogi Berra had in mind when he said, "No one eats there any more—it's too crowded." I once received a rejection slip from John Frederick Nims, then the editor of *Poetry*, saying that he was returning a sestina I had sent him because "sestinas are a dime a dozen." In fact, however, poets continue to write sestinas that are amazingly fresh and inventive. I recently read a fine one by Meg Kearney in *Ploughshares*. In the same magazine a year or two ago appeared a splendid sestina by Jonah Winter that had one end-word for all 39 lines: "Bob."

After a stimulating gossip session with Jim Cummins, who had set a precedent by writing a sestina using "Gary Snyder" as one of his six recurring end-words, I wrote "Sestina," choosing as end-words the names of poets (Walt Whitman, Ted Berrigan, Anne Sexton, Marvin Bell, Philip Levine, and a variable). The poem was written with malice toward no one. I had just happened to read an interview with Ted Berrigan in which he was asked to state his opinion of Rod McKuen. He said something like, "I don't mind McKuen, I begrudge no man his right to make a living. My idea of a bad poet is Marvin Bell." This seemed an extraordinary statement, implying that competent mediocrity was more of a sin than true badness. So I put it into the sestina as part of the mix, without prejudice.

Comedy, wit, humor, satire, japes and jibes—all are valid. What's more, the comic or ironic impulse can heighten the tragic as in *King Lear*. When I was a freshman in college, I wrote a paper on the funny parts of "Paradise Lost." This was considered a brash and eccentric thing to do, as "Paradise Lost" is thought not to have any funny parts. The comic is underrated and complicated. Comedy affirms, but comedy can also express (or cunningly conceal) savage indignation. Wit as a term encompasses not only clever wordplay, skill at repartee, a flair for a turn of phrase, but also a way the intelligence has of apprehending the world.

I see wonderful examples of humor in contemporary poetry. For *The Best American Poetry 2000*, Rita Dove chose Paul Violi's "As I Was Telling David and Alexandra Kelley," which resembles a shaggy dog story with a cruelly ironic ending that makes people laugh out loud. For *The Best American Poetry 2001*, Robert Hass selected Bernard Welt's "I stopped writing poetry . . . ," an outstanding instance of how telling the truth sometimes requires a humorous disguise.

Give yourself assignments. These can be exercises in form (sonnet, villanelle, pantoum, prose poem) or in imitation of masters (Donne, Coleridge, Williams, Stevens). I enjoy distributing a poem in a language foreign to the students and asking them to translate it without the help of a dictionary. The mistranslation assignment invariably generates interesting work.

When I began teaching poetry writing in the mid-1990s after ten years of not doing it, I noticed that many students were writing poems based on experience, so I devised assignments to emphasize the possibility that poetry could be linguistically generated, that you could arrive at truth or beauty or both without being fully aware of what you were up to. In fact, the conscious mind may get in the way. Therefore it is useful to occupy the conscious mind with something it can profitably do, like solve a word puzzle. Sometimes writing a poem is as much about solving a problem or puzzle as it is about resolving a crisis. A poem is a collaboration with language.

I like doing the same assignments I give to students. In 1997 I asked my students at the New School to write a poem or prose poem in a form adapted from a public mode of discourse not usually associated with poetry, like a menu or recipe. When I did the assignment, I chose the errors column in the *New York Times* as my model. "Corrections" resulted.

The newspaper is an underrated source of poetic inspiration. Another assignment I like giving myself and others is to write a poem that does the work of an obituary. "A shilling life will give you all the facts," Auden wrote about a certain type of biography. I wanted to give not all the facts but some striking ones, and some fancies too, in a biographical poem, "Wittgenstein's Ladder."

Can an epitaph become an epigraph? When Ginger Rogers died in 1995, a lot of obituaries repeated Katharine Hepburn's analysis of the success Fred

Astaire and Ginger Rogers had enjoyed as a dancing duo. "He gave her class, she gave him sex," Hepburn said. What an epitaph. The syntax itself seemed irresistible, like a one-line form that you could use to analyze relationships anywhere. That's the thought that set "The Gift" in motion. In the poem "February 10" from *The Daily Mirror,* I revived the he/she syntactical mechanism, this time seeing if I could create a narrative out of an alternation of simple sentences.

The poet's chief obligation is to keep poetry alive. Poetry, if genuine, is a resistance manifested against what would conspire against it. Wallace Stevens has the phrase "the pressure of reality" in one of his essays. He talks about the imagination pressing back against this pressure. The best way to manifest resistance is not by writing a poem that narrowly protests a particular injustice, but, on the contrary, by writing a poem that on the surface has no bearing on that injustice, a poem that renews the possibility of human imagination in a sphere where that is endangered.

At the University of Cincinnati, where I taught as the Elliston Poet-in-Residence in 1995, I was asked what advice I would give to young writers. I looked at the bright, eager faces in the room, and I said—I didn't know I was going to say this, it was just what I felt at that moment—that they should remember that poetry is not life. That there will come a time when all of them will feel envy and resentment, because somebody got a job that they were better qualified for, or won a prize that should have gone to them, or some other injustice, of which there is plenty in the poetry world. How are they going to fend off the bitterness and resentment? Because those things are the enemies of poetry. Those things are not real—not real in the sense that grief and love are real. Unfortunately, it's all too easy to succumb to competitive envy. And that is why it is important to remember that poetry is not the whole of one's life, but a part of it, and that we should not put too great a burden on the poetry that we love. Keeping it alive, poetry and the possibility of poetry, is the great thing.

> *"Keeping it alive, poetry and the possibility of poetry, is the great thing."*

Writing Suggestions

1. Write a villanelle, a sestina, or a ballad. Resurrect this old form by doing one or more of the following: (1) utilizing a heap of pop culture references and allusions, (2) using a slang-filled, colloquial voice, or (3) making humor an integral part of the poem. Do what you have to in order to make these old forms new and exciting, uniquely yours. Challenge the form and your expectations of it. Discover the form's range and potential.

2. Reread Lehman's poems as well as his commentary very closely. Keeping in mind his ideas, style, structure, and voice, write a poem that could be added to his body of work. If you feel resistance at "copying" another's work, remember that becoming a master in a trade occurs in three steps: (1) as an apprentice one learns the necessary crafts and skills directly from a mentor/master, (2) the apprentice imitates the mentor/master and in doing so *learns the craft firsthand*, (3) and after a period of time, the apprentice is given a title, respect, and the freedom to embark on their own. What are the challenges in adopting someone else's style, voice, etc.?

3. Write a list poem that orbits a central topic, such as family, a specific relationship, a season, a school shooting, or some other event/situation. Use specific details and images rather than just a string of nouns and verbs. Reread "The Gift" and "February 10" for variations on the list poem.

4. Find a picture of one of your parents, grandparents, or close relatives as an adult, but at a time *before* you were born. Study the picture. What is the emotion most apparent in the picture? What sort of personality does the person seem to exhibit? Brainstorm about their fears, goals, ambitions, and abilities at that time in their life. Now write your poem in response to this picture. For inspiration, consider looking at Raymond Carver's poem "Photograph of My Father in His Twenty-Second Year," Sharon Olds's "Photograph of the Girl," or Gary Soto's "Photo, 1957."

> *"Poetry begins for me where certainty ends. I think the imagination is an ambiguous and untidy place, and its frontiers are not accessible to logic for that reason."*
>
> —Eavan Boland

Timothy Liu

In Flagrante Delicto

I. Lethe

sound asleep and shadowed by a crumbling pier the body of a stranger
caught in such autoerotic repose and if that rowboat drowned in sand
fails to budge or moonlit sails proclaim the absence of an actual wind
what marriage do we have that thrives on was instead of is to be a kite
washed up on shore blackened shells strewn in trampled grass where
fires last night had been your kiss refused the taste of him ripped deep
inside the salt tide's aftermath inferno streaked eroding all remaining
sense of shore the dawn mere possibility where oarlock gently creaked

II. Like Boys Next Door

channel surfing from baseball scores to late night news for images
of ourselves in vain no faggots here in uniform only shirts that say
repent or perish as closets open wide their flaming doors just try on
the face of a christ that took a lifetime of our suffering to achieve
last-pick sissies striking out foreheads marked with ash as tongues
begin to slide like eels in public parks tempting boys who'd flock
to sport some jockstraps stuffed down throats where teeth had been
knocked-out a pack of trading-cards some drag from base to base

III. Just Some Boys

tossing frisbees in the eucalyptus scented air equidistant to the site
of old catastrophes waterlogged under a bridge our bodies pulled
to the center where it sags with years of connubial bliss and hardly
an hour's peace on unpaved roads that lead to a drive-thru window
where shrooms were tucked in a happy meal why not spy on boys
who spread their legs under leaves so green you'd think it was a set

heaving in the heat forget that homeless voice that kept on shouting
how many easter eggs you want up your ass the two of us pushing

IV. Roman Fever

gripped by a cell-phone panic day-trading shares a load more fun
than getting drunk on Jersey sky awash in amaretto light as I vespa
through the Palisades dependent more on Wall St. than the voice
of Pasolini now walling out all canyon echo clandestine rest-stop
action darting through the shrubs in search of Armani-suited cock
pack-muled through crevices at dusk patrol-car love winking past
that dogstar all aglitter over Ostia falling into the hands of rough
trade *che gelida manina* thread-bare boxers pulled down to our heels

V. Home of the Brave

reduced to rubble our democratic vistas unable to outlast far-right
terrorists who plan to poison water supplies as we wine and dine
in whistle stops trying to outbully operatic regicides curled inside
the tail of a treble clef floating on the outskirts of a forgotten town
where patriots bored from shooting at paper targets put complete
bomb-making guides online while orphans playing stick ball sift
through cases of crackerjack hit lists faxes anthrax sold by mail
some triggers and detonating fuses left inside that local ballot box

VI. Heavy Freight

a handprint fossilized on a child's startled face a bout of fisticuffs
as witness to love's excess straddling another bride as the bouquet
flies ferruginous tresses spilling over marble fonts into some abyss
eleemosynary grunts instead of sermons on the mount as grounds
for divorce where orphaned souls stampede down ungulated clefts
bikini wax ripped off depilatory forms to appease an ultramontane
satrap instructed in orthography by missionaries caught red-handed
in compromised positions trying to micturate into the rutilant night

VII. Requiem

a prayer pooling on our lips while semen spurts across the room
into the laps of virgins hitched in stirrups all of 'em ready to ride
some heavenly horse out of life while candles drip into sockets
of candied skulls that crown a gravestone pulverized by lichen

in a field where couples lean against a crumbling wall the sound
of iron sandals drawing near Andrei Rublev on a board between
two ladders erecting icons in the dark even as Cocteau's woman
wanders onto a set with eyes painted on her eyelids that are closed

VIII. Sirens Singing

of a lover's eyes newly-minted in maternal din anxieties complete
with pink fiestaware jarring the hours a hundredfold where vocal
mutilations hover over a violin come unstrung no talk only grunts
washed up on shore all those hag-infested hours redolent with fog
her laughter's rickety bridge seldom crossed emotions clocking in
instead of punching out the taste of it percolating on that stovetop
licked by dawn by way of telegram a truce delivered yet somehow
always the wrong address the come-on instead of a goodnight kiss

Liu on Being Caught Red-Handed in the Act of Writing (An Interview with Myself): A Commentary on Publishing, Audience, and the Possibilities of Form

Q. *What makes you hesitate about selecting work for this anthology?*

A. Do poets really know what their best works are? I mean, are we talking about some kind of "greatest hits" package, or are we talking about poems of such excellence that might serve as our ticket into Parnassus?

Q. *And yet you've chosen "In Flagrante Delicto" from your most recent book.*

A. I suppose the poem is a culmination of investigations over the past twelve years. One's writing life lags behind one's reading life. I started with Plath and moved backwards through the tradition from favorite Modernists (Crane, Pound, Stevens) to favorite Romantics (Coleridge, Keats) on back to the greatest granddaddy of them all, Milton. Somewhere along the line, I was taken in by Dickinson and Whitman, not to mention a book like *The Morrow Anthology of Younger American Poets,* my introduction to contemporary voices which I carried around like a Bible. Poets like Gertrude Stein, Mina Loy, and H. D. were off my radar as were poets associated with Black Mountain and the New York School—they would come later, after I finished graduate school. Every poet bushwhacks their own way into the wilderness of poetry, whether on roads less traveled or not.

Q. *And yet sections of "In Flagrante Delicto" first appeared in such journals as* Denver Quarterly *(Bin Ramke, ed.),* Rhizome *(Standard Schaefer & Evan Calbi, eds.), and* Talisman *(Ed Foster, ed.), not to mention the ezine* Slope *(Ethan Paquin, ed.).*

A. I suppose my poetic journey has been a movement from the center to the margin and back again, a poetics unwilling to eschew either mainstream or avant-garde camps but to somehow do a lyrical dance in that continuum anchored by Seamus Heaney on the one hand and Susan Howe on the other.

Q. *A dance many poets in your generation seem to be choreographing . . .*

A. It's a lively time to be writing. With poets like John Ashbery, Anne Carson, and Jorie Graham holding court, you get offspring like Lucie Brock-Broido, Forrest Gander, and Carl Phillips, poets whose attentions have radically shifted from the concerns of poets in the aforementioned *Morrow Anthology* which at times seems so retro.

Q. *Yet this new generation of poets that you mention would hardly belong in an anthology like Ron Silliman's* In the American Tree *either.*

A. I'd like to see what kind of essay Marjorie Perloff or Helen Vendler could now write about poets such as Joshua Clover, D.A. Powell, Claudia Rankine, Eleni Sikelianos, or Karen Volkman. Maybe they're no longer the ones to do it. Maybe a new criticism is already being ushered in by younger poets like Brian Henry or Stephen Burt. I mean, what a crop of first books in 2001 alone, from Noelle Kocot's *4* and Cate Marvin's *The World's Tallest Disaster* to Spencer Short's *Tremolo* and Sam Witt's *Everlasting Quail*.

Q. *So you'd like to see a poem like "In Flagrante Delicto" considered in such a context?*

A. Absolutely. Better than the context of this year's National Book Award nominees! Now sure, you might think I'm griping because *Hard Evidence* wasn't nominated, but no, I just wish they had chosen better judges (I hereby nominate Rae Armantrout, Michael Palmer, and Gustaf Sobin for starters).

Q *But what if* Hard Evidence *had been nominated?*

A. That would be unlikely since my publisher couldn't afford the entry fee.

Q. *What does any of this have to do with "In Flagrante Delicto"?*

A. Well for starters, I don't think "In Flagrante Delicto" is the kind of poem that would show up on the radars of mainstream judges, just as the poems written by any of them only on occasion have an impact on my own reading life.

Q. *So there are these entrenched constituencies in American poetry . . .*

A. That's right. As a contributor to this anthology, I was asked by the editor to talk about issues like "the genesis of the work," "choices in tone, style, voice" or "revision concerns"—issues that certainly make sense for a college textbook—but at the moment, the editor has withheld who some of the other contributors are, poets whom I might even have already mentioned in this interview.

Q. *Why an interview anyway? So gimmicky!*

A. Maybe I like the idea of both an imaginary dialogue and a way to write around the subject at hand.

Q. *You mean your poem.*

A. I mean my hesitation to participate in this anthology in the first place.

Q. *Well let me try to help. Why is your poem written in eight sections of eight-line stanzas?*

A. "In Flagrante Delicto" is a response to a series called "To Calamus" that appears earlier in *Hard Evidence*. "To Calamus" is a twenty-part aleatory series of floating sonnets (I had originally written ninety of them between

1995–97 as a way to exercise/exorcise my traditional sense of syntax). In "In Flagrante Delicto," I wanted to employ a more capacious line but to limit myself to a ballpark number of words that I normally used for a sonnet in "To Calamus."

Q. *So it's like you squashed the poem, emphasizing the horizontal features of the line over the vertical, altering one's sense of space and time.*

A. And by doing so, I've eliminated the traditional sestet that follows the argument of the sonnet's octet. What's left feels more compressed. There are moments of thesis and antithesis floating within each line—argument becomes encoded in the poem's syntax.

Q. *Can you give us an example?*

A. Sure, take line 4 in the poem's opening section "Lethe":

what marriage do we have that thrives on was instead of is to be a kite

You can read "a kite" as the object of the line's subject (marriage) or as the subject of a new sentence enjambed across the line break: "to be a kite/washed up on shore." Also the question of whether marriage thrives on "was" rather than "is" might suggest the dangerous safety marriages find by way of nostalgia or even forgetfulness.

Q. *I see. So the poem's loosened syntax allows new arguments to be enacted, even if indeterminate.*

A. Poets must be accountable for the grammars that they use, not only their images, narratives and linguistic tropes. A new grammar is a new mind.

Q. *How did you come to order this series?*

A. The use of juxtaposition creates its own arguments whether within individually collaged lines or across the poem as a whole. "Lethe" starts the series off at dawn. Something tragic has occurred that one is trying to perhaps forget beside an ocean. But one remembers channel "surfing" on a previous night in the next poem. Homophobic violence occurs, thus magnifying "the taste of him ripped deep/inside the salt tide's aftermath" of the first poem. The game of baseball in the second poem turns into a game of frisbee in the third. I love the possible readings of the third poem's final line:

how many easter eggs you want up your ass the two of us pushing

Does the verb "pushing" take a truncated object or not? Here we have a terminal verb that delights in both its transitive and intransitive possibilities. The boys in the park become the men cruising after dark in the fourth

"Poets must be accountable for the grammars that they use, not only their images, narratives and linguistic tropes. A new grammar is a new mind."

poem, "Roman Fever," whose title not only alludes to Edith Wharton's short story but to Pasolini's demise. This thread of danger is subsequently magnified in "Home of the Brave" on through the night of "Heavy Freight" and "Requiem," only to thus emerge again in the dawn of the poem's concluding section, "Sirens Singing" with its allusion to Odysseus trying to make his way back home.

Q. *How long did it take you to put "In Flagrante Delicto" together?*

A. The poem is composed out of fragments written over a five-year period in which hundreds of drafts for all eight sections were liberally discarded.

Q. *Why eight sections?*

A. Well, as you know, the seventh day is the day of rest. Hence, the seventh section of the poem is "The Requiem." But after God has finished creating the world, it is up to his creations to carry on working in a new dawn. Adam and Eve were of course the first couple to be caught "In Flagrante Delicto" and were banished from paradise, a condition necessary for them to bring forth their own creations into the world. But what of gay men who can't procreate? Might there be a substitute in the act of writing poems? And a hope, perhaps, for some kind of redemption.

Writing Suggestions

1. Write a poem about homonyms, words that sound the same but have different meanings (bear and bear, lie and lie, write and right, wear and where, to name just a few). Think of a life situation where these two words might interact. Encounter these words in concrete ways in the poem. Deal with each word individually, then bring them together in the poem's conclusion. A wonderful example of this type of poem is Brenda Hillman's "Cleave and Cleave," which takes great leaps to intellectually bridge two decidedly unlike words.

2. Write down your two favorite poetry words, those words you love for their sound or imagery, their meaning or ambiguity. Get two poetry friends to share their two favorite poetry words with you. Write a poem of at least fourteen lines that uses at least four of these six words.

3. Write up at least two pages of Q&As with yourself on a poem you feel particularly satisfied/dissatisfied with. Ask yourself the hard questions, then answer them honestly. Don't show the Q&As to anyone, if that helps.

4. Look through all the poetry collections nominated for the National Book Award in a single year within the past five or even ten years. Which book

would you have selected to win the award? Why? Who were the judges that year? Can you identify editorial biases/views in terms of those collections that were/weren't selected? What does this say about the future of poetry? Is it fair to say that the editorial biases/views are prescriptive or descriptive?

"*A poem, as a manifestation of language and thus essentially dialogue, can be a message in a bottle, sent out in the—not always greatly hopeful—belief that somewhere and sometime it could wash up on land, on heartland perhaps. Poems in this sense, too, are under way; they are making toward something.*"

—Paul Celan

Adrian C. Louis

Indian Summer Gives Way to the Land of the Rising Sun

Memory is malleable.
Memory is a scar.
Because all things return
to their source,
grace is possible.

***

Lakota makoce and I've been on it
nearly twenty stumbling years.
Pine Ridge is bathed in dusk.
From a bed in the IHS hospital, I
watch clouds smoke over red earth.
They look real, like clouds in those
paintings, those oil landscapes by
that artist on PBS, that white guy
with an afro, the one who spoke
with a hillbilly drawl and used
two-inch house brushes to
daub his little masterpieces.
He died from cancer a while back,
but has been reborn in re-runs.

***

Darkness, sneaking Marlboros
on the balcony, bugs crawling
down the back of my hospital gown.
Under the parking lot light poles,
flying insects swarm, some able
to retain luminosity and fly
so far away with it.

Fireflies? I don't know . . .
A young nurse from Ft. Berthold
says there are fireflies at her home,
but none down here in the wilds
of godless South Dakota.
She puts her hand to my cheek
to check on my fever and
I shudder with loneliness.
I wish I could take her hand
and pull her silently into
the motorized bed with me.
We could share the same cigarette.
The way I feel, it might be my last.

***

Indian macho:
If you're going to get shot,
you might as well have a Marlboro
dangling from your lips . . . enit?
On the road below the hospital,
a young woman is running from
her drunk boyfriend. He pants,
swears and sweats up the hill
after her, but she is too fast,
too sober.

***

Days drag through the unseasonable
warmth of late fall that white
people call Indian summer.
It's Indian summer
all year long around here
and through my medicinal haze
I think I hear the nurse say she'll
cook me a steak when I heal.

Memory is malleable.
Memory is a scar.
Because all things return
to their source,
grace is possible.
The simple vision of a brown
woman cooking over a stove
is a good reason to live.

But I get no steak. Instead, she
thrusts a tube up my nose and
then down into my stomach.
Ghastly brown liquid bubbles
into a glass cauldron.
I thrash and moan and wonder
who those green men are who
sit at the foot of my bed.

***

I am entering a faraway land.
The Indian Health Service ambulance
bumps along the dirt road, exhaust
fumes filling this tin can where I lie
like a fat sardine upon the bed, stench
from the exhaust choking, my stomach
in flames, I'm feverish, the smoking
ambulance rips down the road and up
towards Rapid City like it was in
a Road Runner cartoon.

Then, I'm in Regional Hospital.
The surgeon says the x-rays look
like colon cancer. She smiles.
I smile back and wink and
resign myself to my cliched fate.
I am entering a faraway land.
For all I know, it could be Japan.

***

There are weeks that I know nothing
about when my kidneys shut down,
when my lungs shut down, when
I nearly pass on to the spirit world.
There's no bright light, I do not float
above my bed, but Colleen, you keep
coming back to me, your sweet softness,
the innocent mist you're in now,
this reservation where I found you,
where I look for you, where I cannot
find you, the past, the present all mixed,
mixed in this faraway land, and you're
so soft, wearing a long blue skirt, so soft
and so lost and your family is taking

care of you since I cannot now . . .
but as usual, they're not doing
a good job and they lose you.

***

Somehow the idea comes to write
a book with paintings, watercolors
of Mexican peasant plates, each plate
will tell a story. It's bizarre, but I see
myself forward, out of the hospital
and healing. I'll set up an easel in my
backyard and paint the pictures, each
painting a chapter in my life, each
earthenware plate bordered by bright
flowers and dancing calaveras.

Even in my sickness, I know it's a
crazy idea, but then for a month I waver
between madness and extreme madness.
I believe I have cancer though the doctors
tell me daily that I don't. The thing that
sustains me, keeps me going, is apple juice.
Apple juice grows in the basement of
the hospital where old Jewish women
squeeze the sweet wetness from gray mud.
They dribble it into vials so I drink it and
my life continues. And in this basement
people float like balloons near the ceiling
and one of these people is a little monkey
dressed in a black suit and tophat.
He wears a beard and glasses.
This monkey talks to me.
I don't know why, but I believe
it is a Japanese monkey. Maybe it's
because he screams: PEARL HARBOR!
Frightened by the screeching simian,
I scream back: ENOLA GAY!
and my mad Mexican plates fly
around the room and smash
into smithereens.

***

Every imaginable type of ghost
is dancing in my room.

I'm sick and stoned beyond stone.
Toxic encephalopathy.
My brain, my entire body is poisoned.
I am a toxic half-breed!
A loony and languid viper
hissing on the doorsteps of hell.
What have I done to deserve this?

Hank Williams is under my bed
singing "Rambling Man" and I've
got plastic tubes up my penis
and down my throat, in my wrist
and chest and stomach. A huge
stitched trench runs from my
solar plexus to my belly button.
My American river of madness
pisses against all reason, flowing west
from Reno to San Francisco and then
east to Rapid City to St. Paul and then
into Cambridge, Mass. All these
cities merge into brick sameness.
All these cities are America and all
the red bricks are dried Indian blood.
In this city called "America" there
is a small tavern in the fog
named the Ribeltad Vorden or maybe
the Plough and Stars and it's filled
with derelicts, Indians, and artists.
I buy a pint of good Irish whiskey
and drop it in the pocket of my raincoat
where it clinks up against a chrome .45
and my brother-in-law Duane is there
in an ill-fitting, itchy tweed suit.
Duane's a tribal detective so I ask
if the Japanese doctors who implanted
the golden wire from the base of my brain
to my coccyx have cured the cancer
and he says yeah, hell yeah.
I give him the chrome automatic and tell
him I plan to give one to all his brothers.
And how is sweet-crazy Colleen I ask.
Waiting, he says. She's waiting for you.

***

The flights to Japan were killers.
And the Japanese not only cured me,
but they harvested a kidney
without my permission.
Like it was me who raised
the flag on Iwo Jima . . .

The jets were long and lean lungfish.
Like some mad, mutant mixture
of Ahab and Jonah, I was
the only rider on most trips.
The aisles were windswept
and cellophane overhead ran
the length of the plane.
A howling wind whooshed the plastic
making me cry each time we landed.

On one flight, an ancient lover, now gray
and beaten, sat behind me and drooled.
She said they stole her kidney too.
Said she was a bag lady now!
That it was all my fault.
That if only I had stayed within
the realm of her sweet and mothering
love such disasters would never
have befallen us and all I can do
is nod, stare into her eyes, and cry.

***

Strange, how it took me a month
to believe I didn't have cancer,
and had never been to Japan.
They did remove a huge chunk
of my colon and gave me a colostomy
bag that I'd have to wear for six fragrant
months, but I never had cancer,
I never had the fucking Big C . . .
I didn't, did I?

***

Now, it's a year later and
somewhere in this airless

examining room I can almost
hear my young red-headed surgeon
and her young surgeon husband
doing the dirty deed atop
this Danish modern furniture.

It's now been one year since surgery.
My vibrant MD enters, all smiles, and
says, "You're lookin' good!" But, there
are many other things she tells me,
as she looks at my chart, things I do not
recall at all like how I stood atop my
bed and screamed I was a poet.
How I ripped loose my colostomy
bag and beaned a nurse with it.
How they tied me down for weeks,
stuck a tube down my soul,
and fed me life.

I'm embarrassed, but I am alive.
I thank the spirits for deleting
those memories. Memory is
malleable. Memory is a scar.
Because all things return
to their source, grace is possible.
One of these days I just might fly
to the land of the rising sun
and thank those doctors.
Domo arigato!
Sushi?
Banzai!
Remember Pearl Harbor?

Adiós Again, My Blessed Angel of Thunderheads and Urine

Ah, so there you are, somewhere between
the Demerol and the morphine, silently
emptying my catheter jug. Don't do that, I want to say,
but my voice is lost from two weeks on the
ventilator. Baby Girl, I want to say hello,

say I know your name, say how much I've
always loved you, but only a rasp comes
and then you are gone forever again.

I know I've got a crinkled picture of you
boxed somewhere in my shuttered house.
The image is as foreign as it is faded.
Somewhere west of Tulsa, you are leaning
against a black VW Bug, smiling and pointing

at a remarkable formation of thunderheads
that tower and bluster miles past heaven.
Your long, black hair dances below your waist.
Your worn Navy bell bottoms are snug against

your perfect legs, your strong, loving hips.
And after I snap the photo, you tell me
you're going back to nursing school.
Me, I'll wander in the wilderness for thirty years
before I see you again, and then it will be
only for a minute while you empty my urine bucket
and I try to cough up words that will not
come like the flashing pain beneath
my sutures that signals healing and wonder.

One Man's Opinion: Louis's Commentary on Madness and Inspiration

Let me tell you what I do know. I love poetry, but to me there is nothing more boring than to hear poets wax on about what they think poetry *is*, and what is even worse is to hear them talk about how they "created" a particular piece of work. The two poems of mine included in this anthology derive mainly from a madness that transcends poetry, and it is hard for me to appreciate the fact that somehow they became poems. The madness I refer to is not the romantic anguish of the broken artist, but something more mundane. These two poems come from a time when I nearly died because of physical dysfunction, and they come with a background of the Canadian country singer Shania Twain singing, "You're The One."

The year was 1997 and I was in the hospital with a bowel obstruction. The doctors told me it was cancer and they'd have to operate. I was filled with bravado and drugs and tough guy that I was, I said go ahead and do what you gotta do. They operated and it was a success and I awoke the next day and called friends and family and said, "The old dog is gonna live." Well, two days later I descended into madness from all the poison in my system and remained in a strange comatose world for nearly four weeks. The doctors later told me the syndrome was called "toxic encephalopathy." They had to strap me down because I was so violent. I had a strange, lasting vision that has remained with me to this day. That is pretty much detailed in the poem "Indian Summer Gives Way to the Land of the Rising Sun."

I can't say much about Shania Twain's song except it was piped in over the airwaves one night at the same time a Chicano orderly was checking on me, and I sensed he was Mexican and I blathered on to him in the tongue of one of my grandfathers and he gave me great comfort. Now this poem itself is strange in that it seems to implicate the Japanese for a great many of this country's difficulties. It is not racist, but only points out that Japan is a country that caused many American deaths. I truly believed that I had cancer instead of a diverticular abscess and that I was flown to Japan to be cured. They implanted a thin gold wire from my brain to my butt-bone and it cured me. But they harvested a kidney without my permission. Perhaps that is what fostered my seeming anger at the Land of the Rising Sun.

> *"Is it a good poem? I can't answer that question, nor should any poet be forced to answer such a question because poets like to lie. . . . Sometimes I read poems I wrote years ago and am ashamed to be able to see through the lies that they are."*

What I say in this poem is what I believed and still believe. There was much more that happened in my sick brain such as a whole episode with Jewish/ Indian cowboys and a whole "Star Wars" battleship episode with bombers crashing into aircraft carriers in Boston Harbor and my brother-in-law in his ancient Navy whites, but that is a whole different story. To make a long story short, the poem is basically a narrative of what I saw to be the truth, deranged as I was at the time. Is it a good poem? I can't answer that question, nor should any poet be forced to answer such a question because poets like to lie. It is a good poem in my mind only because it is somewhat recent and thus believable to me. Sometimes I read poems I wrote years ago and am ashamed to be able to see through the lies that they are.

The other poem I include is also true, maybe more true than the first. I don't know how many of you have been in the hospital and have been loaded up on drugs after having a huge chunk of your body excised by surgeons' switchblades, but . . . as they say, this one came to me intact.

"Adiós Again, My Sweet Angel of Thunderheads and Urine" came to me exactly as it is. It came moments after I saw this nurse and I wrote it down at the time, which is somewhat amazing to me. I thought—as did the doctors—that I had had some serious brain damage during this time because of the massive infection. Not only that, I fell badly on the way to take a piss, landed squarely on the back of my head and they had to take me down for scans, the works. Anyways, this beautiful woman dream unto me, emptying my piss jug. She was a woman I used to love, yes, it *was* her! An incredibly soothing and painful vision.

But at the time I had no voice because of the weeks of being on a ventilator! As soon as she left me, I wrote down the poem and have not changed a word of it. I never saw her again. I don't know what else to say about it. It's kind of a holy mystery. I should be sharing this stuff with only those of you who have licked the rough tongue of death and are still able to babble on about it. What is even more incredible about this whole episode is that I was more concerned with the care of the one I love (who is suffering from Alzheimer's dementia) than I was with myself. But hey, that's another tale for another time.

Writing Suggestions

1. Write a long poem (100 lines minimum). Select a "touchstone" subject with which you begin, stray from, and return to at different intervals, à la Louis's poem "Indian Summer Gives Way to the Land of the Rising Sun." What are some of the challenges particular to the long poem? Is it easier to write it directly from personal experience as Louis did?

2. Write a medium-length poem (thirty to sixty lines) in which an element (image, phrase, specific voice, etc.) is returned to again and again, but each time it appears let it be altered, or mean something slightly different. A refrain would be an exact duplication, but this is asking to go one step further. If done well, the recurrences of the element you've chosen will become

part of the poem's music. Two good examples of this type of poem are Stephen Dobyns's "How to Like It" and Mark Strand's "Elegy For My Father."

3. Take a decent-size paragraph out of your local newspaper and type it up. Break up the syntax of the sentences into fragments of poetry. The words you choose to end on might transform the line's meaning or emphasize (reinforce) it. What else can a line break do to the meaning of a poem? Of an individual line? Of the line that follows it?

4. Research a topic/idea/person you've always wanted to know more about. Write a short (twenty- to thirty-line) poem in response, using any form, structure, style, or voice you think is appropriate for your topic. Let the reader share your enthusiasm without telling them to.

"My compositional process almost always begins in a kind of despondency usually born of a conviction that I will never write again, that I'll never again feel that I am at the throat of the dog, that I'm at something essential."

—Louise Glück

Campbell McGrath

CAPITALIST POEM #5

I was at the 7-11.
I ate a burrito.
I drank a Slurpee.
I was tired.
It was late, after work—washing dishes.
The burrito was good.
I had another.
I did it every day for a week.
I did it every day for a month.
To cook a burrito you tear off the plastic wrapper.
You push button #3 on the microwave.
Burritos are large, small or medium.
Red or green chili peppers.
Beef or bean or both.
There are 7-11s all across the nation.
On the way out I bought a quart of beer for $1.39.
I was aware of social injustice
in only the vaguest possible way.

ALMOND BLOSSOMS, ROCK AND ROLL, THE PAST SEEN AS BURNING FIELDS

Across the highlands farmers are burning their fields
in the darkness. The fleet, infernal silhouettes of these men
and the owl-swift birds scared up from the chaff
flicker briefly against the silken curtain of flame as we pass,
an image from Goya cast once before our eyes
to be lost as the road swerves up to alabaster
groves of olives and white-knuckled *almendros*.

Hungry, exhausted, driving all night, there are four of us
hunched in the shell of the beaten, graffiti-winged bug
that we scalped for sixty dollars in Berlin,
no shocks, bald tires, a broken starter so that
we have to pop the clutch every time, dashing like fools
through the streets of Amsterdam and Barcelona—
Hank with no accent, Dave with no license
except for his beard, Ed with the box turned all the way up,
playing over and over the only two tapes we have left
since the night of the lurid Basque luau
and street riot in San Sebastian. For whatever reason
we are insanely happy. Wild and lost, speed-mad,
high on the stale bread and cold ravioli we've eaten for days,
giddy with smoke and the echoes of flame leading south,
El Greco fingers of blue chalk and turtle dove moonlight
at rest on the soft wool mantillas of distant sierras,
rock and roll working its harmonic convergence,
odor of diesel and wild cherry, almond blossoms
settling like ash to the asphalt—. No. Wait.
It wasn't four. There were three of us left
after Hank stayed behind with that girl in Madrid.
And it was ash. Just there, where the highway
carried the flame's liquid insignia, an ash-blizzard
swirled and impelled itself irretrievably
into the melted tar. It was like a county road in Colorado
I once drove, coming to a place where milkweed
or dandelion spores confounded the air
and fell into the fresh-laid black top, embedded there,
fossilized, become the antediluvian kingdom
another era must decode. For us, all of Spain was like
anywhere else, driving the Great Plains or Inland Empire,
Los Banos, Buttonwillow, Bakersfield,
familiar rhythm and cadence of the road,
another car, another continent, another rope of lights
slung the length of the San Joaquin Valley.
I don't know if the rush we felt was culturally specific,
though it was the literal noise of our culture we rode
like Vandals or Moors toward a distant sea,
but that feeling was all we ever desired, that freedom
to hurtle madly against the sweet, forgiving flesh of the world,
urged on by stars and wind and music,

kindred spirits of the night. How the past
overwhelms us, violent as flood waters, vivid as war.
Now Ed wears a suit and tie, Dave deals used cars
in L.A., "pushing iron," as the salesmen say.
My wife and I walk home from the grocery store
through streets of squirrels and school busses
bathed in late October sunlight, musky odor of paper bags
and fresh cheesebread from the Baltic bakery,
when the smell of someone incinerating fallen leaves
brings back a landscape of orchards and windmills,
the inscrutable plains of Castile and Estremadura.
I don't even know what they were burning out there
but it must have been the end
of the season. The symphony of years glissades
like tractors tracing figure-eights across a muddy slope,
sweep and lull of machetes in the sugar fields,
Fiji or Jamaica, places Elizabeth and I have travelled since,
smelled the candied stink of smoldering cane.
But what concerns me most is not so much the smoke,
the resin and ash of human loss,
but rather how glibly and with what myopia
we bore the mantle of individual liberty across the continents,
as if our empowerment entailed no sacrifice in kind,
no weight of responsibility. I guess it was a sign
of the times. That jingoistic, re-election year
a spirit of such complacent self-congratulation reigned
that even Paris seemed a refuge from the hubris.
At the Olympic ceremonies in Los Angeles
they chose to reenact the national epic, westward
expansion, only due to certain staging restrictions
the covered wagons full of unflappable coeds
rolled from west to east, a trivial, barely-noticed flaw.
It is America's peculiar gift and burden, this liberation
from the shackles of history. And we were such avatars.
We took what was given and thought, in all innocence,
that the casual largesse we displayed in return
was enough. When we parked for good in Algeciras
we left the doors unlocked, key in the ignition.
You see, the brakes were gone and it wasn't our country.
Immense in the heat-shadowed distance loomed
the glittering, mysterious mountains of Africa,

and though we stood in the very shadow of the Rock of Gibraltar
we never even noticed it. That's how I picture us still,
me and Ed and Dave on the ferry to Tangier,
laughing in our sunglasses, forgetting to look back.

Delphos, Ohio

is where we turned around, surrendered to fate, gave in to defeat and
abandoned our journey at a town with three stoplights, one good mechanic
and a name of possibly oracular significance.

Which is how we came to consider calling the baby Delphos.

Which is why we never made it to Pennsylvania, never arrived to help J.B.
plant trees on the naked mountaintop he calls a farm, never hiked down the
brush-choked trail for groceries in the gnomic hamlet of Mann's Choice, never
hefted those truckloads of bundled bodies nor buried their delicate rootling
toes in the ice and mud of rocky meadows.

Blue spruce, black walnut, white pine, silver maple.

And that name! Mann's Choice. Finger of individual will poked in the face of
inexorable destiny.

Which is how we came to consider calling the baby Hamlet, Spruce or
Pennsylvania.

But we didn't make it there. Never even got to Lima or Bucyrus, let alone
Martin's Ferry, let alone West Virginia, let alone the Alleghenies tumbled
across the state line like the worn-out molars of a broken-down plow horse
munching grass in a hayfield along the slate-grey Juniata.

Because the engine balked.

Because the shakes kicked in and grew like cornstalks hard as we tried to
ignore them, as if we could push that battered blue Volvo across the wintry
heart of the Midwest through sheer determination.

Which is foolish.

And the man in Delphos told us so.

Fuel injector, he says. Can't find even a sparkplug for foreign cars in these parts. Nearest dealer would be Toledo or Columbus, or down the road in Fort Wayne.

Which is Indiana. Which is going backwards.

Which is why they drive Fords in Ohio.

Which is how we came to consider calling the baby Edsel, Henry, Pinto or Sparks.

Which is why we spent the last short hour of evening lurching and vibrating back through those prosperous bean fields just waiting for spring to burst the green-shingled barns of Van Wert County.

Which is how we came to consider calling the baby Verna, Daisy, Persephone or Soy.

By this time we're back on the freeway, bypassing beautiful downtown Fort Wayne in favor of the rain forest at Exit 11, such is the cognomen of this illuminated Babel, this litany, this sculptural aviary for neon birds, these towering aluminum and tungsten weeds,

bright names raised up like burning irons to brand their sign upon the heavens.

Exxon, Burger King, Budgetel, Super 8.

Which is how we came to consider calling the baby Bob Evans.

Which is how we came to consider calling the baby Big Boy, Wendy, Long John Silver or Starvin' Marvin.

Which is how we came to salve our wounds by choosing a slightly better than average motel, and bringing in the Colonel to watch "Barnaby Jones" while Elizabeth passes out quick as you like

leaving me alone with my thoughts and reruns

in the oversized bed of an antiseptic room on an anonymous strip of indistinguishable modules among the unzoned outskirts of a small Midwestern city named for the Indian killer Mad Anthony Wayne.

Which is why I'm awake at 4 a.m. as the first trucks sheet their thunder down toward the interstate.

Which is why I feel my unborn child kick and roll within the belly of its sleeping mother, three heartbeats in two bodies, two bodies in one blanket, one perfect and inviolable will like a flower preparing to burst into bloom,

and its aurora lights the edge of the window like nothing I've ever seen.

The Prose Poem

On the map it is precise and rectilinear as a chessboard, though driving past you would hardly notice it, this boundary line or ragged margin, a shallow swale that cups a simple trickle of water, less rill than rivulet, more gully than dell, a tangled ditch grown up throughout with a fearsome assortment of wildflowers and bracken. There is no fence, though here and there a weathered post asserts a former claim, strands of fallen wire taken by the dust. To the left a cornfield carries into the distance, dips and rises to the blue sky, a rolling plain of green and healthy plants aligned in close order, row upon row upon row. To the right, a field of wheat, a field of hay, young grasses breaking the soil, filling their allotted land with the rich, slow-waving spectacle of their grain. As for the farmers, they are, for the most part, indistinguishable: here the tractor is red, there yellow; here a pair of dirty hands, there a pair of dirty hands. They are cultivators of the soil. They grow crops by pattern, by acre, by foresight, by habit. What corn is to one, wheat is to the other, and though to some eyes the similarities outweigh the differences it would be as unthinkable for the second to commence planting corn as for the first to switch over to wheat. What happens in the gully between them is no concern of theirs, they say, so long as the plough stays out, the weeds stay in the ditch where they belong, though anyone would notice the wind-sewn cornstalks poking up their shaggy ears like young lovers run off into the bushes, and the kinship of these wild grasses with those the farmer cultivates is too obvious to mention, sage and dun-colored stalks hanging their noble heads, hoarding exotic burrs and seeds, and yet is it neither corn nor wheat that truly flourishes there, nor some jackalopian hybrid of the two. What grows in that place is possessed of a beauty all its own, ramshackle and unexpected, even in winter, when the wind hangs icicles from the skeletons of briars and small tracks cross the snow in search of forgotten grain; in the spring the little trickle of water swells to welcome frogs and minnows, a muskrat, a family of turtles, nesting doves in the verdant grass; in summer it is a thoroughfare for raccoons and opossums, field mice, swallows and black birds, migrating egrets, a passing fox; in autumn the geese avoid its abundance, seeking out windrows of toppled stalks, fatter grain more quickly discerned, more easily digested. Of those that travel the local road few pay that fertile hollow any mind, even those with an eye for what blossoms, vetch and timothy, early forsythia, the fatted calf in the fallow field, the rabbit running for cover, the hawk's descent from the lightning-struck tree. You've passed this way yourself many times, and can tell me, if you would, do the formal fields end where the valley begins, or does everything that surrounds us emerge from its embrace?

The Orange

Gone to swim afer walking the boys to school.

Overcast morning, mid-week, off-season,

few souls to brave the warm, storm-tossed waves,

not wild but rough for this tranquil coast.

Swimming now. In rhythm, arm over arm,

let the ocean buoy the body and the legs work little,

wave overhead, crash and roll with it, breathe,

stretch and build, windmill, climb the foam. Breathe,

breathe. Traveling downwind I make good time

and spot the marker by which I know to halt

and forge my way ashore. Who am I

to question the current? Surely this is peace abiding.

Walking back along the beach I mark the signs of erosion,

bide the usual flotsam of seagrass and fan coral,

a float from somebody's fishing boat,

crusted with sponge and barnacles, and then I find
the orange. Single irradiant sphere on the sand,
tide-washed, glistening as if new born,
golden orb, miraculous ur-fruit,
in all that sweep of horizon the only point of color.
Cross-legged on my towel I let the juice course
and mingle with the film of salt on my lips
and the sand in my beard as I steadily peel and eat it.
Considering the ancient lineage of this fruit,
the long history of its dispersal around the globe
on currents of animal and human migration,
and in light of the importance of the citrus industry
to the state of Florida, I will not claim
it was the best and sweetest orange in the world,
though it was, o great salt water
of eternity,
o strange and bountiful orchard.

McGrath on Creating Your Own Rules

Capitalist Poem #5

Note: This is the poem in which, for the first time, I identified with my essential "subject." While I had invested myself quite seriously in poetry for years, I had mostly written in my dutiful modes, on received topics, and without a great sense of personal urgency. Poetry seemed an important undertaking, but beyond the beauty of language I wasn't sure how to connect the craft to my life, to the world I knew and inhabited. In essence, I was a late-twentieth-century imperial American, a creature of cities, cars, TV, McDonald's, and yet I had never seen this everyday landscape as material for my poetry until, like a vision, like a flaming bush, the image of the 7-11 burned before my eyes! The 7-11 became the emblematic icon of my first book, a figure for the culture that had created me and was busily re-creating the entire planet in its image.

"Poetry seemed an important undertaking, but beyond the beauty of language I wasn't sure how to connect the craft to my life, to the world I knew and inhabited."

Note: I sing the body eclectic.

Note: Another lesson I learned here, is that the poetic grail of "finding one's voice" can sometimes be a matter of unlearning, of stripping down the furniture rather than applying more gilt and polish. Having been schooled in formal, aloof, and intellectualized poetic traditions, it was a great relief to toss all that baggage out the window in favor of simplicity. Just write it, I remember telling myself, as clearly and simply as possible. In lines. In sentences. Like William Carlos Williams, Slurpeefied.

Note: People will say—"But 7-11s are so stupid, foolish, trivial, jejune! They are so culturally specific! They are not universal! How is anyone going to understand this poem in Guatemala or Tibet?" It seems to me that the only universal of the human condition is the absolute unique particularity of each individual life; bearing witness to the specific is, therefore, a means of honoring the universal. Don't be hoodwinked by those who would have you believe that the actual, quotidian, earthly, or spiritual texture of your life is not every bit as fit material to be fashioned into poetry as were the earthly textured lives of Whitman and Neruda, the spiritually textured lives of Rumi and Emily Dickinson.

Note: Never be afraid of appearing stupid, foolish, trivial, or jejune.

Almond Blossoms, Rock and Roll, the Past Seen as Burning Fields

Note: The texture of an individual life, yes, but also a sense of historical context, how my world bordered or overlapped other worlds, other cultures, other social orders—this was the larger notion that gives the poem its multifaceted, symphonic, overstuffed quality.

Note: 1984 was an apex year for a certain kind of American arrogance. As much as I would have liked to be held accountable, I felt myself to be complicit, at the very least, a willing passenger on the currents of the zeitgeist. Documenting that, thinking it out on the page, gave the poem its essayistic skeleton. *Thinking it out on the page:* what this really means is to make the narratorial consciousness itself one subject of the poem, to textualize not merely the sensory data but the processes by which the intellect interprets and comprehends the world.

Note: I was also learning about the complex, figurative magic of metaphor: those three young men so fueled by youthful self-certainty that they can overlook the existence of the Rock of Gibraltar were true to my personal experience, and could also symbolize the nation's larger historical blindness—how cool is that?

Note: Formally, the language is lush, romantic, ornate; there's a lot of assonance and alliteration; the line is a variable, unstructured equivalent of blank verse—the poem is pretty much haunted by the ghost of William Wordsworth, and perhaps by the ghost of Lynda Hull, as well. Lynda's work was new to me then, and strongly influenced several of the poems in my second book—I wanted to match her energy and verve, follow her model in creating updated, extended lyric poems in the Romantic tradition.

Note: Lynda Hull's untimely death in a traffic accident still seems to me a grievous loss to contemporary American poetry.

Delphos, Ohio

Note: The poem evolved from the sight of those towering signs for motels, gas stations, and restaurants visible miles away down the highway, designed to lure you off the road at their exit. Now a familiar part of the interstate landscape, they were fairly new to the world then—sometime in the late 1970s the technology for those slim metal poles must have evolved to support such fantastic heights. At any rate, one day, driving through the Midwest, I was suddenly struck by the pathos of them; how they speak, in a purely American way, of the age-old desire to elevate one's name into the sky, a hunger for recognition that resonates with biblical fervor to which we are commonly blinded by their commercial vulgarity. What's in a name? Suddenly, expecting our first child, the question positively buzzed with relevance, which surely accounts for my heightened susceptibility to the entire notion of the poem.

Note: Formally, I was trying to open up the prose poem into what I thought of as "sculptural fragments," a means of investigating the lost realm between the prose paragraph and the line of verse; I have since come to identify this as "strophic" structure, following a causal chain through Robert Hass to Czeslaw Milosz and back into the mists of Greek prosody.

Note: Power of the image!

Note: Dare to be funny.

Note: The baby was named Sam.

The Prose Poem

Note: Essays, parables, fables, nature sketches, travelogues—great poetic models, all.

Note: Having previously written prose poems intuitively and somewhat haphazardly, I undertook to explore the form more systematically in my fourth book. Writing such a sequence, thinking about it rigorously, I inevitably began to teach the prose poem in a graduate seminar on poetic form. One day in class, seeking to define the differences—and the even more important similarities—between poetry and prose, the metaphor of two farmers tilling neighboring fields suggested itself. The sheer delight of developing the metaphor, with the help of those terrific students, drove the entire process, and the finished poem is in part a testament to that communal creative effort. To paraphrase: thinking cartographically, we tend to identify prose as one distinct territory, and poetry as another: where they come together is just a line on the map, a border lacking dimensionality—there is no *there* there. So the prose poem, at a purely definitional level, is homeless. As is so often the case, the error of categorial abstraction can be rectified by moving from the theoretical to the practical, from the clean colors of the map to the muddy marshlands of the real world.

"The prose poem is such a rich and flexible form, a great strategic choice to help overcome one of the inherent weaknesses of lyric poetry—namely, its difficulty in accommodating large amounts of information."

Note: Beware of false dichotomies.

Note: The prose poem is such a rich and flexible form, a great strategic choice to help overcome one of the inherent weaknesses of lyric poetry—namely, its difficulty in accommodating large amounts of information.

Note: After writing a number of prose poems you are likely to experience great homesickness for the line; you can go home again, but don't forget to write.

The Orange

Note: When I first read this poem to an audience here in Miami, several friends who happen to be the mothers of some of my childrens' school friends, heard it, and were troubled, perplexed, even alarmed, that I had "eaten" the orange. How could I ever again be entrusted with the welfare of small children if I was prone to such egregious lapses in judgment?

Note: Poetry should not be mistaken for autobiography.

Note: Mostly, poetry is hard work. It is a salt mine, a logging camp, an assembly line, a phone bank. Inspiration is wonderful, but the long complex, obsessively detailed labor of revising what inspiration offers towards its necessary perfection—line after line, draft after draft, day after month after year—is a lonely, daunting, Sisyphean task. Mostly, yes, but sometimes—sometimes the world rolls a poem right up to your feet!

Note: If it's so hard, and the material rewards are small, why do we do it? Fun, necessity, gratitude, obligation, love of language, the joy of creation, to make sense of existence, to give shape to chaos, flexible hours, high job satisfaction, no risk of layoffs or downsizing when you control the means of production.

Note: Go ahead, eat the orange.

Writing Suggestions

1. Write a list poem describing an emotion other than love. Call upon all five of the senses, and use imagery, innuendo, memory, and voice to add meaning. What are some of the challenges inherent in the list poem? What are some of the advantages? Which of McGrath's poems included here might be considered a variation on a list poem?

2. Select one (or more) icon of popular culture and write a poem about your relationship with it. Look deeply into what the icon represents, the social mores, the hidden messages, why it's an icon at all. McGrath does this quite effectively with 7-11, Denise Duhamel has an entire Barbie series, and Wanda Coleman populates the universe of her poems with a multitude of pop culture references and figures. How are they handling pop culture differently than you are? What might you learn from their examples? What might they learn from your example?

3. Use the Internet to find a poem in a foreign language that you do not speak or read. It's easy to find a foreign language poem—just use a search engine and type in the name of a poet like "Czeslaw Milosz" or "Miroslav Holub" or "Pablo Neruda" and scroll through your findings. Odds are you'll have your

pick of poems in their original language. Print up a copy of this poem and then translate it. Use your imagination and creativity versus a dual-language dictionary. Make educated guesses. When you're through, see if you can find a professional translation of the poem. How close is yours? What components of the poem "translated" well despite the language barrier? (Variation: Try this with a foreign language that has many cognates with English, such as Spanish. Then try this with a language that's very different from English, such as Russian or Swedish).

4. In the spirit of Robert Pinsky's Favorite Poem Project, select a contemporary poet (someone who has been writing and publishing since 1950) who *is not* included in this book, read at least one of their books in its entirety, and share your findings with friends, a writing class, an informal writing group, or anyone else you know who appreciates literature. In your brief presentation/discussion, include a short bit of biographical information as well as your response to and critique of this collection. How does learning more about another poet's work help you as a writer? As a student of literature?

> *"Everybody has their own idea of what's a poet. Robert Frost, President Johnson, T. S. Eliot, Rudolf Valentino—they're all poets. I like to think of myself as the one who carries the lightbulb."*
>
> —Bob Dylan

Peter Meinke

Ode to Good Men Fallen Before Hero Come

In all story   before hero come
good men from all over set forth
to meet giant ogre dragon troll
and they are all killed every one
decapitated roasted cut in two
their maiden are carted away and gobbled like cupcake
until hero sail across white water
and run giant ogre dragon troll quite through

Land of course explode into rejoicing
and king's daughter kisses horny knight
but who's to kiss horny head of slaughtered
whose bony smile are for no one in particular
somewhere left out of story somebody's daughter
remain behind general celebration
combing her hair without looking into mirror
rethinking life without Harry who liked his beer

I sing for them   son friend brother
all women-born men like one we know
ourselves   no hero they no Tristan
no St. George Gawain Galahad Sgt. York
they march again and again to be quartered and diced
and what hell for them never attempt to riddle
I'm talking about Harry Smith caught in middle
who fought pretty bravely for nothing and screamed twice

The Poet, Trying to Surprise God

The poet   trying to surprise his God
composed new forms from secret harmonies
tore from his fiery vision galaxies
of unrelated shapes   both even & odd
But God just smiled   and gave His know-all nod
saying   *There's no surprising One who sees*
the acorn   root   and branch of centuries
I swallow all things up   like Aaron's rod

So hold this thought beneath your poet-bonnet:
no matter how free-seeming flows your sample
God is by definition the Unsurprised
'Then I'll return' the poet sighed 'to sonnets
of which this is a rather pale example'

Is that right?   said God   *I hadn't realized . . .*

Rage

Eighteen below: the black-capped chickadee
bangs on the suet in front of the cat
pressing against the pane   The woodpile
sprawls below the porch   the woodsmoke shadow
solid as the snow   the emptiness
where the old elm used to be: all frozen forever
in this scene   by these words   on this page:
a poor farmhouse broken down by age

And rage   too   will never go away   never
Your disappointment   bitter as ash   more
murderous than this weather
is part of what we'd taste like now
if whatever's in the woods got in the house
You're sleeping now: you never had it better

Liquid Paper

Smooth as a snail   this little parson
pardons our sins   Touch the brush tip
lightly and   *abracadabra!*   a clean slate

We know those who blot their brains
by sniffing it   which shows
it erases more than ink
and with imagination anything
can be misapplied . . . In the army
our topsergeant drank aftershave   squeezing
my Old Spice to the last slow drop

It worked   like Liquid Paper   in his head

until he'd glide across the streets of Heidelberg
hunting for the house in Boise Idaho
where he was born . . .   If I were God
I'd authorize Celestial Liquid Paper
every seven years to whiten our mistakes:
we should be sorry and live with what we've done
but seven years is long enough and all of us

deserve a visit now and then
to the house where we were born
before everything got written so far wrong

Scars

Subject - Scars
other layer-
father
Internal scars
struggle of
life

When I was young I longed for scars
like my father's   They were the best
scars on the block   startling   varied
pink as a tongue against his whiskey skin

The longest bolted from his elbow
finger-thick where the barbed wire plunged in
a satin rip thinning toward the wrist
I read the riddle of my father's body

like a legend punctuated by pale hyphens
neat commas   surgical asterisks and exclamation
points from scalp to ankle   His tragic knuckles
spoke violence in demotic Greek

My silent father said little   too little   it seems
but after the divorce he told me   tracing
the curved path on his skull where hair never grew

'It's the ones you can't see that kill you'
and it's true our doctor said his liver
which did him in   was scarred like an old war-horse
Still   the mark I knew best I gave him myself   hitting
a pop fly straight up and swinging the child's bat again

with all my might as the ball descended
over the plate   He had to run in to catch it
and the bat cracked him under his chin   dropping
my father like a murdered king   peeling a wound

no butterfly bandage could cover   I was too stunned
to move   but the look my mother gave me proved
no matter what happened later   this man bleeding
like Laius on the ground was the one she loved

The Secret Code

Bach was rising from another room

like a secret code in a mathematician's castle
when you came toward me in a summer dress
light slatted through the oaken banister
like a secret code in a mathematician's castle

floating down the stairway in the afternoon
light slatted through the oaken banister
an idea of harmony made manifest
floating down the stairway in the afternoon
striping your slender body like a strobe
an idea of harmony made manifest

The music wound you in a golden braid
striping your slender body like a strobe
and Bach and April and undying youth

like music wound you in a golden braid
conspiring until I knew the dream
of Bach and April and undying youth

would cling across the downward years
conspiring until I knew that dream

despite the disharmonic tarnishing of time
would cling across the downward years
and fuse our lives together like a fugue
to spite the disharmonic tarnishing of time

Then all turned mysterious and blessed
and fused our lives together like a fugue
when you came toward me in a summer dress
turning all mysterious and blessed

while Bach was rising from another room

Seven & Seven

Looking back at it now he
can see what a fool he was
but life's not a damn exam

and if being a dunce and
disgrace has dragged him to where
he kneels in this sweltering

sagging house with the shutters
hanging like drunks from a frayed
merry-go-round a pen or

a drink in his hand and her
reading a book while the dogs
circle outside maniacs

running the land no matter
which way we vote he can say
at least we tried and this the

road we took: *twisting below*
the oaks the vines sucking their
trunks where unearthly shadows
mix with the smell of salt and
decay and the swollen threat
of rain warps the cypress boards
and softens the porous ground
until the house tilts like a

monk tipsy beside a stream
that murmurs the drunkard's dream:

Everything can be fixed O
Lord anything can be fixed

A Meditation on You & Wittgenstein

Wittgenstein never met you face to face
but fancied someone like you when he said
The world is everything that is the case

a maxim hard to fathom   Nevertheless
its rhythms tug like Ariadne's thread:
the world *is* everything that is the case

the world's *everything*   that is the case
(you for example sleeping in my bed)
Although Wittgenstein never met you face to face

he guessed logic lies in poetry's embrace
and from the same dark labyrinth has fed
the world being everything that is the case:

for love or dreams of love curls at its base
and if you miss it your heart's bled and dead
I wish he could have met you face to face

An ounce of loneliness outweighs a pound of lace:
what strange equations winding through my head!
Poor Wittgenstein never met you face to face
The word is only everything: *that's* the case

Assisted Living

Hunching at the adult center
like aluminum crickets
on the ground-floor hallway
outside the arthritic elevator
our chrome appendages clanking

and hooking each other we stuff
ourselves in the box and turn around

Language is queer: adult movies
mean fucking but adult centers
mean dying though both mean
without dignity in front of others
In the elevator our spotted hands
and heads shake like mushrooms in rain

Not one in here who hasn't had
adventure We've cried out
in bed and staggered home at midnight
sung songs and lied making
hellish mistakes and paid for them

or not: it makes small difference Life
is gravity dragging all together:
the sparkiest eye the delicate breast
the sly hand the harsh laugh . . .

If there were humor left in the this small band
it would raise its dying voice and shout
knowing most are deaf: *Going down!*

But no one says a word so we wait
nodding fungily for someone

to press our number

Zinc Fingers

Though scientists inform us that criminals
have insufficient zinc I've always believed
it's insufficient gold and silver that gets
them going The man who slipped his hand into
my front pocket on the jammed Paris Métro
wasn't trying to make friends His overcoat
smelled greasy and it was unpleasant holding
hands above my wallet pressed in on all sides
like stacked baguettes There was no way to move or

take a swing   Still   some action on my part seemed
to be called for: we stood   nose to nose   I tried
to look in his eyes but he stared at my chin
shy on our first date   so after a while as
we rattled along toward the Champs-Élysées

I lost concentration and began to think

of our scholarly daughter working at Yale
on a project called Zinc Fingers   scanning a
protein with pseudopods   each with a trace of
zinc   that latch on to our DNA and help
determine what we become   This brought me back
to *mon ami*   the pickpocket: I wondered
how he chose his hard line of work and if as
a boy he was good at cards for example
or sewing and for that matter what choice did
I have either so when we reached our stop and
he looked up from my chin at last I smiled at
him and his eyes flashed in fear or surprise and
I called *It's OK!*   as he scuttled away
Tout va bien!   though I held tight to my wallet

Meinke on the Potential of Form

Looking at the ten poems I chose as my "best," I realize that they aren't my most popular, which tend to be freer, funnier poems like "Supermarket," "The Magic Kingdom," "Chicken Unlimited," and "Artist of the Heart." The ones I like best are the ones I've worked on a long time, like prodigal children, to get "right": if not entirely formal, they're more shapely. Four of them are title poems for my books. Included in the ten are two sonnets ("Rage" and "The Poet, Trying to Surprise God"), two syllabics ("Zinc Fingers" and "Seven & Seven"), two in original "shapes" ("Assisted Living" and "Liquid Paper"), an ode ("Ode to Good Men Fallen Before Hero Come"), a pantoum ("The Secret Code"), a villanelle ("A Meditation on You & Wittgenstein"), and unrhymed quatrains ("Scars").

Philosophically, I don't hold formal poetry higher than free verse, and about half my poems are "free" ("loose" might be a better adjective), but practically I think form has a great deal to offer. When it works, it's more memorable (the poems I've memorized over the years tend to be formal: Shakespeare, Donne, Keats, Dickinson, Frost, Nemerov). When a poet becomes comfortable in forms, from long reading and writing, he or she is often more original for the simple reason that form has a mind of its own, whereas in free verse you're winging it alone. In writing a formal poem, you begin by following your own thought, but sooner or later the form itself suggests a sound, a word, a rhythm that changes and enriches your own idea.

"In free verse you're winging it alone. In writing a formal poem, you begin by following your own thought, but sooner or later the form itself suggests a sound, a word, a rhythm that changes and enriches your own idea."

For example, after reading a fine novel, *Wittgenstein's Mistress*, I began thinking about what I remembered about that logician's philosophy, and all I could think of was "The world is everything that is the case" (which isn't in the novel). I recognized that as an iambic pentameter line, and I wrote, right off, the beginning of a love poem:

Wittgenstein never met you face to face
but fancied someone like you when he said
The world is everything that is the case

My "idea" was to write a classical love poem whose theme might be paraphrased, à la John Donne, as "You're my everything." But the possibility of a villanelle (I thought immediately of a title, "Wittgenstein's Villanelle"—alliterated dactyls!—which I later discarded as too cute) led to all kinds of ideas I wouldn't have thought of otherwise. Looking for a rhyme with "said" led to "Ariadne's thread," which led to the "dark labyrinth" and "equations winding through my head." It also brought into my mind the saying, "A pound of feathers equals a pound a lead" which gradually morphed in the poem to "An ounce of loneliness outweighs a pound of lace." I could write a whole chapter on the number of things that happened because this poem, later published in *The Georgia Review*, "wanted" to be a villanelle.

My poems start in all sorts of ways, but usually with an image that seems somehow verbally interesting. "Their maiden are carted away and gobbled like cupcake," "The black-capped chickadee/bangs on the suet in front of the cat," "We know those who blot their brains/by sniffing it, which shows/it erases more than ink," and "When I was young I longed for scars/like my father's" are typical poem-starters that I wrote down in my notebook, which I now transfer to the computer.

"My practice, when I get a line attached to an idea, is to push the poem through to the end, or as far as I can, including all kinds of things that even then I know I won't keep, but that might suggest different turns later on."

My practice, when I get a line attached to an idea, is to push the poem through to the end, or as far as I can, including all kinds of things that even then I know I won't keep, but that might suggest different turns later on. For example, in "Rage" (first called "The Farmhouse") I was describing a winter scene outside our kitchen window after a snowstorm—I was teaching that January at Hamilton College. When I wrote the line "a poor farmhouse broken down by age," the sound suggested the next line, and the poem turned: "And rage, too, will never go away . . ." Following this lead, writing fast, I wrote:

your disappointment, bitter as ash, colder
than this weather, is part of what we'd taste like now
if cannibals appeared and cut us up.

Even as I wrote it, I knew that cannibals were ridiculous in the poem (and in upstate New York!)—but I knew I had plenty of time to rewrite it. Eventually, long after the cannibals departed, the poem became a kind of free-verse sonnet—because the "turn" occurred in the ninth line—and was published in *The New Yorker*.

Robert Frost said that one of the keys to writing good poetry was recognizing "happy accidents." In "Rage," the black-capped chickadee was just there, outside our window; only later, as I recognized how the poem was developing, did it take on darker connotation, along with the cat watching it. After that, I added—made up—touches that fit the darkening mood: the frozen woodpile, the cut-down elm. And although it doesn't appear directly, I think the ending was influenced by a poem that came to mind as I was working, Browning's mordant "Porphyria's Lover."

In a general way, most of my changes are done for sound. Although I'm a great believer in clarity, and feel that far too many of our poets write poems so obscure that no reasonable person would be interested in them, I believe also that the music of a poem supersedes its meaning, or narrative (ideally, they merge). So, in "Scars," for example, among the changes I made was "startling" in the third line, to go with "scars," "father," and "block." The last two lines of the third stanza originally read:

points from knee to brow. His eloquent
knuckles told tales out of school.

This became, for "sound" reasons:

points from scalp to ankle His tragic knuckles
spoke violence in demotic Greek

To write simply about changes in poems is always to tell a lie, because everything is happening all at once: sound, meaning, form, shape, tone. In addition, most successful poems take turns that their author didn't foresee, which gives them a certain tension and unpredictability. When Peter Davison accepted "Scars" for *The Atlantic Monthly*, he wrote that he liked its modern treatment of the Oedipus myth. But that came late to the poem (our family was German/Irish, not Greek); only after I remembered the incident, more or less true, with the bat, did I think of it, leading to the addition of words like "legend," "riddle," and "war-horse," and the last two lines with "Laius"—Oedipus's father—picking up all those "l's" and "a's":

no matter what happened later this man bleeding
like Laius on the ground was the one she loved

It's always difficult to know when a poem is "finished," but working in forms, or shaping a poem, helps a great deal. First I try to put down as clearly as possible what I'm feeling and thinking, what I'm passionate about, as uncritically as possible. Then I like to give the poem a little time, and after that begin to work on it like an object, turning it this way and that, trying to understand it and strengthen it at the same time.

> *"To write simply about changes in poems is always to tell a lie, because everything is happening all at once: sound, meaning, form, shape, tone. In addition, most successful poems take turns that their author didn't foresee, which gives them a certain tension and unpredictability."*

"Zinc Fingers" began after a man attempted to pickpocket me in the Paris Métro; at first it was a not-very-interesting poem about the pickpocket; it had more description of him, and included the students who were with me, and my wife's reaction (she thought I'd gone crazy, staring at this sleazy character pressed against me). Later that semester I read an article that claimed prisoners often had in common some sort of zinc deficiency, and I made a remark to my wife that now more or less begins the poem. And that reminded me (still later) of a project at Yale our scientist daughter had worked on. Now I had plenty of material for an interesting poem but had to organize it.

The first thought I had was to break the poem in two, to slow it down, and while doing that I saw that more or less in the middle was the line "I lost concentration and began to think." When I isolated that, I liked the idea: to me, it matched the train going between the Left and Right banks of Paris. At first the lines were uneven in both number and length but I worked on getting them down to fourteen lines each, sonnet length. As I rewrote the lines I could see they were becoming close in syllable count, and I liked that idea, too, in a poem with a slight scientific bent. In the end, "Zinc Fingers" was published in the Catholic magazine *America* as a 25-line syllabic poem, eleven syllables per line. No one cares, or should care, much about this, except the writer; but when it finally worked out in that shape I thought, Well, it's as finished as I'm ever going to get it. I felt I had found the right shape.

Similarly, when I stumbled on the stanzaic shapes for "Liquid Paper" (3-7-1-7-3) and "Assisted Living" (7-6-5-4-3-2-1) and the syllabic count (7) for "Seven & Seven," it helped me close them out. Again, this isn't the most important thing about these poems; I hope they sound both natural and inevitable: but working this way often lets me hear the "click" that Yeats said he heard when a poem was finished.

A slightly different case is "The Secret Code," which I wrote as a pantoum and love poem to Jeanne, whom I met in 1955 when she came down the stairs at Syracuse University. Although it worked fairly well as a "regular" pantoum—seven quatrains—I wasn't satisfied with it because the stanza breaks didn't match the flow of the narrative. So I experimented by breaking the stanzas closer to the natural sense of the lines, gradually shaping it in a different, but balanced, order, still 28 lines but now 1-4-6-3-3-6-4-1: a kind of disguised pantoum, a secret code in itself, published in *The Georgia Review*.

"The Poet, Trying to Surprise God" is an attempt to talk about this subject—the relation of form to vision—and frame it so the form carries the "meaning": God's exclamation finishes the poem and makes it—a happy accident?—a sonnet. First published in *Yankee*, it became the title of my second collection.

The freest poem I've chosen is "Ode to Good Men Fallen Before Hero Come" (published in *The New Republic* during the Vietnam War). I wanted to write about Vietnam without mentioning—and therefore limiting—it, and suddenly just began writing in a kind of pidgin English, a slight hint of an Asian accent. Even this irregular poem is in eight-line stanzas, ending with an envelope rhyme (diced/riddle/middle/twice) .

I've no doubt said both too much and too little about these poems, which, after all, might not be my best. A good friend of ours claims that poets should never read their own poems, on the grounds that they don't understand them. There's some truth in that. But I hope these few remarks have been helpful or interesting, or both, to readers and writers.

Finally, I might add a word of encouragement: despite popular opinion, writers are often happy! Our two main occupations are the ones which most lose our human curse of self-consciousness: writing and reading. Everything else is a hassle.

Writing Suggestions

1. Arnaud Daniel "discovered" the sestina. Giacomo da Lentino "invented" the sonnet. Jean Passerat "created" the villanelle. "Discover" your own poem form other than one that you know already exists. Write a poem in that form. Establish the "rules" of this form and see if these "rules" suggest words, images, sounds that you didn't expect. (Variation: Get a friend to "discover" a poem form, too, then switch so you try a poem in their form and they try one in yours.)

2. Meinke is an admitted fan of William Carlos Williams—so much so that many of his poems might properly be called homages. A number of other poets were so influenced by William Carlos Williams that they wrote their own poetry homages to him, as well. Denise Levertov wrote "Williams: An Essay." Robert Creeley wrote "For W. C. W." C. Dale Young wrote "Homage to Williams Carlos Williams." Write your own homage to William Carlos Williams, Meinke, or any other poet whose work you've greatly enjoyed. Use a structure they've employed; use a voice reminiscent of theirs; or use a topic or theme they cover in one of their poems. Explore any aspect of their work that "speaks" to you. The homage poem is not copying, but a time-honored and crucial aspect of many poets' education. Feel free to use the Interent to do further research on your poet in order to find more possibilities for your poem.

3. Take a poem of yours that you feel is complete and cut out all the punctuation—all of it. How does this change the poem? What if you put back in only the commas? Do you need to rebreak lines or alter stanzas to keep meaning? Are more meanings now suggested through ambiguity? What's the difference between ambiguity and confusion? Between mystery and muddle? Pay attention to the things that for you have become automatic. Be willing to experiment and challenge yourself, even on what seems to be the simplest level.

4. Whether he's writing in free verse or forms, Meinke loves the rhythm of language, the almost-there rhyme. Listen to his selections on the audio CD, then record one of your own poems on tape, CD, or a computer file. Listen to yourself reading your poem, paying particular attention to rhythm and the cadence of language. Do your lines roll off the tongue? Is there a

syncopation, a jazz beat to your words? Try rearranging the stanzas in print, then rerecord it. Did that affect how your read the poem? Be aware of the possibilities and potential of rhythm.

"A poem convinces us not just with words—the meaning of words—but the sound of them in our mouths, the way they increase our heart-beat or not, the amount of breath it takes to say a sentence, whether it will make us breathless at the end or whether it gives us time for repose or contemplation."

—Rita Dove

Lisel Mueller

When I Am Asked

When I am asked
how I began writing poems,
I talk about the indifference of nature.

It was soon after my mother died,
a brilliant June day,
everything blooming.

I sat on a gray stone bench
in a lovingly planted garden,
but the daylilies were as deaf
as the ears of drunken sleepers
and the roses curved inward.
Nothing was black or broken
and not a leaf fell
and the sun blared endless commercials
for summer holidays.

I sat on a gray stone bench
ringed with the ingenue faces
of pink and white impatiens
and placed my grief
in the mouth of language,
the only thing that would grieve with me.

The Triumph of Life: Mary Shelley

The voice addressing us is that of Mary Wollstonecraft Shelley (1796–1851), daughter of the radical philsopher William Godwin and the feminist Mary Wollstonecraft, who died as a result of her birth. She eloped with Percy Shelley, who was married to Harriet Westbrook at the time, and became his second wife after Harriet committed suicide. Shelley and Mary lived a nomadic life, moving around England and the Continent, never settling down anywhere for long. Three of their four children died in infancy. Their eight years together were a series of crises, many of them brought about by Shelley's restlessness and the drain of outsiders on their emotional and physical resources. After Shelley's accidental drowning, Mary, who was twenty-four at the time of his death, supported herself and their surviving son by her own writing and by editing and annotating Shelley's work. She published the first complete edition of his poems. Her own works consist of essays, short stories, and six novels, of which Frankenstein, *written when she was nineteen, is the most famous. Her journal has been an important biographical source for Shelley's and her life together.*

1
My father taught me to think,
to value mind over body,
to refuse even the airiest cage

to be a mouth as well as an ear,
to ask difficult questions,
not to marry because I was asked,
not to believe in heaven

None of this kept me from bearing
four children and losing three
by the time I was twenty-two

He wanted to think I sprang
from his head like the Greek goddess

He forgot that my mother died
of my birth, *The Rights of Women*
washed away in puerperal blood,
and that I was her daughter too

2
I met him when I was sixteen
He came to sit at my father's feet
and stayed to sit at mine

We became lovers
who remained friends
even after we married

A marriage of true minds
It is what you want
It is what we wanted

We did not believe in power
We were gentle
We shared our bodies with others
We thought we were truly free

My father taught us there was a solution
to everything, even evil

We were generous, honest
We thought we had the solution

and still, a woman walked
into the water because of us

3
After that death I stopped
believing in solutions

And when my children died
it was hard not to suspect
there was a god, a judgment

For months I wanted to be
with those three small bodies,
to be still in a dark place

No more mountain passes
No more flight from creditors
with arms as long as our bills

No more games to find out
who was the cleverest of us all
No more ghost stories by the fire
with my own ghosts at the window,
smiles sharpened like sickles
on the cold stone of the moon

For months I made a fortress
of my despair
"A defect of temper," they called it
His biographers never liked me

You would have called it a sickness,
given me capsules and doctors,
brushes and bright paints,
kits for paper flowers

4
An idea whose time has come,
you say about your freedom
but you forget the reason

Shall I remind you of history,
of choice and chance, the wish and the world,
or courage and locked doors,
biology and fate?

I wanted what you want,
what you have

If I could have chosen my children
and seen them survive
I might have believed in equality
written your manifestos

Almost two hundred years
of medical science divide us

5
And yet, my father was right
It was the spirit that won in the end

After the sea had done
what it could to his flesh
I knew he was my husband
only by the books
in his pockets: Sophocles, Keats

The word survives the body

It was then I decided
not to marry again
but to live for the word

6
I allowed his body to be burned
on that Italian beach
Rome received his ashes

You have read that our friend
snatched his heart from the fire
You call it a grisly act,
something out of my novel

You don't speak of the heart
in your letters, your sharp-eyed poems
You speak about your bodies
as though they had no mystery,
no caves, no sudden turnings

You claim isolation, night-sweats,
hanging on by your teeth

You don't trust the heart
though you define death
as the absence of a heartbeat

You would have taken a ring,
a strand of hair, a shoelace
—a symbol, a souvenir

not the center, the real thing

7
He died
and the world gave no outward sign
I started a Journal of Sorrow

But there were the words, the poems,
passion and ink spilling
over the edges of all those sheets
There was the hungry survivor
of our bodily life together

Would it have lasted, our marriage
if he had stayed alive?

As it was, we fed each other
like a pair of thrushes
I gave his words to the world
and they came back to me
as bread and meat and apples,
art and nature, mind and flesh
keeping each other alive

His last, unfinished poem
was called *The Triumph of Life*

8

You are surprised at my vision,
that a nineteen-year-old girl
could have written that novel,
how much I must have known

But I only wanted to write
a tale to tremble by,
what is oddly called a romance

By accident I slid
out of my century
into yours of white-coated men
in underground installations,
who invent their own destruction
under fluorescent lights

And in a few more decades,
when your test-tube babies sprout,
you will call me the prophet
of ultimate horror again

It was only a private nightmare
that dreamed the arrogance of your time

I was not your Cassandra
In any age, life has to be lived
before we can know what it is

Mueller on Persistence

Although "The Triumph of Life" was not written until 1975, its seeds were sown about twenty years earlier, long before I had any inkling that I might write a poem about Mary Shelley one day. I was reading a biography of the poet Percy Shelley—not his wife Mary—by Andre Maurois, a popular biographer of the early 1900s. This book was completely unlike contemporary biographies, which tend to be extremely long, heavily focused, and as impartial as possible. Maurois's biography, written in 1923, was about the length of a medium-size novel, and it read like one. His stance toward Shelley was decidedly sympathetic, so much so that I was entranced by this genius and firebrand, whose best-known lyric poems I had read in college. I admired him for his rebellious spirit, his disavowel of the religious pieties and rigid social conventions of the time, as well as for his poetry. Like his mentor, the radical philosopher William Godwin, who was to become his father-in-law, he risked ostracism and poverty by publishing his unpopular views in the English press.

"Although 'The Trimph of Life' was not written until 1975, its seeds were sown about twenty years earlier, long before I had any inkling that I might write a poem about Mary Shelley one day."

I could empathize with the 16-year-old Mary Godwin for falling in love with the 21-year-old Percy and eloping with him, though he was still legally married to his first wife, Harriet Westbrook, from whom he had separated and by whom he had two children. Reading this in America in the conservative 1950s, I was fascinated by the nomadic and communal lifestyle of the Shelleys in Switzerland and Italy, by their stream of long-term visiting poets and writers and the triangular relationship of Percy, Mary, and Mary's stepsister Claire. I was touched by Shelley's generosity in helping troubled friends and relatives, even though he and Mary had troubles of their own: serious debts, Mary's frequent illnesses, and, most tragically, the deaths of three young children and the suicide of Shelley's first wife. (After her death the Shelleys were legally married and applied for custody of Harriet's children, but their request was denied.) Finally, there was Shelley's death at age 29, when the boat he had hired for Ian Errand capsized off the coast of Italy. The boat was named *Ariel*, which seemed so right to me for this worshiper of ideal beauty, who had done an astonishing amount of writing in his short life and left much of it for Mary to edit and publish.

Percy Shelley was the hero of Maurois's book, and Mary, although ever-present, remained shadowy except for the sensation of her gothic novel *Frankenstein*, written when she was nineteen and begun on an evening when the circle of friends decided each of them should write a ghost story. All except Mary's were abandoned, and her spectacular book became a best-seller upon publication in England in 1818. At that time no one saw it as a futuristic novel, nor did I, in the 1950s, imagine that it would turn out to be a prophecy for our present-day technology.

I did not think seriously about Mary Shelley again until twenty years later, when the burgeoning feminist movement produced several books on Mary's mother, the heroic and tragic Mary Wollstonecraft (1759–97). She too was a radical and dissenter, and her two most famous books were *A Vindication of the Rights of Woman,* in which she advocated full property and other legal rights for women, and *Thoughts on the Education of Daughters,* which held that the education of women should be equal to that of men. She spent several years in France, where she observed and wrote about the French Revolution, and where she met an American writer, who fathered her daughter Fanny, and who abandoned her when she returned to England. She went to live with William Godwin and married him shortly before the birth of their daughter Mary, the future Mary Shelley. She died a few days later from complications of Mary's birth.

I was extremely moved by Mary Wollstonecraft's story and the irony of her fate. Here was a woman of spectacular intellect and courage, two centuries ahead of her time, who nevertheless could not escape the two almost stereotypical female tragedies of her time: seduction and abandonment, for one, and death in childbirth, for another. I was a happy wife and mother of two healthy children by then, and I became acutely aware of my historical good luck, to be living in a time and place which had given me rights and choices and a reasonable expectation that my children would survive for many years to come.

I would have liked to write about Mary Wollstonecraft, but with all the recent attention given to her, that would have been redundant. Instead I started thinking about the Godwins's daughter and her legacy. What would it have been like to be a motherless child, educated at home by a famous father to be an intellectual and free spirit and at age sixteen become the lover and companion to one of England's greatest poets? To be part of a brilliant circle and yet be frequently excluded because of the sicknesses that accompanied one's pregnancies? To endure four such pregnancies and have only one child survive the earliest years? I read her *Journal* (to which Percy also contributed) and became acutely conscious of the long lapses in the entries after these deaths, caused by what we now recognize as depression. Here again was a woman whose mind belonged in our century, but who was trapped in hers by its abysmal lack of medical knowledge.

So in the end it was the daughter, rather than the mother, who became the subject of my poem. Because of her lack of public announcements and the reticence of her *Journal,* she remained somewhat mysterious and intriguing to me, and this gave me more freedom to speculate about her thoughts and feelings. The question was how to frame the poem. I wanted it to be a poem of homage, an address to Mary in my own voice. I started to work on the poem, but it was lifeless and getting nowhere. Finally I realized that what I was doing was reciting the circumstances of her life back to her who had lived them, which made no sense. I abandoned the poem, unable to think of any alternative. Then one day, out of the blue, it came to me: let Mary be the speaker, let *her* address *me,* address all of us, the women of our time, as if she had been clairvoyant.

This idea came to me in a flash, and I began writing in a white heat, never considering that this mixture of straight biography and fictional clairvoyance would require a suspension of disbelief on the part of readers. If this poem illuminates the life of Mary Shelley vis-à-vis our present lives, I trust such a suspension is justified.

Once I had made this decision, the poem virtually "wrote itself." The rhythm of the short, speechlike lines was in my head, as if it had been a real, conversational voice telling a life history.

And in a few more decades
when your test-tube babies sprout,
you will call me the prophet

I heard her voice speaking in a rush, trying to get it all said, to tell me what was significant in her life and different from mine. You might say she was dictating her history to me in an urgent voice, one episode at a time. As a result the poem quite naturally fell into sections, each a separate segment of information and comment, remembrance and reflection. Of course there remained the work of polishing and sharpening the language as well as arranging the sections into an approximately chronological order, but that was pure pleasure because I knew I had finally written the poem I had wanted to write for twenty years.

While I felt that I needed a few commas for clarity, I decided not to use periods. The poem is constructed of very short, simply, declarative sentences, brief units of speech that are perfectly comprehensible without the periods that would have boxed them in. Instead I decided to open up the poem by means of frequent stanza breaks, which I hoped would suggest the ebb and flow of natural speech. I want this poem to be *heard,* if not physically, then in the mind.

"I decided to open up the poem by means of frequent stanza breaks, which I hoped would suggest the ebb and flow of natural speech. I want this poem to be HEARD, if not physically, then in the mind."

At the time I wrote this poem, work on the development of what is now known as in vitro fertilization was just beginning. I greatly underestimated the time it would take for these experiments to become standard practice. It did not take decades, but only a few years.

Writing Suggestions

1. Select a historical figure who interests you and write a persona poem in the voice of that person. Be aware of the audience, he/she/they whom this historical figure is speaking to. Consider doing research for verisimilitude and authentic, significant details. (Variation: Write this same type of persona poem as an epistolary poem. Begin it with Dear ________. Address it to

someone specific and let the historical figure say what they need to say to this person.)

2. Write a letter poem. Address it to a living person who is a stranger. Begin with Dear __________ and end with a closing such as Yours, Sincerely, Love, or perhaps With Affection. Ground yourself in the occasion of the letter—give the "I" a reason to write to the "you." Say what the "I" has always wanted to say, to the "you," to anyone. Brainstorm a bit to understand who the "I" is and what their desires, fears, and dreams are. These details may not come up in the poem, but in knowing them you'll be better able to write convincingly in the voice of the "I."

3. Choose any ten- to twenty-line poem in this book. Type out the poem, triple-spacing between the lines. Fill in the gap between the original poem's lines with lines of your own that are based on or vaguely reminiscent of the original lines. Cut out all the original lines and work to make what you have left cohere. Add or subtract lines, imagery, or individual words as needed. (Variation: When first adding your own lines, don't work *with* the poem, work *against* it. Violently, if necessary. Your poem will be the antithesis of the original, which may feel more like "your own" poem.)

4. Mueller is one of only a few American poets to have won both the National Book Award and the Pulitzer Prize for poetry. Use the Internet or a good reference book to find out who some of the others who've won both are. Locate some of these other critically acclaimed poets' works on-line or in your local library or bookstore. Carefully read through a few of their poems. What is it about their work (or Mueller's) that merits two of the top literary honors an American can receive for poetry? Is there a similarity in theme, structure, voice, style, imagery, mood, tone? Can you make an educated guess on which writer in this book is likely to win one or both of those awards? Why?

"It took me years to admit that the poem is smarter than I am."

—Charles Simic

Sharon Olds

I Go Back to May 1937

I see them standing at the formal gates of their colleges,
I see my father strolling out
under the ochre sandstone arch, the
red tiles glinting like bent
plates of blood behind his head, I
see my mother with a few light books at her hip
standing at the pillar made of tiny bricks with the
wrought-iron gate still open behind her, its
sword-tips black in the May air,
they are about to graduate, they are about to get married,
they are kids, they are dumb, all they know is they are
innocent, they would never hurt anybody.
I want to go up to them and say Stop,
don't do it—she's the wrong woman,
he's the wrong man, you are going to do things
you cannot imagine you would ever do,
you are going to do bad things to children,
you are going to suffer in ways you have not heard of,
you are going to want to die. I want to go
up to them there in the late May sunlight and say it,
her hungry pretty face turning to me,
her pitiful beautiful untouched body,
his arrogant handsome face turning to me,
his pitiful beautiful untouched body,
but I don't do it. I want to live. I
take them up like the male and female
paper dolls and bang them together
at the hips like chips of flint as if to
strike sparks from them, I say
Do what you are going to do, and I will tell about it.

The Missing Boy
for Etan Patz

Every time we take the bus
my son sees the picture of the missing boy.
He looks at it like a mirror—the dark
blond hair, the pale skin,
the blue eyes, the electric-blue sneakers with
slashes of jagged gold. But of course that
kid is little, only six and a half,
an age when things can happen to you,
when you're not really safe, and our son is seven,
practically fully grown—why, he would
tower over that kid if they could
find him and bring him right here on this bus and
stand them together. He sways in the silence
wishing for that, the tape on the picture
gleaming over his head, beginning to
melt at the center and curl at the edges as it
ages. At night, when I put him to bed,
my son holds my hand tight
and says he's sure that kid's all right,
nothing to worry about, he just
hopes he's getting the food he likes,
not just any old food, but the food
he likes the most, the food he is used to.

Little Things

After she's gone to camp, in the early
evening I clear our girl's breakfast dishes
from the rosewood table, and find a small
crystallized pool of maple syrup, the
grains standing there, round, in the night, I
rub it with my fingertip
as if I could read it, this raised dot of
amber sugar, and this time
when I think of my father, I wonder why
I think of my father, of the beautiful blood-red
glass in his hand, or his black hair gleaming like a
broken-open coal. I think I learned to

love the little things about him
because of all the big things
I could not love, no one could, it would be wrong to.
So when I fix on this tiny image of resin
or sweep together with the heel of my hand a
pile of my son's sunburn peels like
insect wings, where I peeled his back the night before camp,
I am doing something I learned early to do, I am
paying attention to small beauties,
whatever I have—as if it were our duty to
find things to love, to bind ourselves to this world.

The Race

When I got to the airport I rushed up to the desk,
bought a ticket, ten minutes later
they told me the flight was cancelled, the doctors
had said my father would not live through the night
and the flight was cancelled. A young man
with a dark brown moustache told me
another airline had a non-stop
leaving in seven minutes. See that
elevator over there, well go
down to the first floor, make a right, you'll
see a yellow bus, get off at the
second Pan Am terminal, I
ran, I who have no sense of direction
raced exactly where he'd told me, a fish
slipping upstream deftly against
the flow of the river. I jumped off that bus with those
bags I had thrown everything into
in five minutes, and ran, the bags
wagged me from side to side as if
to prove I was under the claims of the material,
I ran up to a man with a white flower on his breast,
I who always go to the end of the line, I said
Help me. He looked at my ticket, he said
Make a left and then a right, go up the moving stairs and then
run. I lumbered up the moving stairs,
at the top I saw the corridor,
and then I took a deep breath, I said

Goodbye to my body, goodbye to comfort,
I used my legs and heart as if I would
gladly use them up for this,
to touch him again in this life. I ran, and the
bags banged against me, wheeled and coursed
in skewed orbits, I have seen pictures of
women running, their belongings tied
in scarves grasped in their fists, I blessed my
long legs he gave me, my strong
heart I abandoned to its own purpose,
I ran to Gate 17 and they were
just lifting the thick white
lozenge of the door to fit it into
the socket of the plane. Like the one who is not
too rich, I turned sideways and
slipped through the needle's eye, and then
I walked down the aisle toward my father. The jet
was full, and people's hair was shining, they were
smiling, the interior of the plane was filled with a
mist of gold endorphin light,
I wept as people weep when they enter heaven,
in massive relief. We lifted up
gently from one tip of the continent
and did not stop until we set down lightly on the
other edge, I walked into his room
and watched his chest rise slowly
and sink again, all night
I watched him breathe.

The Knowing

Afterwards, when we have slept, paradise-
comaed, and woken, we lie a long time
looking at each other.
I do not know what he sees, but I see
eyes of quiet evenness
and endurance, a patience like the dignity
of matter. I love the open ocean
blue-grey-green of his iris, I love
the curve of it against the white,
that curve the sight of what has caused me

to go over, when he's quite still, deep
inside me. I have never seen a curve
like that, except our sphere, from outer
space. I don't know where he got
his kindness without self-regard,
almost without self, and yet
he chose one woman, instead of the others.
By knowing him, I get to know
the purity of the animal
which mates for life. Sometimes he is slightly
smiling, but mostly he just gazes at me gazing,
his entire face lit. I love
to see it change if I cry—there is no worry,
no pity, a graver radiance. If we
are on our backs, side by side,
with our faces turned fully to face each other,
I can hear a tear from my lower eye
hit the sheet, as if it is an early day on earth,
and then the upper eye's tears
braid and sluice down through the lower eyebrow
like the invention of farming, irrigation, a non-nomadic people.
I am so lucky that I can know him.
This is the only way to know him.
I am the only one who knows him.
When I wake again, he is still looking at me,
as if he is eternal. For an hour
we wake and doze, and slowly I know
that though we are sated, though we are hardly
touching, this is the coming that the other
brought us to the edge of—we are entering,
deeper and deeper, gaze by gaze,
this place beyond the other places,
beyond the body itself, we are making
love.

The Promise

With the second drink, at the restaurant,
holding hands on the bare table,
we are at it again, renewing our promise
to kill each other. You are drinking gin,

night-blue juniper berry
dissolving in your body, I am drinking Fumé,
chewing its fragrant dirt and smoke, we are
taking on earth, we are part soil already,
and wherever we are, we are also in our
bed, fitted, naked, closely
along each other, half passed out,
after love, drifting back
and forth across the border of consciousness,
our bodies buoyant, clasped. Your hand
tightens on the table. You're a little afraid
I'll chicken out. What you do not want
is to lie in a hospital bed for a year
after a stroke, without being able
to think or die, you do not want
to be tied to a chair like your prim grandmother,
cursing. The room is dim around us,
ivory globes, pink curtains
bound at the waist—and outside,
a weightless, luminous, lifted-up
summer twilight. I tell you you do not
know me if you think I will not
kill you. Think how we have floated together
eye to eye, nipple to nipple,
sex to sex, the halves of a creature
drifting up to the lip of matter
and over it—you know me from the bright, blood-
flecked delivery room, if a lion
had you in its jaws I would attack it, if the ropes
binding your soul are your own wrists, I will cut them.

5¢ a Peek

The day my class was to go to the circus,
I went into the bathroom, early,
and stood on tiptoe, into the bottom
corner of the mirror, and leaned on the sink,
and slowly cut off my eyelashes
down close to the eyelid. I had no idea what I was
doing, or why, I studied the effect
—not bad, a little stark—but when I saw the effect

on my mother, not just anger, but pity
and horror, I was interested.
I think I had almost given up on being
a girl, on trying to grow up to be a woman like my mother,
I wanted to get disadopted
and go home to the baby with a calf's head,
home to that birth-mother the bearded lady,
my father the sword-swallower stopped mid-swallow,
one with the sword. I had tried hard to act normal
but when the inspiration came
I felt I was meant to act on it,
to look at my mom with my gaze trimmed to a seer's
and see her see me for an instant, see
her irises contract. I did not
imagine I could ever leave my mother,
mostly I *was* her, in distorted form,
but at least for that second the itsy scissors
spoke to her with their birdy beak,
skreeek, skreeek, witch whinge. And when
my lashes grew back, no thicker no thinner no
shorter no longer, my mother sat me
down and taught me to bat them, to look
sidelong, blindly, and shudder them at seven beats a second.

His Costume

Somehow I never stopped to notice
that my father liked to dress as a woman.
He had his sign language about women
talking too much, and being stupid,
but whenever there was a costume party
he would dress like us, the tennis balls
for breasts—balls for breasts—the long
blonde wig, the lipstick, he would sway
his body with moves of gracefulness
as if one being could be the whole
universe, its ends curving back to come
up from behind it. Six feet, and maybe
one-eighty, one-ninety, he had the shapely
legs of a male Grable—in a short
skirt, he leaned against a bookcase pillar

nursing his fifth drink, gazing
around from inside his mascara purdah
with those salty eyes. The woman next door
had a tail and ears, she was covered with Reynolds Wrap,
she was Kitty Foil, and my mother was in
a tiny tuxedo, but he always won
the prize. Those nights, he had a look of daring,
a look of triumph, of having stolen
back. And as far as I knew, he never threw
up, as a woman, or passed out, or made
those signals of scorn with his hands, just leaned,
voluptuous, at ease, deeply
present, as if sensing his full potential, crossing
over into himself, and back,
over, and back.

The Space Heater

On the ten-below-zero day, it was on,
near the patients' chair, the old heater
kept by the analyst's couch, at its end,
like the infant's headstone that was added near the foot
of my father's grave. And it was hot, with the almost
laughing satire of a fire's heat,
the little coils like hairs in Hell.
And it was making a group of sick noises—
I wanted the doctor to turn it off
but I couldn't seem to ask, so I just
stared, but it did not budge. The doctor
turned his heavy, soft palm
outward, toward me, inviting me to speak, I
said, "If you're cold—are you cold? But if it's on
for me . . ." He held his palm out toward me,
I tried to ask, but I only muttered,
but he said, "Of course," as if I had asked,
and he stood and approached the heater, and then
stood on one foot, and threw himself
toward the wall with one hand, and with the other hand
reached down, behind the couch, to pull
the plug out. I looked away,
I had not known he would have to bend

like that. And I was so moved, that he
would act undignified, to help me,
that I cried, not trying to stop, but as if
the moans made sentences which bore
some human message. If he would cast himself toward the
outlet for me, as if bending with me in my old
shame and horror, then I would rest
on his art—and the heater purred, like a creature
or the familiar of a creature, or the child of a familiar,
the father of a child, the spirit of a father,
the healing of a spirit, the vision of healing,
the heat of vision, the power of the heat,
the pleasure of the power.

Silence, with Two Texts

When we lived together, the silence in the home
was denser than the silence in the home
after he left. Before, the silence
had been like a large commotion or industry
at a distance, like the downroar of mining. When he went,
I studied my husband's silence like an almost
holy thing, the call of a newborn born
mute. Text: "Though its presence is detected
by the absence of what it negates, silence
possesses a power which presages fear
for those in its midst. Unseen, unheard,
unfathomable, silence dis-
concerts because it conceals." Text:
"The waters compassed me about, even to
the soul: the depth closed me round
about, the weeds were wrapped about
my head." We lived alongside him, in his hush
and patience, sometimes we teased him, calling his
abstracted mask "Dad's alligator look,"
seeking how to love him as
he was, under the law that he could not
speak, and when I shrieked against the law
he shrinked down into its absolute,
he rose from its departure gate.
And he seemed almost like a hero, to me,

living, as I was, under the law
that I could not see the ones I loved
but only consort with them as beings
fixed as elements. In the last
weeks, by day we moved through the tearing
apart, along its length, of the union,
and by night silence lay down with blindness,
and sand, and saw.

Olds on Rhythm and Revision

Probably what I hope for most in a poem of mine is a feeling of aliveness. Since I'm a formal poet, that hoped-for aliveness or immediacy or sense of "realness" is going to be in some tension with the structure of the poem. Sometimes, from where form and freedom touch on each other, a small curly spark of energy might pop out for a moment from a work of art. I love those little rare jets of life force (and of tension between life force and the still power of the grid).

I tend to talk nonsense when I try to talk about my poems! I don't know what to say. I'm an old-fashioned storyteller poet. I write with a ballpoint pen in wide-lined grocery-store notebooks. I did not plan to be a formal poet or know that I was one. But here are all these four-beat lines (many of them in rough four-line "quatrains" though not in visible stanza form) with all this enjambment—a spider weaving a round web on a square grid.

"When I'm asked for the one piece of advice in craft that I think is the most important, I tend to say, 'Take your vitamins, exercise, no drugs. Poetry is joyous work, and it's good to keep our tools well cared for!'"

And not a drunken spider! When I'm asked for the one piece of advice in craft that I think is the most important, I tend to say, "Take your vitamins, exercise, no drugs. Poetry is joyous work, and it's good to keep our tools well cared for!"

I have put these ten poems in chronological order—I love chronological order (part of the mortal grid)—and I have included a variety of characters and subjects: parents, children, love, death, loss, fear, joy, and the general oddness of ordinary life.

I Go Back to May 1937

The way those two first *I's* are lined up shows me that I had not yet been told (fifteen or twenty years ago, when this was written) that I use the *I* too much!

Over the years of reading this aloud, I changed the *never* in line 18 to *have not* (mistrusting the melodrama of *never, always, no one,* and so on), and I took *blank* out of line 21 and *blind* out of 23—too corny and inexact.

It still makes me a little nervous to read that last line aloud. Some small part of me still slightly expects to be hit by lightning for it.

The Missing Boy

I like this one for what the child says. And as I read it over now I see the four-beat lines, often with a caesura: the controlled church-hymn rhythm with the sentences rappelling down it.

Little Things

I like the speaker's repetition of *I think of my father,* and I know I like the change in meter—two dactyls, a spondee, then seven trochees. (Of course I was not scanning it in any conscious way while writing it!)

> *glass in his | hand, or his | black hair | gleaming | like a*
> *broken- | open | coal. I | think I | learned to*

The Race and The Knowing and The Promise

These I chose for their ordinary subjects in ordinary language (with here and there a lozenge, a nomad, a lion).

5¢ a Peek

Strange species! Cheerful momentum!

His Costume

Less jumpy, more meditative: resolving.

The Space Heater

I chose this one for the last six lines—which of course I had no idea were coming. I did not know where this poem might go, but once the central object (and action) came into my mind I sat down and began to write.

Silence, with Two Texts

When I read those two passages cited in the poem (one from philosophy, one from the Old Testament), the poem began—or was made in me. Then it was my job to try to draw it out while changing it for the worse as little as possible!

If you were to ask me an hour after a poem was written how it started in my head and then how I became aware it had gotten started, I could probably tell you. I think it's usually a matter of noticing that my mind/heart is half-working on a scene or image; that something is gathering. Then often are the false starts—how to get in? How to begin? Without being untrue to the *life feeling* of it, or to the pattern/shape/music.

Maybe I'll close with a word on how I revise—every poet I know has a different way! When I like a poem, I type it (on my portable manual typewriter—

almost as old as I am—which I carry on my back). Then I try to remove what's irrelevant, or merely personal, or boring, or overly rich in vocabulary, or pretentious, without hurting the meter, the life-force feeling of the poem's breath and heartbeat. I tinker with the counterpoint, the cut-and-thrust (old rock and roll dance term?), the caesura, the do-wop of the ends and beginnings of the lines. I always save every draft in a pile, so I can look back and check if I've unknowingly revised the life out of the poem.

Writing Suggestions

1. Write your own version of "The Missing Boy." Let what's missing be anything but a person. Use your imagination to think of the emotions felt, the ache of need, the ramifications of loss. Specific, concrete details will help. (Variation: Think of people who are missing or at one time were, such as Jon-Benet Ramsey, Jimmy Hoffa, or the Lindbergh baby, to name just three. Select one whose situation speaks to you, and write "The Missing ______" from the point of view of a loved one who deeply misses this person. Some research might help, but rely mainly on inspiration and imagination.)

2. Some writers best write of self—uninhibitedly so—in their poems. Write a brutally honest, autobiographical poem that depicts an experience you had, an idea you believe, and/or a love from your past. See if the images, language, and structure can suggest a life beyond the poem, a history of events and experiences and people and stimuli. Think of this poem as being in lieu of an "author's biography" on the dust jacket of your best book.

3. Write a short (fourteen- to twenty-line) poem that does what Sharon Olds's "Little Things" does—that is, write a poem that focuses on small, usually unnoticed details. This attention to small details will also serve you well in all of your other poems as it provides verisimilitude, which is much needed in poetry today. (Variation: Take a poem that you've already written and rework it with the high attention to details that Olds shows here in her own poems. See how much mileage you can get out of a few select choices.)

4. Take a break from poetry and writing for a while. Purposefully go and do something you haven't done for a long time, something that has nothing at all to do with writing. Play Wiffle ball with your cousin. Skip stones across a pond. Pretend you're a child again and roll in the mud. Go to an ice-cream shop and get two cones, then eat them both yourself. An hour or three days later, reflect on what you did and find a way to use it in a future poem. Writers don't stop writing, even without a pencil or word processor in hand.

There's a famous anecdote about James Thurber where he's standing among friends in the middle of a cocktail party, and he goes suddenly quiet for a moment—his wife storms up and hisses into his ear, "Thurber! Stop writing!"

"I still harbor the rather quaint idea that poems have things to teach me, and one of those things is how to write a poem. Because of that I try as much as possible to let the poem have the reins."

—Sherod Santos

Lee Ann Roripaugh

PEARLS

Mother eats seaweed and plum pickles,
and when the Mormons come knocking
she does bird-talk. I've never seen
an ocean, but I'd swim in one to look
for secrets. She has a big pearl
from my ojii-san, says it will be mine
when she's dead. It's in a drawer
hidden with silver dollars. I hope
she doesn't buy a ticket, go back
to her sisters and leave me.

With stinging strokes, she brushes
my hair, pulls it into pigtails
that stretch my face flat. I walk
to school across sagebrush while
she watches from her bedroom window.
Once I found a prairie dog curled
sleeping on the ground and I brushed
away ants on his eyes. Mother
saw me dilly-dally, told me not
to touch dead things.

I have a red box in my desk
with a dragon lid that screws on
and off. It smells sweet from face
cream and I keep a kokeishi doll
inside for good luck. Wishing
for more colors in my crayon pail,
I make up stories about mermaids

and want a gold crayon to draw hair,
silver for their tails. But
we can't afford lots of kid junk.
I have piano lessons. She says
I'll be a doctor someday
but I think I'd like to be a fireman
or maybe a roller derby queen.

One day when I was walking home
some boys on bikes flew down
around me like noisy crows.
They kept yelling *Kill the Jap!*
I ran fast as I could but fell
in the dirt, got up and fell.
My mother came running to me.
She carried me home, picked out
the gravel, washed off blood,
tucked me into her bed and let
me wear the ring for awhile.

I wish I had long, white skinny
fingers, gold hair and a silver
tail. I'd gather baskets
of pearls. But my hair is black,
my fingers stubby. Mother
tells me they're not found just
floating underwater. She says
oysters make them, when there's
sand or gravel under their shells.
It hurts. And the more it hurts,
the bigger the pearl.

The Woman Who Loves Insects

If you stand outside my gate
    and peer between the slats
you might see me in the shrubs,

gathering up the caterpillars
    who disguise themselves
as bird-droppings, to tuck into

my kimono sleeves. I will not be
    the kind who makes pets
of butterflies. They only leave

a glitter of dust on my palm
    that makes me sneeze,
and they climb at night inside

my rice-paper lanterns, quick
    as I can snap my fingers,
explode into a curl of bitter-

smelling incense. (Even Buddha
    would wrinkle his nose).
And if you take care not to

trample the garden beetles, tear
    the spider's glistening veil,
you may come up to my window

and leave me a token—a snail,
    a locust, a cockroach.
I know the dragonfly's song,

the war-cries of grass-crickets,
    and will sing them to you
through a chink in the blinds.

And if my favorite caterpillar
    should accidentally drop
from my kimono sleeve and brush

past your face—and you do not
    let him break open
against the pebbles, but unfold

your fan in time to catch
    his fall—then I
will be the praying mantis,

who wears a mask on her wings
    to scare off birds.
I will pull away the mantle

from my face, and if you
    are not afraid of my fierce
eyebrows, my disheveled hair,

my unblackened teeth that give me
    a white, barbaric grin,
I will feed you tender leaves,

nestle and stroke you in the palm
    of my hand until you
are plump with nectar. Kawamushi,

my hairy caterpillar.

My honeybee.

My centipede.

Octopus in the Freezer

What could you possibly have been dreaming of
as you slumbered coiled there, tentacles
furled about your large soft brow, bashful
and pink, ruminating in the back corner
beneath an arched shelf of antelope ribs—
snugged between headless-bodied broods
of sage grouse, the icy bright pillows
of Shur-Fine lima beans and the buttered
currency of carrot medallions? What were
you thinking down there in my parents'
basement, blue blood's pulse stilled to a wiry
tangle of navy ribbon, the syncopated bongo
drum thump and thrum of your three hearts
on break between sets and resting silent
on the stage? By what *unlikelihood*
were you frozen solid in this tightly-wound
pose, like a multi-limbed Hindu goddess
in lotus position, riding the plains by freight
truck to Sakura Square in Denver, where
my mother admired the brawny circumference
of your arms, the snow-white firmness

of your inner flesh, the rubbery erect grip
of your suction cups? And what were the odds
that you'd be packed in dry ice by the ojii-san
behind the counter, tucked into our avocado-
green Igloo ice cooler and driven home
across the state line to Wyoming? You remain
frozen in time in my parents' freezer—totemic,
statuesque, infinite and apocryphal, even though
you've been eaten many times over, one arm
at a time, sliced thin into cross-sectioned slivers
for sushi on birthdays and holidays. As a child,
I used to think the dull muffled thud and clunk
of the furnace firing into life at night was the sound
of your head bumping up against the freezer lid,
the cold grate and clash of meats shifting,
scraping against one another in the wake
of your thrashing tentacles' lash and whip.
What error in judgment took you from your cozy
niche, your eclectic garden arranged with such
compulsive precision: the slender-necked
and lush-hipped wine bottles; the shiny winking
bits of mirror startling back your placid mild eye;
the pickle jar whose lid you loved to screw
and unscrew, dangling in a tapered arm—
your exquisitely sensitive, ganglia-rimmed
suckers quivering—to check for tasty things
to eat? Did you become snarled in a fisherman's
net, or clasped tight in the steel embrace
of a lobster trap—caught in the careless
kleptomania of your endless lust for crustacea?
And did your chromatophores pulse first white,
then red, to semaphore the blushing flush
of fear flaming to anger? Were you caped
in a smoky swirl of spewed blackness dispersing
the way sumi-é ink curls away from
the tornado whirl of a horsehair brush
being twirled clean in water? Today the snow
just falls and falls, and I think of you
as the relentless volatile wind lifts the flakes
into blinding, shimmering white veils that spiral
and mist—so cold the fine spray delicately
burns for one moment against the skin,

and frozen feathery etchings are flung up
against the windows like splayed bits
of goosedown. Cars and trucks cough and come
to a halt, my back door freezes shut.
The barometer drops and empty wine bottles
line the kitchen counter like bowling pins.
How odd, I keep thinking to myself
as everything around me creaks and groans
and shivers, then stills to ice and frost.
How odd that it has all come to this.
And then I wish for someone, anyone at all,
to dream of me, if only for a moment,
to unfurl my rigid aching limbs and melt down
all my hearts, taste my salt on their tongue,
let ice transubstantiate to breathing flesh,
and resurrect me back into the living again.

Roripaugh on Revision and Love

"Pearls," was very much a "breakthrough" poem for me as a graduate student in creative writing. It was one of the first poems I'd written that felt as if it had a strong sense of voice—in this instance, the voice of a five-year-old child (ostensibly a re-creation of *my* voice as a five-year-old child). At that point in time, I'd been struggling with attempting to write poems of childhood memory exploring issues of race, racism, culture, and identity that didn't lapse into melodrama, didacticism, or *overt* sentimentality. During that same period in time I had also been reading and admiring both Randall Jarrell's poem, "The Truth," and Yusef Komunyakaa's wonderful poem, "Venus's-flytraps"—both of which are poems narrated by five-year-old child speakers. I loved how the child's voice in these poems created a sense of simplicity, directness, and clarity that established a piercingly emotional resonance. I was particularly intrigued by the way in which the gap between the child speaker's understanding/comprehension of the events being narrated and the adult reader's understanding/comprehension of these events allowed this adult reader to shape, interpret, and formulate the implications of the narration on his/her own. It also struck me that it was this gap between child speaker's and adult reader's understanding/comprehension of narrative events that created the emotional space in which the real pathos of these poems emerged, without ever having to resort to sentimentality or heavy-handedness.

My goal was to achieve a similar effect, then, in "Pearls." To create the sense of an authentic five-year-old's voice in this poem, I used simple declarative sentences, with a basic palette of "primary colors," so to speak, in terms of vocabulary. There are occasional repetitions, and the voice is open, loquacious, and somewhat tangential. The child speaker simply reports the events, leaving the subsequent interpretation of these events up to the adult reader. As in any sort of monologue, in which the poet must create a sense of an authentic voice, there is a fine balance between artifice and realism—the voice must seem natural, conversational, and believable, while at the same time the poem must still function *as* a poem imagistically, sonically, and rhythmically.

> *"The poet must create a sense of an authentic voice [where] there is a fine balance between artifice and realism—the voice must seem natural, conversational, and believable, while at the same time the poem must still function* AS *a poem imagistically, sonically, and rhythmically."*

I am very much attracted to the challenges of poems that work with voice, particularly monologues, because in these poems the speaker does not stand outside of the poem and comment on the contents inside the poem's frame, but rather the speaker emerges from *inside* the poem and communes directly with the reader. "Pearls" was a rare "thank you" poem for me, in that it seemed to write itself in close-to-finished form in one sitting. I should add, though, that this happens very rarely to me, and most poems require an extended period of drafting and revising. I frequently begin public readings with this poem. It is, in many respects, an extremely personal poem, and in reading it I feel as if I have opened myself up completely to my audience.

"The Woman Who Loves Insects" is based on a traditional Japanese fairy tale in which there are two women characters—one of the women loved butterflies and made pets of them, while the other woman loved insects. Interestingly, in the fairy tale, the woman who loved insects was always being compared unfavorably to the woman who loved butterflies. The woman who loved butterflies was continuously characterized as being pleasingly "feminine"—not only in her choice of butterflies over insects, but in her personal demeanor, dress, and behavior. The woman who loved insects, on the other hand, was characterized as displeasingly "unfeminine" and completely unmarriageable—eccentric, stubborn, with unblackened teeth (at one time it was considered aesthetically pleasing for aristocratic women in ancient Japan to blacken their teeth), bushy eyebrows, and wild hair. Of course, I immediately identified with the woman who loved insects—her eccentricity, her love of insects, her wild hair and odd ways—and decided that I wanted to write a poem in her voice. One of the pleasures of exploring a voice taken from myth or fairy tale—in other words, a voice that is further removed from the confines of reality—is that one is not restricted to the conventions of a modern-day colloquial vernacular.

"One of the pleasures of exploring a voice taken from myth or fairy tale—in other words, a voice that is further removed from the confines of reality—is that one is not restricted to the conventions of a modern-day colloquial vernacular."

As a result, when I write poems in the voices of characters based on Japanese myth or fairy tale, the voices are much more lyrical, the images frequently very lush, and I try to create a very musical effect in terms of sound and rhythm.

This type of poem is consequently very appealing to me because it allows me to explore my interest in voice/monologue, while simultaneously pursuing my love for lush, sensual imagery and musical phrasings within the line. In terms of sound and rhythm, I am attracted to the musical possibilities of the line break, assonance (or internal rhyme) within the lines, and the music created by the juxtaposition of different types of words as they rest against one another. To my ear, words at the end of the line, as well as at the start of the line, receive an extra bit of prominence, both visually and aurally by virtue of the line break, and so I frequently try to choose words which seem deserving of this extra attention or emphasis to place at the starts and ends of lines.

This poem is composed in stanzas of three lines apiece, concluding with three single-line stanzas to create a *ritardando,* or a gradual slowing down, at the end of the poem for extra emphasis and effect. Frequently I will write poems in three-line stanzas in set syllabic patterns (i.e., 10 syllables, 6 syllables, 10 syllables), both as an homage to traditional syllabic Japanese forms such as the haiku or tanka, as well as for the subsequent rhythmic effects that are created. I also like the creative challenge imposed by working within the strictures of this type of form. This is not the case here, however.

In many ways, I think that this is a feminist poem in that it centralizes the voice and character of the traditionally "unfeminine" woman who loves insects and celebrates the very traits for which she is criticized in the traditional fairy tale. Ultimately, though, this is also a poem about the mortifying processes of the courtship/dating ritual. In this instance, the suitor who comes to woo the woman who loves insects must approach her on her own terms—leaving her the kinds of tokens that she will specifically appreciate (i.e., snail, locust, cockroach), exhibiting care and compassion toward insects, and accepting her wild hair, fierce eyebrows, and unblackened teeth. The moment in which the suitor unfolds a fan in time to catch the fall of a favorite caterpillar is a play on the traditional Japanese courtship ritual of presenting love poems to a beloved written on carefully chosen paper, exquisitely decorated and folded, then offered to the beloved (by being presented underneath the screen behind which she is ensconced for privacy) on an outstretched, unfolded fan.

I wrote "Octopus in the Freezer" more recently than the first two, and it perhaps provides an indication of some of the new directions that I'm currently exploring in my poetry. Clearly, it is a much longer poem, with extremely dense, rich, and lush imagery. The poem was inspired by a single auditory image—the sound of a furnace violently clanking, thumping, and bumping in the middle of the night as it fires into life during winter in an extremely cold climate. This is a sound very familiar to me from my childhood, but one that I hadn't heard for a number of years after leaving home for college and living in Indiana and Ohio. During my first winter in South Dakota, however, I was awakened in the middle of the night by this very same sound, catapulting me back into my childhood in Laramie, Wyoming, where I used to think the sound of the furnace coming on in the basement was the sound of frozen octopi in the freezer bumping their heads up against the freezer lid. The poem is addressed to and spoken directly *to* the octopus.

The challenge that I wished to explore in this poem was how to achieve a very radical shift in tone between the start of a poem and its ending without this tonal shift becoming disruptive or obtrusive. I envisioned this process as being somewhat similar to making a left turn in a very large and long truck. The opening tone in the poem is light, humorous, and whimsical, but by the end of the poem the tone has become much more serious, dark, and passionately wistful. I start making the tonal "left turn" in the poem with the lines beginning with "What error in judgment . . . ?" I attempt to make this tonal shift as gradually as possible, with each subsequent line building in tonal intensity and taking on darker shadings and nuances. By the end of the poem, it becomes apparent that the speaker of the poem, stranded alone in her house during a winter of heavy snowstorms, is heavily identified with the persona of the octopus and that she, too, feels trapped, frozen, and out of her element. The speaker wishes that, in the same way she has resurrected the octopus from the deep freeze of childhood memory and brought it back to flesh and life, someone will also think of her and resurrect her from the deep freeze of loneliness, isolation, and alienation.

Writing Suggestions

1. As Lee Ann Roripaugh does in "Octopus in the Freezer," start a poem with one tone and end convincingly with another. Try to make this change as subtle and subdued as possible. Think of Roripaugh's analogy of turning an eighteen-wheeler—you don't just yank the wheel and hope for the best, you coax, nudge, inch towards your goal.

2. Retell a story from myth or legend in a poem. Feel free to break from colloquial vernacular and use language as lush and dense or terse and wild as you see fit. Let the language reflect the actions/themes from your myth or legend. Reread Lee Ann Roripaugh's "The Woman Who Loves Insects" or Peter Meinke's "Ode to Good Men Fallen Before Hero Come" for inspiration.

3. Take a poem you've already written and change the speaker to a five-year-old child. How does this change the poem? What new observations, ideas, and insights does your speaker have? This is a spin-off on Miller Williams's idea that you ought to be able to explain a poem to a five-year-old, a wonderful idea that encourages clarity.

4. Do some genealogical research to find out what it was like to live in your grandparents' time, or your grandparents' grandparents' time. What were the worries of the day? The dreams? The daily routine? Write a poem that chronicles a moment in that place and time with the type of attention to detail and verisimilitude that you'd write a poem about contemporary America. Dream up what you can't find out through research, and blend fact and fiction until your poem "reads true."

> *"If a poem has an air of spontaneity, it has that air because the poet has been careful, in his slow and choosy writing of the poem, to keep in touch with its original impulse. And one must try to do that, one must try to keep the poem seeming sudden and abrupt even though it has been slowly contrived."*
>
> —Richard Wilbur

Kay Ryan

The Excluded Animals

Only a certain
claque of beasts
is part of the
créche racket

forming a
steamy-breathed
semicircle
around the
baby basket.

Anything more
exotic than
a camel
is out of luck
this season.

Not that the
excluded animals envy
the long-lashed
sycophants;
cormorants
don't toady,
nor do toads
adore anybody
for any reason.

Nor do the
unchosen alligators,
grinning their

three-foot grin
as they laze
in the blankety waters
like the blankets on Him.

Blandeur

If it please God,
let less happen.
Even out Earth's
rondure, flatten
Eiger, blanden
the Grand Canyon.
Make valleys
slightly higher,
widen fissures
to arable land,
remand your
terrible glaciers
and silence
their calving,
halving or doubling
all geographical features
toward the mean.
Unlean against our hearts.
Withdraw your grandeur
from these parts.

Star Block

There is no such thing
as *star block*.
We do not think of
locking out the light
of other galaxies.
It is light
so rinsed of impurities
(heat, for instance)
that it excites
no antibodies in us.
Yet people are

curiously soluble
in starlight.
Bathed in its
absence of insistence
their substance
loosens willingly,
their bright
designs dissolve.
Not proximity
but distance
burns us with love.

The Pass

Even in climes
without snow
one cannot go
forward sometimes.
Things test you.
You are part of
the Donners or
part of the rescue:
a muleteer in
earflaps; a
formerly hearty
Midwestern farmer
perhaps. Both
parties trapped
within sight
of the pass.

Failure

Like slime
inside a
stagnant tank

its green
deepening
from lime
to emerald

a dank
but less
ephemeral
efflorescence

than success
is in general.

Swept Up Whole

You aren't *swept up whole,*
however it feels. You're
atomized. The wind passes.
You recongeal. It's
a surprise.

Mirage Oases

First among places
susceptible to trespass
are mirage oases

whose graduated pools
and shaded grasses, palms
and speckled fishes give
before the lightest pressure
and are wrecked.

For they live
only in the kingdom
of suspended wishes,

thrive only at our pleasure
checked.

Crustacean Island

There could be an island paradise
where crustaceans prevail.
Click, click, go the lobsters
with their china mitts and

articulated tails.
It would not be sad like whales
with their immense and patient sieving
and the sobering modesty
of their general way of living.
It would be an island blessed
with only cold-blooded residents
and no human angle.
It would echo with a thousand castanets
and no flamencos.

The Hinge of Spring

The jackrabbit is a mild herbivore
grazing the desert floor,
quietly abridging spring,
eating the color off everything
rampant-height or lower.

Rabbits are one of the things
coyotes are for. One quick scream,
a few quick thumps,
and a whole little area
shoots up blue and orange clumps.

Turtle

Who would be a turtle who could help it?
A barely mobile hard roll, a four-oared helmet,
she can ill afford the chances she must take
in rowing toward the grasses that she eats.
Her track is graceless, like dragging
a packing-case places, and almost any slope
defeats her modest hopes. Even being practical,
she's often stuck up to the axle on her way
to something edible. With everything optimal,
she skirts the ditch which would convert
her shell into a serving dish. She lives
below luck-level, never imagining some lottery
will change her load of pottery to wings.
Her only levity is patience,
the sport of truly chastened things.

Impersonal

The working Kabbalist
resists the lure of
the personal. She
suspends interest
in the Biblical list
of interdicted shell fish,
say, in order to
read the text another way.
It might seem to some
superficial to convert
letters to numerals
or in general refuse plot
in favor of dots or half circles;
it might easily seem
comical, how she
ignores an obviously
erotic tale except for
every third word,
rising for her like braille
for something vivid
as only the impersonal
can be—a crescent
bright as the moon,
a glimpse of symmetry,
a message so vast
in its passage that
she must be utterly open
to an alien idea of person.

Ryan on Brevity, Teeth, Cartoons, and Sound

When you are a young writer it is so ridiculous; you have no idea what *your* poems sound like, so you have to blunder around writing all sorts of poems. Most of your early poems just don't fit, even if they might be decent efforts in somebody else's voice, or in the ambient style of the day. But pretty soon you start stumbling onto things that give you private pleasure (and private pleasure is really just about your only guide to how to write). It's as though you have to be a miner—nobody knows why you have to be a miner, but you do. You have to go down in the tunnels and labor as hard as you can. *However, you have no idea what ore looks like.*

In time, I was able to sort out some aspects of language use that brought me particular happiness.

- brevity
- teeth
- something cartoonlike
- sounds bound up like a rubber band ball

"It's as though [when you're a young writer] you have to be a miner—nobody knows why you have to be a miner, but you do. You have to go down in the tunnels and labor as hard as you can. HOWEVER, YOU HAVE NO IDEA WHAT ORE LOOKS LIKE."

Brevity

Brevity is of course *not* the soul of wit, because brevity by itself is without soul. Brevity lends itself to asperity or rudeness as easily as to wit. Brevity is always in danger of being ungenerous and that is a great challenge for the poet. In a poem, brevity can't be imposed; there must be an ease in the brevity. One of my favorite essayists, Annie Dillard, once said something in a lecture that troubled me, opining that much poetry which goes unread could be unpacked to become lovely essays which *would* be read. I am recalling this, and of course paraphrasing, but I think I have her sentiment right. I think this feeling of hers touches on something deep in the nature of poetry. Brevity is central to poetry. But in a wonderful poem, brevity feels like space; it doesn't feel stripped down or cramped up. If a poem *does* feel like it should be "unpacked" into the more generous form of an essay, as Annie Dillard suggests, then it just wasn't a good poem.

Teeth

Poems are ferocious. You don't know what they'll do because they aren't tamed and can't be tamed. A poem may be very calm, but there is always that sense that it could get up suddenly. It's the wildness in the language, even in rest. Similarly you always sense teeth in a poem.

I have two kinds of bad dreams; I dream I lose my teeth and I dream about big cats—tigers and leopards—dying. I see them lying in the road, too still, breathing shallowly.

Something Cartoonlike

In cartoons, a few lines in combination with a few words do the work. I greatly admire the art of cartooning. Recently I have been thinking that I would like to be Ben Katchor, the creator of several extended comic strips including my favorite, *Julius Knipl, Real Estate Photographer.* I once dreamed—or thought—this phrase: "The cartoonlike nature of higher truth." Cartoons make me laugh, but I don't want you to assume I laugh because they are funny; they may or may not be funny. Think about when you finally get the answer to something that you have been worrying about for a long time. The answer is always so clear and so *simple* that a laugh escapes from you. And isn't that an interesting thought—"a laugh *escapes* from you." Maybe that is what is stuck in us: laughs. I am astonished at how a great cartoon alters me. Am I radically destabilized, like a molecule when a new particle is introduced? Or am I instantly simplified, as if a troublesome itchy extra particle has been removed, leaving me suddenly *more* stable? Whatever it is, this quick alchemy should be in poems too.

Sounds Bound Up Like a Rubber Band Ball

Unlike cartoons, rhyme is *always* funny. I love this about rhyme, but the funniness also makes rhyme tricky to use. Rhyme is such a big show-off. Most twentieth-century poets seem to have felt burned by the garish excesses of Victorian rhymers (who didn't seem to know rhyme was funny). As a result, for many years now poets have shied away from rhyme altogether. This is a great pity; rhyme is one of our deepest and earlier pleasures. Rhyme is also just plain useful in a poem. Through its kind offices, some bits of sound adhere to other bits, and the poem coheres to itself. I delight in the whole diapason of rhyme, I celebrate all the keys on the great instrument of rhyme, whose black keys are sublime and whose white keys are ridiculous—and which are always played as chords. Puns are rhymes too, rhymes right on top of themselves. It has been my particular pleasure to hash up sounds so that there is a sense of rhyming which is often rather like a sneeze threatening.

"Most twentieth-century poets seem to have felt burned by the garish excesses of Victorian rhymers (who didn't seem to know rhyme was funny)."

Writing Suggestions

1. Write a "postcard poem." Take a plain, 3" x 5" postcard, turn it vertically, and write a skinny poem that ends when it hits the bottom of the first side. (Variation 1: Write this first draft without using any internal or end rhyme. Then flip the card over and do a different version of the same poem, but

with internal or end rhyme.) (Variation 2: Use 4x6 note cards, if you feel the need to write longer poems.)

2. Write your own poem that begins with the lines "There is no such thing/as _________" and let your imagination loose. If you get stuck, write the lines "There is no such thing/as _________" again but this time fill in the blank with a different thing than you used the first time. Let it operate as a kind of refrain.

3. Retype one of Kay Ryan's poems as a piece of prose. Without looking back at the original, put it back into poem form by breaking lines where you think they should be broken. How close is your new version to the original? What claims can you make about your own tendencies with line breaks? With Ryan's line breaks?

4. Spend an hour in an urban setting that's somewhat foreign to you. A laundromat. A bus terminal. A French pastry shop. Record your observations and thoughts. Spend another hour in a rural setting, such as a chicken farm, apple orchard, or fishing hole. Record your observations and thoughts. Write a poem about the urban setting that uses words, ideas, and images exclusively from your rural setting, and then write a poem about the rural setting that uses words, ideas, and images exclusively from your urban setting. Does forcing yourself into using unusual vocabulary choices allow you greater freedom? Does it make intuitive leaps easier? How might this translate into your other poems?

"The poem is not a vessel for thought, a receptacle for what I have previously known. The poem is a way of thinking, a vehicle for that thinking, a way to write toward what I do not know."

—Eric Pankey

Vivian Shipley

Black Hole

Was your mind vacant like Harlan county mine shafts or dark
as the lake in Mammoth Cave when the tour guide flicked

off light? I grabbed for you, Uncle, but you leaned back
in the boat's seat. Your silence taunts me; I can't let go

of the quarrel you would not join in last summer when I blurted
out I couldn't help it you weren't a father, that I was not the boy

you wanted. Showing how much science I had learned anyway,
I repeated a lecture about black holes, dense clumps of mass

in outer space with a gravitational force so strong that stars,
meteors, gas clouds and even light were sucked in as I was

by hope of even a nod from you. You were fingering the top
you'd whittled but I continued right on hoping to startle you

with a list of statistics, how the hole might contain well over
two billion suns, that Albert Einstein predicted them in 1915

even though he had no way of proving the identity of one
until the Hubble Space Telescope could spot the distant whirlpools

of stars as they were snuffed out. Certain as the scientists
of density I couldn't see, sure there must be a black hole behind

leathered furrows about your eyes, I tried to settle my hook
with talk of *Star Trek* and how time and space could be stretched,

twisted, torn or looped to take trips into other eras and dimensions.
Not even waiting to hear the grand finale, how the only way

to escape a black hole was to travel faster than the speed
of light, you called out to Uncle Paul, in from the back field,

that, finally, you had figured out how to pick out Queenie's
hunting mouth from her treed mouth. When you slumped

gray faced over the tractor, you made no sound, left no word
for me resting on the tip of your tongue like communion cubes

before the preacher gives the congregation a signal to swallow
the bread, transformed into flesh by the human need for love.

May 17, 1720: Superiour Court Justice Counsels Elizabeth Atwood in His Chambers Before Sentencing Her to Hang

> *If any woman be delivered of any issue of her body, male or female, which, if it were born alive, should by law be a bastard and that she endeavor privately to conceal the death thereof that it may not come to light, whether it were born alive or not, but be concealed, in every such case the other so offending shall suffer death as in case of murder, except such mother can make proof by one witness at the least that the child whose death was by her so intended to be concealed was born dead.*
> Massachusetts Provincial Laws, 1692–93, Chapter 19, Section 7

In the final conversation about Judgement, you will be the first
to get to give your version. Quivering to hear your name
Elizabeth, remember scarlet in the live oaks was blinding
that first day when the bench you sat on was just a bench.

Hair thin as dune grass, I believed I had roots, that your beauty
would not be small waves coming in with the tide, sucking
my clothes. I left, came back. Left. Came back, hiding under
branches so God would not see me, thinking how cool, green

the garden must have been. Michael Wigglesworth, I wrote
in my diary, *For admiring myself, I loathe myself.* Your house
a whistle only I could hear, the gray cat was the other life I saw.
Pressing my stomach against your spine, your breasts cupped

in my palms were better than any hope of afterlife. I fell asleep
in your bed, awakened to a gull startling me like a rusty hinge.
Fog hung like a bedsheet. I was in the wrong house, could not
find my clothes, my wife. The first time, I told her I had been

praying deep in briar, then it was the bay gleaming like tar,
the smell of the Atlantic that drew me. Those dawns spread like
a rash but sunset was your menstrual smear until there was snow
filling, white, white, swelling to banks. I never wanted the child

to be the sum of our parts, rounded into an irregular face almost
human. Even under oath, I knew you would not name me father.
This court will never prosecute me for fornication, or adultery
but our bastard's red hair with my earlobes would have spoken

my sin in each street of Ipswich. Refusing to kill what our love
had created, I had to do what you should have done. Surely,
Elizabeth, you must want to leave me in peace. When we go out
of this room, it will be time for you to say what you have to say.

The courtroom stilled by our entry, even God will be looking
down with interest. Like ships resting in Salem's harbor or dogs
with their heads cocked, Essex County's women are hushed
to hear loneliness, hurt, a poem you might have written. Spinster,

twenty eight, you slept with no husband's arm across your hip.
Ipswich's men understand you were filled with sin, with desire.
I am trying to give you a defense. Plead insanity or overwhelming
emotional stress during pregnancy. Crazed by pain, you didn't

know what you were doing. Whisper ignorance, delirium,
or illness at birth. All are legal excuses for fatal neglect. Fitting
the weak nature you share with all women, claim inexperience.
Because of incessant crying, you dropped our son or placed him

in an unheated attic, fell asleep and had no money to pay for
a doctor. You could have overlaid such a small body, smothered
it in bed. Just last year, I acquitted an exhausted mother because
her infant slipped from her unsteady grasp, fell into the privy.

Using gloves, I was careful, did not leave marks on our son's neck
that would condemn you. There is no recorded testimony. The boy
was already dead when your stepmother came and cleared herself
by giving this court the date of birth. February the 20th is branded

into me. Willful, unrepentant, you wear your stained dress
to court, will not acknowledge your sin. Elizabeth, how can I
save you? Don't ask me for what purpose and quote St. Paul, I
Corinthians 15: *Flesh and blood cannot inherit the kingdom*.

Ink dripping from my pen, you give me no choice but to date
your death warrant: June 23, 1720. As the chief magistrate
for the Massachusetts Superiour Court of Judicature, Assize
and General Goal Delivery, it's my duty to lead you to Mile Lane

and High Road, watch Sheriff Denison hang you at gallow's lot
on Pingrey's Plain. Elizabeth, raise your hand to me now,
uncurl it slowly, release me at least from your judgment. Think
of my days closed up in this room after you are gone. Imagine

the ache in my lungs, like a right whale wheezing in dark, each
breath in deep water held a very long time. Spring will resurrect
our mornings but I will peer from attic slats, not knowing
one day to the next if I will stride around a judge, vivid like God,

shoulders in the clouds or be staring into that little elastic face.
If I take a walk into a pasture, the scent of milk on your breasts
might come to me. Think of the place in my body where the past
with you will thorn, rise sharp as the question of what will

happen to me if I am found out. Sins deducted from graces,
you will go to heaven but I will be roped to this earth knotted
by memory, by the fear of last breath: the noose on your throat,
my hands like a chain of baptism circling the neck of our son.

Number Fifty Two: Winifred Benham, Hartford, Connecticut, October 7, 1697

Joseph, my husband, couldn't hold his tongue,
said selectmen were no more fit for office than dogs,
threatened to shoot a neighbor who'd named me witch.
Ours was prime land on the east side of Main Street
just south of Center Street in Wallingford. Watching

the surveyor and tax assessor finger pears, spit grape
seeds around my orchard, I knew to train for holy water.
Lowered into a barrel, life, our six acres would be taken
if I was damned, gnawed by demons that caused me to rise.
Pulled down to blackness, encircled by the hand of God,

three minutes would prove my innocence. My accusers
rehearsed their lines: John Moss, 15, only grandson
of Wallingford's commissioner and Elizabeth Lathrop,
19, daughter of the New London Court judge testified
I had frequently and sorely afflicted parts of their bodies

too private for inspection. Charges were posted: I read
Shakespeare, not scripture; I appeared as apparitions,
allowing Satan to take my form. Stripped in court,
searched for signs of possession, stretch marks where
the devil must have suckled were found that matched

rows of spots that appeared while bathing the corpse
of the infant son of Joseph Royce, a founding father
in Wallingford. Other physical evidence was Winifred,
my daughter. At thirteen, she could be only a child
of the devil being born so late when I was forty five.

Attending more than thirty trials, I had seen women
who could not sink, struggling upward to surface
for air the rope would suck away. I witnessed women
forgotten a minute too long. Innocent, but hanging
in holy water, no breath of an angel for breeze, dresses

undulated as if to Purcell. I prepared for the judge
whose brother lived across the street from us to become
distracted, say by a fit of coughing or a baby teething.

Declared unclean like the cormorant in *Deuteronomy*,
I learned from gutting the bird how the rounded sea

pebbles in its stomach served as a diver's weight.
Forgetting my skill as seamstress, the judge didn't slit
braiding on my skirt for rocks or prod the oval panels.
I had prepared my answer: bombast, your honor, cotton
stuffing inserted to bulge my dress in Elizabethan fashion.

In bed, I practiced kicking with feet tied, learned how
to count out three minutes, studied where women's
fingers rested when bound to their sides. Burning,
lungs were about to consume me, I pulled two threads
I left hanging next to my hands to release slip stitches

binding smooth stones. I kicked to surface, to salvation.
Under holy water, thinking of the judge above me, I found
a darkness I would grow into. Unable to nail my world
back into shape as I did the arbor in my garden the judge
could not confiscate in God's name, I craved a reason,

an explanation to justify my trial. Reading Milton's
description of Satan in *Paradise Lost* who *sat like*
a cormorant in the Tree of Life preparing to work
mischief in the Garden of Eden, I slicked my hair
back like a tulip, used India ink to cover the gray.

Deliberate as Joseph unbuttoning my blouse each
night, I reached up to pick out stars and then bent
to uproot ferns with shovels, sometimes with spoons.
Crushing bottles in my hand to seed the garden,
I thought of my neighbors, swelling nerves, joints

aching as they swiveled like my hatred working its way
into their hearts. Rubbing my belly while mixing tea,
I added herbs for stomach venom, fever to shake
awake mouths blubbering in sleep. Time surely will
swallow up my place in history as the last witch tried

in Connecticut, but the sight of a cormorant, shining
like a black angel struggling to fly, will keep alive
the cry of a believer fallen. With no final word, unable

to make up one truth to give my daughter a sliver
of comfort, each October, I tell her to imagine God

at an easel, painting leaves sunflower, crimson, ochre,
copper, sienna. Freezing them to edge in crystal, a master
with a trained eye, the artist stands back deciding what
to crop from the canvas, which stand of forest should be
cut and which trees will move to the center of the frame.

Kachino, Russia: Perm 36

But I will find him when he lies asleep,
And in his ear I'll holla 'Mortimer!'
Nay,
I'll have a starling shall be taught to speak
Nothing but 'Mortimer,' and give it him
To keep his anger still in motion.
—Henry IV, Part I

Vasyl Stus, were guards reading Shakespeare outside
your cell door? Fearing your poems more than bricks,
they may have learned power in a word from Hotspur

as he trained a starling *to gall and pinch* Bolinbroke.
Touring Perm 36, a stop on a summer boat tour
of the Gulag and a fifty mile bus ride from Lysva,

I see why Stalin never allowed photographs or films
of Soviet labor camps. Vasyl Stus, a guide will not allow
me to sandpaper my hand on cement walls of a punishment

cube where you died. No cause, just: September 4, 1985.
No death camp like Kolyma or Magadan, you did not
expect to be killed one month before the Nobel Prize

you were nominated for was announced. Buoyed
by hope your poems would speak for you in Stockholm,
you did not live to hear the name Claude Simon called.

Ukrainian, you earned the Russian title for inmate, *zek*—
a badge I can't pin on. Your body tied you to earth, hooked
as if on a rod held in hands slowly reeling you to a death

that must have been your salvation. Blackened with rot,
wooden shacks cluster at Perm 36. Green on green,
painted guard towers seem to be the only life in this camp.

Natan Sharansky, Sergei Kovalyov, Vadimir Bukovsky
and Sevko Lukyanenko. All ghosts, all vanished
like you, Vasyl Stus. Hanging over rails of a tour boat,

I saw no sign of the twenty million other bodies
bulldozed or smothered by snow drifts in the chain
of prisons and labor camps that link the Gulag, wind

Ural Mountains like lights on an evergreen. Walking
into a maximum security room, a tourist, I can't imagine
being starved, flayed, my eyes being toed like glowing

coals by boots and my legs, a forest fire being
stamped out. Like an unrecorded voice without throat
to channel, memory of a name thickens to amnesia,

then vanishes if there are no words to hold it, no starling
Hotspur coached to speak it. Each morning, four to six men
from each cell crossed this narrow corridor where I stand

to finger workroom bars as if feeling for a weak spot.
Vasyl Stus, when you were a free man, you walked about,
opened, closed books, sat down in a chair, then another,

fingers hooking a pen. Here in Perm 36, your hands hung,
meaty growths from your shoulders. With no thought
to scissor it, each day was like the next, pointless. Rubbing

thin striped-cotton uniforms you wore even when cold
pared down to your bone, I sit down on an iron bunk bed
you might have coiled on, kneel at the hole that served

as both sink and toilet. In the exercise yard, six by six feet,
my neck cranes, I try to spear sky silvering the crosshatch
of barbed wire. Vasyl Stus, did wood splintering a nail

remind you of light around a star, of what you would not
see again, moon washing a field to bronze, show of deer,
light from a bar over the street? What can I know of what

is done in cement-walled rooms to break a man's spirit,
what is done to break a man's body? What can I know
of what was done to you, how your breath was taken

in this room I visit? I see the wall you saw before you
passed out. A starling, a construction worker's wolf whistle,
I will call, arousing every ear that sleeps. Vasyl Stus,

Vasyl Stus, Vasyl Stus, echo and anger, still.

Barbie, Madame Alexander, Bronislawa Wajs

I told Jerzy Ficowski if you print my songs in *Problemy*,
my people will be naked, I will be skinned alive. Desperate
to reclaim my ideas, my words, I rushed to Warsaw, begged

the Polish Writer's Union to intervene. At the publishing house,
no one understood me. I went home, burned all of my work,
three hundred poems. Ficowski used my real name, Bronislawa

Wajs, even though I'm known by my gypsy name, Papusza
which translates to doll. That did not matter to the Baro Shero,
I was *magerdi*, defiled. Punishment was irreversible: exclusion.

It's raining again, a cold prickly rain that makes the window
look like a Spielberg effect on TV. If only my memories could
dissolve one luminous dot at a time but the mud season has

begun with snowmelt. The mantle of the earth is mush, sucking
off my boots when I try to walk away. Water stains, etching
the ceiling like an antique map of my heart. Thirty four years,

alone, shunned by nieces, nephews, unknown to their children,
I'm discarded, mute as my name, Doll. My family's voice, I still
hear it in my voice which is my mother's, my father's voice.

The older I have gotten, the more I recall although I will allow
no one to listen to my poems or songs. Harpists, my people
hauled great stringed instruments upright as if they were sails

on wagons carting us from northern Lithuania to eastern Tatras.
If we stopped for more than a day, I'd steal a chicken, take it
to another villager to exchange for reading and writing lessons.

Another chicken or two, I got a book or paper. When my father
or brothers caught me, I was beaten, my books, poems buried.
Married at fifteen to Dionizy Wajs, revered as a harpist but old,

I had a work station in a courtyard corner, a tin tub on wood.
Pour in boiling water: rub, rub, rub. The rhythm in my poems
was born in blankets and rugs, the words in my unhappiness.

I was the youngest wife, a *boria,* who got up before everything
even the *khaxni,* the hens. In the sooty light, I followed the rules:
move in silence, collect wood, build the fire, heat water, coffee,

do not speak to a man in the morning before he washes his face.
All day I talked about sheep parts: brains, balls, guts, organs,
glands, skinned heads, joints. I would pinch other girls' breasts

in greeting, in play. None of my hard work was mentioned when
I was pronounced *magerdi* and then banished from the *kumpani.*
The charges spoken were that I had no children, that I invented

long ballads to lament being poor, impossible love, rootlessness,
lost freedom and the *lungo drom,* or long road. A gypsy, I had
ou topos, no place to dream about, no homeland to yearn for.

Tinsmiths, blacksmiths but no Romulus and Remus, no Aeneas
wandering to do battle for me. No anthem or Holocaust memorial
because no names were recorded. Papusza, I sang my poems

in Romani called the cant of thieves, argot of liars, but changing
words meant survival depending on secret laws that could never
be written in order to hide the past, to make a hedge to protect us

from the *gadje,* the non-Gypsies. I blackened pages with elegies
for our nomadic life spread out like skeletons of carp wrapped
in a map of Europe. For thirty four years, I have hidden my face,

afraid to thumb books or open newspapers, see Ficowski's face
who'll ask *So now where is your poetry?* Silenced by exclusion,
living in a well, no voice called down, Papusza. Romani echoes.

Marime, Magerdi is still warm as the spot where Baro Shero
touched the finger I had used to write down our gypsy songs.
Sentient, my hands kept memory, could not let go, could not ball

to a fist, penetrate the hedge. Papusza will be closed over; *death
date unknown* will be my final sentence. I told Jerzy Ficowski
if you print my songs in *Problemy*, I will be skinned alive, my

people will be naked. My words did not even light a tiny flicker,
but mouth to ear, voices I remember that will be buried with
me have more than the sound of one lifetime, more than my own.

Shipley on Re-envisioning the Past

In *The Sacred Wood,* T. S. Eliot observed: *The only way of expressing emotion in the form of art is by finding an 'objective correlative'; in other words, a set of objects, a situation, a chain of events which shall be the formula of that particular emotion; such that when the external facts, which must terminate in sensory experience, are given, the emotion is immediately invoked.* People who are the subjects of poems I consider to be my best work become an objective correlative for me. In order to avoid reducing their lives to a historical summary, I try to re-create what my subjects may have thought or remembered based on my near-death experience. In *What is Art?*, Leo Tolstoy defines artistic achievement as a "human activity, consisting in this, that one man consciously, by means of external signs, hands on to others feelings he has lived through, and that other people are infected by these feelings, and also experience them." In order to achieve Tolstoy's definition of art, a major decision I need to make in each poem is who will voice the narrative and where the voice will be located. Like the mythical figure of Antaeus, the giant whose strength was based on having at least a foot on a specific patch of ground, my poems get power from location, place. The spirit in a landscape is a compelling force and often can be the critical factor in shaping individuals. In my poem about the Ukrainian poet, Vasyl Stus, I want the reader to picture Perm 36 where Vasyl Stus was killed. Compelling creative work needs to embed its characters in a matrix of location, values, beliefs, thought; in short, it must give them identities. I believe my poems about women and men who were silenced succeed because of my interest in accurate detail. To preserve lives and voices, I utilize town records, historical societies, and local libraries to collect information that enables me to resurrect spirits of women and men, to capture the dailiness of their lives.

> *"I believe my poems about women and men who were silenced succeed because of my interest in accurate detail. To preserve lives and voices, I utilize town records, historical societies, and local libraries to collect information that enables me to resurrect spirits of women and men, to capture the dailiness of their lives."*

In order to follow Eliot and Tolstoy's advice about how to interest an audience, I need to be aware of how close emotionally I am to the subject, to the material in the poem. In Kentucky where I was raised, my cousins and I would have a contest to see who would find a pond with first ice which was one notch harder than unready rubber ice. In poems I write that involve strong feelings, I strive to find that first ice in a metaphor or an individual subject that will skate me over sentiment created when emotion is not controlled. A series of poems I did about a former student, Eve Cummings, were difficult for me to write because I cared very deeply for her. I attempted to avoid making her pathetic as I gave the details of her hard life by allowing readers to imaginatively inhabit her home in Fair Haven, Connecticut, and to draw their own conclusions about why Eve's poetry did not surface in a permanent way. Because I had more emotional distance from the subject, it was easier for me to write and revise a poem about Charlotte Mew, the British poet who ended her life by drinking Lysol. Like Eve, she was worn down by the harshness of daily living and silenced by poverty. I was delighted when poems about them were awarded the Reader's Choice Award from *Prairie Schooner*, because the recognition helped to preserve the names, Charlotte Mew and Eve Cummings, and develop an awareness of their difficult lives as poets.

Another reason I am drawn to the subject of lost voices is because of my heritage. My Kentucky relatives, whose days were corseted by unending struggle, taught me that silences of the body do not necessarily correspond to silences in the heart. I wrote "Black Hole" to show the pain a failure to talk can cause. In eastern Kentucky, people are cut off from the world by a lack of literacy and technology. Many still live in mountain "hollers" where the sun does not show itself before noon, and die never having seen, or talked to anyone in the world beyond the Appalachian Mountains. Nonetheless, they are spirited men and women even if they come from a humble background. They are my relatives who have been destined by their location to endure difficulty and tragedy. Their dignity, pride, and decency have been lost because they have been stereotyped as "hillbillies."

Whether gathering oysters in Fair Haven, or mining coal in Harlan County, hard work ground down the spirit men and women needed to communicate. In addition, attitudes about sexual roles in Kentucky also caused the loss of women's voices. I was raised to believe that the only time a woman's name should be in print was in notices of her birth, marriage, and death. As a consequence, I am particularly interested in using women as subjects of my poems on silences. Even though women made major contributions to our national heritage in every state, details of particular lives are often lost. Public records and history books are dominated by accounts of men. A pigeon can roost on the bronze head of several men in each state, but most states do not have even one public statue for a prominent woman. Standard state travel guidebooks contain historical sites for very few women. In the forward of *The Extraordinary Tide,* an anthology of new poetry by contemporary American women edited by Susan Aizenberg and Erin Belieu (New York: Columbia University Press, 2001), Eleanor Wilner observes, "The unsaid and unseen have always been poetry's driving necessity, its images corresponding not just to what hasn't yet been seen, but to what can't be seen or said or known another way. So we may suppose that it is the huge reservoir of unspoken inner life of the female past that drives and energizes the extraordinary tide of contemporary poetry by women."

To honor a woman's voice that was silenced, Eavan Boland chose my poem about the hanging of Elizabeth Atwood for the *Eclectic* prize from the University of West Georgia. Her commentary about the poem summarizes why I believe it is one of my best: "I think this poem is so successful because of a deft, witty and dark mixing of decorum with savage intention. This man who hands down judgment, in a closed world of language and faith, is the deadly enemy of the woman he speaks to with such respect." Hopefully, poems like Elizabeth Atwood or the one I have written about Winifred Benham, the last woman to be tried for witchcraft in Connecticut, will keep alive the legacy of New England women before histories of their lives are swallowed up and replaced by Wal-Mart, Burger King, and Domino's. The success of these poems can be measured by the reader's ability to intellectually and emotionally inhabit the locations, the lives of women I try to record.

Another poem about a Gypsy woman poet who was silenced by her tribe, Bronislawa Wajs, won the Lucille Medwick Award from the Poetry Society of America. The judge, Pattiann Rogers, commented on its strength: "The poem speaks of the desire for self-realization in conflict with community pressure for conformity to its structures. The complexities of this conflict as the poem suggests, include struggle against the native community yet loyalty to the native community: love of the community of birth along with the love of that which is outside the community of birth: anger and resentment toward both; and the longing for identification with the land; a place, a home." With no records, diaries, letters, or poems like Emily Dickinson's kept in trunks, this anthology with my poems can keep the names of Vasyl Stus, Charlotte Mew, Elizabeth Atwood, Winifred Benham, and Bronislawa Wajs from being as anonymous as grave markers on the open plains.

Writing Suggestions

1. Write a poem about a recent dream. Recreate it in all its vividness and wildness and (possibly) incomprehensibility. Remember to explore all five senses to make it real for a reader. Does it help to root a poem about a dream in reality? Is it better to throw away all notions of reality (laws of physics and science, etc.) and let the poem have free rein?

2. Think of your favorite fairy tale, then write a poem that updates and contemporizes it. Fill your poem with details relevant to modern culture and times, and oddly enough, the more you bring in contemporary references, the more timeless your poem will be. Remember, too, what fairy tales are about: persistent fears, desires, ideals, and possibilities. Let your poem be about these essential human impulses.

3. Consider for a moment your ideal audience. Who are you thinking of when you're writing your poems? Write a very short poem (fourteen lines maximum) that's geared toward complete strangers. Now do a different version of that same poem specifically for friends and family, people who know you well. Does the way you present (essentially) the same material change when your audience changes? Does it help to think of a specific audience when you're writing?

4. Write a poem of preservation. Think of the life of a relative, a semifamous person, or a historical figure that very little is known about and then find out all you can about this person via research. Let your poem recreate their voice, their dreams, their fears. Give them the voice that history and/or society wouldn't let them have. Tell their story in their own voice, or from the point of view of someone who knew them intimately, meaningfully. (Variation: Write a poem about a figure who *was not* silent in their life [Martin Luther King Jr., Abe Lincoln, Malcolm X, etc.] and bring back their voice now, in a contemporary setting. Do they have something different to say than before? Do they speak/act in the same way? If they're different now, how so?)

> *"Most of my poems are bound to specific objects, places, persons, or circumstances, and these are usually places or people who are part of my experience. That is not to say that I rely only upon my life or the facts of life. The most important thing I have tried to learn as a poet is to follow and trust my own imagination."*
>
> —Larry Levis

Elizabeth Spires

Easter Sunday 1955

Why should anything go wrong in our bodies?
Why should we not be all beautiful?
Why should there be decay?—why death?
—and, oh, why damnation?
—Anthony Trollope, in a letter

What were we? What have we become?
Light fills the picture, the rising sun,
the three of us advancing, dreamlike,
up the steps of my grandparents' house on Oak Street.
Still young, my mother and father swing me
lightly up the steps, as if I weighed nothing.
From the shadows, my brother and sister watch,
wanting their turn, years away from being born.
Now my aunts and uncles and cousins
gather on the shaded porch of generation,
big enough for everyone. No one has died yet.
No vows have been broken. No words spoken
that can never be taken back, never forgotten.
I have a basket of eggs my mother and I dyed yesterday.
I ask my grandmother to choose one, just one,
and she takes me up—O hold me close!—
her cancer not yet diagnosed. I bury my face
in soft flesh, the soft folds of her Easter dress,
breathing her in, wanting to stay forever where I am.
Her death will be long and slow, she will beg
to be let go, and I will find myself, too quickly,
in the here-and-now moment of my fortieth year.
It's spring again. Easter. Now my daughter steps
into the light, her basket of eggs bright, so bright.

One, choose one, I hear her say, her face upturned
to mine, innocent of outcome. Beautiful child,
how thoughtlessly we enter the world!
How free we are, how bound, put here in love's name
—death's, too—to be happy if we can.

Cemetery Reef
Grand Cayman Island

Walking down the beach, I took your arm.
The treatments were over. Your hair was growing back.
For a week, time lay suspended. And yet, too fast,
too soon, everything was changing to memory.
But your arm was real when I touched it, real flesh and blood.
We were talking about doctors when I saw the blowfish,
green as the greenest apple, puffed-up and bobbing in the shallows.
But when I looked again, it was only a pair of bathing trunks,
ballooning out, aimlessly knocked back and forth by the tide.
Ahead, the cruise ships lay at anchor in the harbor.
At noon they'd slip away, like days we couldn't hold onto,
dropping over the blurred blue horizon to other ports of call.
The hotels we were passing all looked out to water,
but no one sat there early in the morning. And no one
slept in the empty hammock at the Governor's House,
where workmen in grey coveralls raked the seaweed into piles,
until the sand was white and smooth, like paper not yet written on.

All lies in retrospect now: how, each afternoon,
we put on masks and fins and swam to Cemetery Reef.
The coral looked like brains and flowers, like unreal cities
of melted peaks and towers, pointing up to where the sun,
flat and round as a host, lay dissolving on the water.
Schools of fish, bright as neon, ragged as flags,
drifted directionless with the tide, or swerved
and hid from our reaching hands in beds of waving kelp.
We breathed through snorkels, did the dead man's float,
the hollows rushing sound we heard inside our heads
our own frail breath going slowly *in* and *out*. Farther out,
the shallow reef dropped off to chasm, the waves
choppy and thick, the calm clear water darkening to ink.
How far could we swim before exhaustion took us,

before a shark or barracuda rounded a cornerless corner
to meet us eye to eye? My mind circled back to our dinner
in the Chinese restaurant: the waiter bringing six cookies
on a plate, alike in every way, except that one, just one,
contained a different fate. *Wealth, long life, happiness,*
the plate was passed around. Then your turn came.
You chose one, broke it open, read aloud,
Soon you will cross the great water, dropping it, as if stung.

And then, too quickly, it was the last day.
Dreaming, we all came to. We were back at Cemetery Reef,
walking a narrow path of broken shells toward the shining water.
Off to one side, a low stone wall squared off the cemetery,
the dead buried aboveground in white weathered slabs,
their plots neatly surrounded by smooth white stones.
Morning of all mornings, you swam out to the reef alone,
came back. Gathering our things to go, what made me say,
When we come back . . . . All lies unanswered now.
I remember how the flowers on the graves were red
and white plastic, the color of flesh and blood, of regret,
of paper not yet written on. Put there, *In Memory.*
In a colder place, we would soon—unwilling, stunned—
remember you with the kind that always die.

Spires on the Potential of Memory

I began "Easter Sunday 1955" several years ago after watching some home movies made when I was a child. In them, a succession of holidays, birthdays, and anniversaries passed in the blink of an eye, the years spliced together to make a jerky, racing chronology. I couldn't have predicted the mix of emotions I felt at seeing my parents so young, or at seeing my grandparents alive again, a wealth of years still ahead of them. One scene in particular stayed with me: an Easter morning when I was three, a slow parade of relatives ascending the wide steps of my grandparents' house on Oak Street. The scene was shadowed for me by my awareness that time was passing for all of us much to rapidly. It was like peering over the wall into a Biblical Eden and knowing the outcome. The image stayed with me for weeks, but I did not actually begin the poem until, by chance, I came across a passage in a letter by the 19th-century English novelist Anthony Trollope that mirrored the painful emotions I had felt watching those home movies. In his letter, which I decided to use as an epigraph, Trollope voiced in an explicit way what I wanted to show through image and dramatic action.

"My writing process usually involves weeks of revision, and 'Easter Sunday 1955' probably went through a total of fifty or sixty drafts. At one point early on, I had made so little headway that, in exasperation, I threw away most of my drafts."

My writing process usually involves weeks of revision, and "Easter Sunday 1955" probably went through a total of fifty or sixty drafts. At one point early on, I had made so little headway that, in exasperation, I threw away most of my drafts. My two working titles reflected the poem's twin genesis: "Watching Home Moves" and "Five Questions." Oftentimes, I begin a first draft with little more than a few lines, an image of phrase, rough and un-thought-out. My process is associative and intuitive: I begin writing whatever comes to mind, with no concern for bad grammar, sentence fragments, or redundancy. Out of this initially chaotic process comes a slowly developing sense of the poem's music and phrasing, of line length and stanza structure, of dramatic action. Using this cumbersome process, which nevertheless works, it may take me several weeks to finish a poem of thirty or forty lines.

Occasionally, I discover the first line of the poem early on. When this happens, I know there is a good chance I will be able to bring the poem to completion. Why? Because a first line is crucial in establishing a voice, tone, and measure for the poem. In "Easter Sunday 1955," Trollope's five questions led me into two of my own: "What were we? What have we become?" The epigraph suggested the then/now structure: the death and decay of the past existing in a counterpoint to the present's sense of immediacy and renewal. In the finished version, the narrator's childhood is lost in the ongoing rush of time, then recaptured again years later when she experiences the childhood of *her* child. This is the "hope" of the poem, that plays against knowledge of death and decay. The finished poem is certainly not a happy one, but I think it allows for the *possibility* of happiness.

My writing process is dependent upon the belief that the unconscious is the part of us that does the creative, imaginative work that results in a poem. The conscious mind, unfortunately, has a tendency to censor and control the poem's statement. My rule is to allow sufficient time for reverie *and* revision, for deeply buried images, desires, and fears to surface out of the unmapped "nowhere" of the unconscious. It is only over the stretch of days or weeks that it takes me to write and revise that the contradictions and ambiguities inherent in my actual experience coalesce in a way that is truthful to that experience.

> *"My rule is to allow sufficient time for reverie* AND *revision, for deeply buried images, desires, and fears to surface out of the unmapped 'nowhere' of the unconscious. It is only over the stretch of days or weeks that it takes me to write and revise that the contradictions and ambiguities inherent in my actual experience coalesce in a way that is truthful to that experience."*

In contrast to "Easter Sunday 1955," "Cemetery Reef," written more recently, offers scant possibility of renewal in the present moment; rather, the present is experienced as something passing much too quickly to hold on to, like sand rapidly pouring through an hourglass. A poem is an act of remembering, existing *in memory* of a person, a place, an event, an emotion, a state of mind. We remember and write. And we write to remember, the poem becoming, in a sense, a precious artifact. (Apropo of this, Elizabeth Bishop's words in "The Monument" come to mind: "The crudest scrollwork says 'commemorate . . .'"). Like the red and white plastic flowers placed on the island graves in "Cemetery Reef," the poem will outlast the past. That, I believe, may be our primary motive for writing: to leave something of ourselves behind, to cheat time and preserve the vanishing present.

Writing Suggestions

1. Leaf through *The Oxford Dictionary of Quotations* or a similar book and find a quote that interests you. Use that quote as an epigraph for a poem you've been meaning to write, or write a new poem in response to/conflict with/or extension of that quote.

2. Write your own "Easter Sunday 1955" poem. Select (or imagine) a powerful event that happened to you (or to a friend, colleague, schoolmate) years back that meant one thing then and means another thing now. If you gravitate towards a sad event, strive to write a poem about sadness *without* being

a sad poem. Let it have power and resonance, but keep the melodrama and tears out.

3. Type up Spires's poem "Easter Sunday 1955" as one prose paragraph. Now break up the lines as you envision them. Go through every noun, every adjective and alter them (switch, add, subtract) for maximum effect. Compare your version to the original. Which do you think is better? Are there times when understatement works better than overstatement? How do line breaks affect mood? Rhythm?

4. Look through the poems in this book and note how many use epigraphs. Reread those poems. What is the purpose of an epigraph? Does it add an extra voice or another dimension of meaning to the poem? Are epigraphs ever inappropriate? Add an epigraph to a poem you've already written. Does it make your poem better? See how many poems featured on Poetry Daily (www.poems.com) over the past month use epigraphs. What claims can you make about the use of epigraphs in contemporary American poetry? What is or should be the role of epigraphs in your own poetry?

"Twentieth-century poetry has become garrulous. We are drowning not in a sea but a swamp of words. We have forgotten that poetry is not in what the words say, but in what is said between them, that which appears fleetingly in pauses and silences."

—Octavio Paz

Virgil Suárez

Psalm for the Boy Cartographer

Geography is the history of my body,
—Victor Hernández Cruz

Your eyes already in the slant of drifting foam;
Your breath sealed by the ghosts I do not know:
Draw in your head and sleep the long way home.
—Hart Crane, Part V of "Voyages"

What is the secret of buoyancy? Lines? He craves
to know, out this far in the region where
clouds' eyes water. Where his heart echoes,

plunges and rises beneath concave surfaces
of these opaline waters, wreaths of kelp
and seaweed tickle his feet. What he remembers

is the path by which everything drowns, the sky
a big wound, a tongue of fire that swallows
the earth. What rhythms carry in the silence?

Words muted by a constant hiss or air,
how salt dries and riddles tributaries of loss
onto his burnt skin. He remembers his mother's

prayer to Santa Barbara, the Saint of Difficult
Crossings, a chant-like murmur that carries
him further than these currents of constant tug,

pulling him into this recurring dream of rope,
knots, how a quill pen catches on paper,
fire from the mouth of the dead. This upturned,

upside down world now drowns in memory.
What this boy will forever remember is
his mother's litany to *Changó, Changó, Changó,*

a vastness of blue-green in the sea and sky, one
huge mass of empty space, a silent geography
of elements, how sharks rub themselves in mock

caress against his dangling arms and feet, as though
to say we know you, we know your people.
Out here where so much of history is ignored,

those who suffer know, those who are bound
know, those who are lost know, those
who learn to float know—this memory of rough sea,

a nightmare of screaming in the night, a boy,
his dead mother, two countries between
this ebb of hurt and pain. Later as a young man,

he will arrive at the edge of water, plunge in
and swim homeward toward his mother,
there at the bottom of his sleep, waiting, her arms

like welcoming tentacles to guide her boy home.

Those Lost Souls: Florida Strait Tragedy #1

> *When the low, heavy sky weighs like the giant lid*
> *Of a great pot upon the spirit crushed by care,*
> *And from the whole horizon encircling us is shed*
> *A day blacker than night, and thicker with despair.*
> —Charles Baudelaire

1 Out here on the high seas, the ocean is possessed
of a thousand hues between lapis lazuli and emerald,
and on this makeshift raft headed north, another
family prays to Santa Barbara, Holy Mother

of the crossing, to spare the lives of everyone
on board, but it is too late, the sun has taken

its toll on the skin, made the old man Lazaro
dizzy and he's fallen overboard into the water,

swallowed into the dark waters, and now not even
with an oil lamp will the sea return him, a kiss
of night and air on the full moon, the children
have stopped crying, the only sound left is breath

upon a prayer, those who say the sea is the great
mother are liars, it is the great void, a woman says,
and by morning, the storm clouds gather ahead,
a welcoming sign of eternity, the horizon undulates,

sea birds flock heavenward, thoughts of the damned,
a song of the needy, and there is no returning,
no returning, only the promise of another land,
in the distance, always in the distance, broken and blue.

AGUACERO

These downpours of my Cuban childhood
when my father loved to smoke a cigarette
on the patio of the house in Havana
and watch as the sheets of rain bent against
the tin roofs of the shacks in the neighbor's
yard, the way drops hung from the wire
mesh of the chicken coops and fell, one
by one on the dirt, dampening, darkening
as they fell, and he would remove his shirt
after a long day's work feeding the zoo
animals and he would sit on his makeshift
hammock, lean back, blow smoke up
at the rafters, and he listened to all that rain
as it fell on everything. He imagined
it was raining all over the island, his island,
and the sound of it drumming on the plantain
fronds rose all around him like the clamor
of thousands of cattle birds scattered-shot
into the heavens, and when he closed his eyes
he dreamt of a man, his hands buried deep
into fertile earth, seeding a son, a wife,

in new life from which so much hardship
sprouted in this life, in the next, exile
a possibility dripping from his fingertips—
then the song of bullfrogs calling home the night.

Women Who Carry Water from the River

they cloister at the sandy banks to gather water
to bring back to their kitchens,
quench the thirst of household cuys, guinea
pigs, neither pigs, not from Guinea,
staple, gifts, like this water they bend like willows
for, so close to the surface. They catch
their reflections against the slick surface,
mirror magic, they believe in,
stand straight to sniff the wind, tuck a strand
of hair back inside their shawls or hats,
does come for water, egrets and other wader
birds; a carp breaks the water's
surface, then there is silence. I really enjoy this,
says one of the younger women,
others look beyond her at the huts leaning
into the grassy hillsides, the sway
of plantain fronds, shimmered light off everything.
Youth, they say, they were young once,
too, and the men returned from the hunt sooner,
thirsty, hungry, tired from the miles
their feet have traveled. Now they know
the men don't appreciate this hard work,
this fetch of water to fill gourds hung from ceiling
rafters. Hard work indeed.
Now they carry the clay jugs homeward,
slow ascend, water swishes, not a drop
falls, not a drop. They walk steady, strong,
their shadows now in front,
then at their sides, this is the life, they sing,
this close to the river's edge
where so much life thrives.
Necessary this is, so necessary.

Bitterness

My father brings home the blood of horses on his hands,
his rough, calloused, thick-fingered hands; he comes home
from the slaughterhouse where the government places him to kill

old, useless horses that arrive from all over the island. On his hands
it comes, encrusted and etched into the prints and wrinkles
of his fingers, under his nails, dark with the dirt too, the filth and grime,

the moons of his fingers pinked by its residue, his knuckles skinned
from the endless work. Sticky and sweet-scented is the blood
of these horses, horses to feed the lions in the new zoo which is moving

from Havana to Lenin's Park near where we live. Dark blood, this blood
of the horses my father slaughters daily, and loses himself doing so.
I, being a child, ask how many horses it takes to feed a single lion.

This, of course, makes my father laugh. I watch as he scrubs and rinses
encrusted blood from his forearms and hands, those hands
that kill the horses, the hands that sever through skin and flesh and crush

through bone because tough is the meat of old horses. Feed for the lions.
So my father, the dissident, the *gusano,* the Yankee lover, walks
to and from work on tired feet, on an aching body. He no longer talks

to anybody, and less to us, his family. My mother and my grandmother;
his mother. But they leave him alone, to his moods, for they know
what he is being put through. A test of will. Determination. Salvation

and survival. My father, gloomy, under the new zoo tent on the grounds,
doesn't say much. He has learned how to speak with his hands.
Sharp are the cuts he makes on the flesh. The horses are shot on the open

fields, a bullet through the head, and are then carted to where my father,
along with other men, do the butchering. He is thirty (the age
I am now) and tired and when he comes home his hands are numb

from all that chopping and sawing. This takes place in 1969. Years later
when we are allowed to leave Havana for Madrid, to the cold
winter of Spain, we find ourselves living in a hospice. The three of us

in a small room. (My grandmother died and was buried in Havana.)
  My father, my mother and I and next door is a man named Izquierdo
who keeps us awake with his phlegmy coughs. From the other side of the walls,

his coughing sounds like thunder. We try to sleep; I try harder but the coughing
  seeps through and my father curses under his breath. I listen to the heat
as it tic-tacs through the furnace. My father tries to make love to my mother.

I try now not to listen. The mattress springs sound like bones crushing.
  My mother refuses without saying a word. This is the final time
she does so tonight. My father breaks the immense and interminable silence,

saying, "If you don't, I'll look for a Spanish woman who will."
  Silence again, then I think I hear my mother crying.
"*Alguien,*" my father says, meaning someone, "Will want to, to . . . (fuck him.)"

And I lay there on my edge of the mattress, sweat coming on from the heat.
  My eyes are closed and I listen hard and then the sound of everything stops.
This, I think, is a sound like death. Then my father begins all over again.

The room fills with the small noises . . . the cleaver falls and cuts through the skin,
  tears through the flesh, crushes the bone, and then there is the blood.
All that blood. It emerges and collects on the slaughter tables, the blood of countless

horses. Sleep upon me, I see my father stand by the sink in our Havana house patio.
  He scrubs and rinses his hands. The blood whirls and dissolves
slowly in the water. Once again I summon the courage to go ahead and ask him

how much horse meat it takes to appease the hunger of a single lion.

In the House of White Light

When my grandmother left the house
    to live with my aunts, my grandfather,

who spent so much time in the sugar
    cane fields, returned daily to the emptiness

of the clapboard house he built
    with his own hands, and he sat in the dark

to eat beans he cooked right in the can.
There in the half-light he thought of all he'd lost,

including family, country, land, sometimes
he slept upright on that same chair,

only stirred awake by the restlessness
of his horse. One night during a lightning

storm, my grandfather stripped naked
and walked out into the fields around

the house saying "*que me parta un rayo,*"
may lightning strike me, and he stood

with his arms out, the hard rain pelted
his face, and then the lightning fell

about him, and he danced and cradled
lightning bolts in his arms, but they

kept falling, these flashes of white light,
and he ran back inside and brought out

an armful of large mason jars my grandmother
used for pickling, and he filled them

with fractal light. Like babies, he carried
the jars inside and set them all about the house,

and the house filled with the immense
blinding light that swallowed everything

including the memories of how each nail
sunk into the wood, the water level rose

in the well, the loss of this country,
the family who refused to accept him now,

that in this perpetual waking, the world
belonged to those who believed in the power

of electricity, those moments zapped
of anguish, isolation, this clean and pure

act of snatching lightning out of heavy air,
plucking lightning like flowers from a hillside.

Carterista / Pickpocket

After he got caught & sentenced to the sugar
cane fields in Oriente for six months, the last
time, my cousin (the pickpocket) said enough,

he'd had it with this life of emptying pockets,
so he moved to Havana, walked the streets,
slept under the hollows of a stairwell, made deals

with the local Tourist-Only cafes & restaurants
to keep the ashtrays empty & clean, for free,
& they let him. He threw the ashes in one pocket

& the cigar & cigarette butts in the other,
& at the park he sat on the benches or under
the shade of a banyan, looked at the ashen

pigeons & the grimy sparrows while he gutted
cigars & cigarettes, clipped off those with filters,
shredded the tobacco & rolled himself a day's

supply of new smokes, strong, sweetly varied
in taste, the way he liked them. He sat there
for hours until night time when the moon

& stars appeared in the sky, and he thought
of wallets he'd seen bulged in the back
pockets of bus travelers, such sadness in the way

they hung, thick & heavy, & of women tourist
purses, wide like their thighs, & he exhaled
a heavy sigh, smoke clouding his vision, waiting,

a game, when tomorrow he could spell *Pronto*
in this heaven-ward smoke, floating like blue
petals in water, like these visions of the thick wallets,

wallets he's too afraid to open like his mouth, his life.

Suárez on Reworking the Past

I started writing poetry early in my life, around age fourteen, when I first came to the United States from Spain where my family and I spent four years waiting for visas to enter this country. I was born in Havana, Cuba, and lived there for eight years. Those eight years made an obvious impact on my life, and later on in my work as a poet.

I arrived in Los Angeles in the fall of 1974, and life was exploding all around me in my new country. At school I sought refuge in the classroom from the violence of the playgrounds and the hallways. I met a few angels in the forms of teachers who guided me toward books, books that would forever change my life. I read Poe, Dickinson, Emerson, and Thoreau early in my youth, and reread them once I had finally learned English. For months I looked at Whitman's poems, how they spread from margin to margin in such wonderful long lines and I thought of the trains of my youth, the miles of fence post around my grandfather's farm back in Cuba. I fell in love then with the way poetry looked on the page, with the possibilities for filling up white space.

I think the best of my poems show a careful balance between form and content, between line and white space, between positive and negative energy. This is the case with one of my favorite poems I've written in recent years, "Psalm for the Boy Cartographer." Whenever I am writing about water, or the kind of water travesty most Cubans endure—and still endure knowing the odds are one in four of making it to freedom—I cannot help but think of waves, of their movements, their rhythms. Waves make wakes, undulations upon smooth surfaces. They rise in peaks and fall in valleys. As a child I was fascinated by the beaches, by waves coming in and going out, ebb and flow, leaving behind a sheet of froth. I've always been intrigued by residue, by what is left behind, by what lingers.

"Poems, of course, approach slowly from the horizon of the mind. They take their time, but I can always see the headlights of one coming early on. I hear their rumble emerging like distant thunder just before a hurricane is about to burst onto island shore."

For me, a poem will surface and demand to be recognized through the power of recollection, but it's always filtered through the imagination. Poems, of course, approach slowly from the horizon of the mind. They take their time, but I can always see the headlights of one coming early on. I hear their rumble emerging like distant thunder just before a hurricane is about to burst onto island shore. Often it's a quiet but persistent noise—it's like putting your ear to a conch shell, there's always something there if you listen hard enough.

The first four poems, "Psalm for the Boy Cartographer," "Those Lost Souls: Florida Straits Tragedy #1," "*Aguacero*," and "Women Who Carry Water from the River," concern themselves with water, and their lines play an important role on the page. I think of the boy who leaves with his mother to cross the perilous Florida

Straits, his mother quite aware of the odds, and of their moving away from land, floating for days and nights. The mother dies while the boy, it is said, floats on in the right direction, as if by magic, guided perhaps by the moon and a pod of dolphins that swim around him to keep the sharks at bay. Some people believe in miracles, I believe in the poetry of water and what it does to my imagination. I've studied the poetry of the great Caribbean poets like Derek Walcott, Victor Hernández Cruz, Dulce Maria Loynaz—theirs, too, is a poetry born of the elements, of water, fire, earth.

The other poems I've chosen, "Bitterness," "In the House of White Light," and "*Carterista*/Pickpocket," elicit recollection, salvaged moments my mind refuses to obliterate. I am fortunate to have almost come full circle to return to Miami which for Cubans is almost like being home. In its tropical flavors, I find solace. I find an enrichment in my work.

These poems I think are among my best because they come close to capturing the essence of my bilingual, bicultural, hyphenated life. I write poems that often begin with the sound of Spanish words or phrases. I like when the kernel of a poem surfaces due to something I've heard a million times before at family gatherings, words like "*agua*" (water), "*tierra*" (earth), "*luz*" (light)—enchanted words as I call them. I hear them over and over again and they set me off. I use Spanish, Latin, and French in my poetry because it is a way for me as poet to lay the bridgework from one culture to another, from other times to the here and now. I have built poems entirely out of remembering the sound of a word I heard a relative speak, as is the case with the poem "*Carterista*/Pickpocket."

> *"I use Spanish, Latin, and French in my poetry because it is a way for me as poet to lay the bridgework from one culture to another, from other times to the here and now."*

For quite some time I would hear my mother say that my cousin had had trouble back in Cuba because he had a bad habit of picking things out of people's pockets in buses and trucks. Then she said the word in Spanish, pronounced it slowly, and I was hooked. I couldn't run to write the poem down faster than my mind kept thinking of the details. How it feels to have your wallet stolen, slipped out of your back pocket. About why someone would choose to do this. What it meant.

"Bitterness" on the other hand comes out of a particular mood a memory put me in when I remembered those days when we first arrived in Madrid, Spain, and had to share a room at a hostel. Back in Cuba I had my own room. I slept alone, and then I found myself sleeping in the same room with my parents. Proximity in such close quarters breathes strangeness, I think. So the poem is about what I heard my father say. It had to be a narrative because I was remembering many of the details of that moment. I also had to place it into some context for the reader. Why would my father say such a thing to my mother? It was the very first adult conversation I paid close attention to and it devastated me. Memory poems are, for me, necessarily narrative because I feel like I have to set the stage for maximum impact on the reader, and telling a story requires time and a linear movement over lines and stanzas. I tried a number of layouts on the page, but ultimately left it with the form it now has because I wanted the reader to think of waves, think of returning and leaving, a cycle that would keep them reading to the end. It's one of my longest poems, and one of my most successful I think because all elements (language, content, form) work in unison to provide the reader a lasting moment, a picture, the same memory which is forever locked in my mind.

"In the House of White Light" brings us back to water. At a friend's party one night, I saw a picture on the wall very similar to the painting *American Gothic* in which an old man and an old woman stood by a barn with a bunch of mason jars filled with strange, sci-fi-like, broken-up light, like those in Frankenstein movies. The picture captivated me for weeks, months, until I thought of the reasons my mother claimed my grandfather and my grandmother broke off their marriage of fifty years, and she moved out and he stayed behind in an old clapboard house in a hillside in San Pablo, Cuba. I thought of a Cuban deluge, of so much rain everything my grandfather believed about nature and climate would be tested, almost in a religious sense. I thought of those mason jars filling up with light, of someone going out in the rain to collect them. It was a struggle to find the right words to capture the mystery and magic of this moment, and I ended up throwing out three stanzas, but the poem is better for it. I tried to take a luxurious detour via a short reminiscence about a nutty neighbor who found God on her deathbed, but this section ultimately had to go. The poem demanded it.

"I am a strong believer that a poem has to take certain risks and a poet, while writing a poem, has to arrive at a precipice and jump in with eyes wide open. Only then can you get to those moments in poetry that are truly enlightening and made of pure epiphany. You have to risk and take chances, even if it means you fail."

I am a strong believer that a poem has to take certain risks and a poet, while writing a poem, has to arrive at a precipice and jump in with eyes wide open. Only then can you get to those moments in poetry that are truly enlightening and made of pure epiphany. You have to risk and take chances, even if it means you fail.

All poets, I think, need to find their place of meditation, where the work feeds off the daily routines, the daily struggles of people arriving, finding their way into a particular life of longing, desire, memory. These are the essentials for me and my work. These are the elements my work thrives to maintain, uplift, reveal. In some cases, the act of writing a poem for me is as easy as looking out from my eighth-floor balcony off Key Biscayne toward the open water, closing my eyes to the breeze, and seeing how some survive such difficult crossings by day and by night. As immigrants, as poets, as human beings, what guides us in and saves us *is* nothing short of a miracle.

Writing Suggestions

1. Write a poem about water, but do so from the point of view of a person who, like Suárez, is obsessed with water in their own way. An ex-sailor who still loves the sea. A widow whose husband drowned. A child who once was stung horribly by a jellyfish. Imagine that this person is forced through circumstances to reconfront water again. Try to express feelings and mood through concrete details. Control image, sound, and indirect presentation of emotion. Like in good fiction, put the emphasis on showing versus telling. Revisit "Women Who Carry Water from the River" and "*Aguacero*" for inspiration.

2. Suárez's poems often get their power through transformation (of the self, of the other, of inanimate things). Write your own poem of transformation of the self. Begin with an assertion that likens yourself to an inanimate thing (e.g. I am the pinky ring on Mike Tyson's finger, or I am a car radiator). Follow the logic through. Be curious about your previously human attributes and emotions in your new form. Think about love, exercise, greed. Where are your eyes? Where is your left hand? Write with energy and conviction. Remember (or revisit) what Bly writes about assertions.

3. Poem titles can be tricky to get exactly right. A decent one doesn't help or hurt a poem, but a good one adds to a poem's value and meaning. Select three poems you've already written and carefully re-examine the titles. Do any strike you as not quite right yet? As Suárez does in "Women Who Carry Water from the River," let the title be part of the first line of the poem. This technique allows the poem to gather momentum quickly and it clearly establishes the relationship between title and poem. Replace all three titles with part of the first line so that the poem begins with the title and reads straight through from there. Does the pace of your poems change? Does the meaning? Put back the original titles if you want, but remember that a compelling or interesting title will make a reader stop and say "I have to read at least a bit of this poem to see if it's as compelling or interesting as that title." And they will. Poem titles (as with a poem's first line and even first stanza) make a promise to the reader. Make sure your poems fulfill that promise. Make sure, too, that the right promise is promised.

4. Suárez is one of the most widely published poets writing in America today. Use the Internet to find three of his poems, and read them carefully. What themes does he deal with in these poems? How would you characterize the style? The voice? When were the poems you've found written? How do

they compare to Suárez's selections on the audio CD? Does Suárez write exclusively about Cuban or Latino concerns? If you enjoy his poetry, take a moment to look at his home page, www.virgilsuarez.com and send him an e-mail telling him so. Reaffirm your own presence in the literary community.

> *"Poetry is the lifeblood of community; by fostering empathic connections among people, it may indeed remind each of us of our own ongoing process of being alive, of how and why we live."*
>
> —Rafael Campo

Ron Wallace

Oranges

This morning I eat an orange.
It is sour and juicy. My mouth
will tingle all day.
Outside, it is cold. The trees
do not anticipate their leaves.
When I breathe into my hand I smell
oranges.

I walk across the lake.
Ice fishermen twitch their poles until
perch flicker the surface, quick
and bright as orange slices.
The sun ripens in the sky.
The wind turns thin and citrus,
the day precise, fragile.

My mustache and eyelashes freeze.
When I arrive at your house
you are friendly as a fruit seller.
We peel off our clothes, slice through
that wordy rind.
When I lift my fingers to your lips:
oranges.

The Facts of Life

She wonders how people get babies.
Suddenly vague and distracted,
we talk about "making love."

She's six and unsatisfied, finds
our limp answers unpersuasive.
Embarrassed, we stiffen, and try again,
this time exposing the stark naked words:
penis, vagina, sperm, womb, and *egg.*
She thinks we're pulling her leg.
We decide that it's time
to get passionate and insist.
But she's angry, disgusted.
Why do we always make fun of her?
Why do we lie?
We sigh, try cabbages, storks.
She smiles. *That's more like it.*
We talk on into the night, trying
magic seeds, good fairies, God . . .

At Chet's Feed & Seed

The man who is telling me about the chicken
stationery he makes in his backyard trailer
leaves with his beaky wife.
Their voices clabber and scratch.
In the corner, guinea hens, $1.50 each,
scutter and strut in jerky grandeur.
Clyde is pleased to meet me. He
shakes my hand, a 200 lb. feed bag
perched on his left shoulder, his big
arm, glistening in its sleeveless T-shirt,
a mixture of roast corn, oats, molasses, wheat.
The bald woman tied up to her chihuahua,
her son still in Vietnam with the marines,
adjusts her rheumy teeth.
She says he'll be coming back.
Chet says he will, pulls a pencil out of his ear
and takes a dollar off her bill.
She grunts. Chet bleats at Clyde
who whinnies under the weight of the feed sack.
The chicken man and his wife come back.
They're looking at me.

The smell of feed and goodwill is sweet.
I feel so stupid I could almost moo
with approval. So I do.

The Hell Mural: Panel I

Iri and Toshi Maruki are "painting the bomb."
Their painting, they say, will comfort the souls of the dead.
"It's a dreadful cruel scene of great beauty,"
Toshi says. "The face may be deformed but there's kindness
in a finger or a breast, even in hell."
The Hell Mural spreads over the floor.

Iri stretches naked on the floor,
painting. He remembers Hiroshima after the bomb—
the bodies stacked up, arms outstretched toward hell,
nothing he could see that was not dead,
nothing that cared at all for human kindness,
nothing that wept at such terror, such beauty.

Now a brush stroke here, a thick wash there, and beauty
writhes and stretches from the canvas floor.
He wants his art to "collaborate with kindness,"
he wants his art to "uncover the bomb."
But no lifetime's enough to paint all the dead
or put all those who belong there in hell.

"Hitler and Truman," he says, "of course are in hell."
But even those of us who live for beauty
are in hell, no less so than the dead.
(He paints himself and Toshi on the floor.)
"All of us who cannot stop the bomb
are now in hell. It's no kindness

to say different. It's no kindness
to insist on heaven; there's only hell."
Toshi adds bees and maggots to the bomb,
and birds, cats, her pregnant niece, the beauty
of severed breast and torn limb on the killing floor.
"In Hiroshima," she says, "we crossed a river on the dead

bodies stacked up like a bridge. Now the dead
souls must be comforted with kindness.
Come walk in your socks across our floor,
walk on the canvas. (A little dirt in hell
almost improves it.) Can you see the beauty
of this torso, that ear lobe, this hip bone of the bomb?"

Iri and Toshi Maruki, in "Hell," are painting the bomb,
the mural on their floor alive with the thriving dead.
Come walk on their kindness, walk on their troublesome beauty.

In the Amish Bakery

I don't know why what comes to mind
when I imagine my wife and daughters,
off on a separate vacation
in the family car,
crashing—no survivors—
in one of those Godless snowstorms
of Northern Illinois,
is that Amish bakery
in Sauk County, Wisconsin, where
on Saturday mornings in summer,
we used to go—
all powdered sugar and honey in
the glazed caramel air. And O
the browned loaves rising,
the donuts, buns, and pies, the ripe
strawberry stain of an oven burn
on the cheek of one of the wives.
And outside in the yard
that goddamned trampoline
where we'd imagine them—
the whole blessed family in
their black topcoats and frocks,
their severe hair and beards,
their foolish half-baked grins,
so much flour dust and leaven—
leaping all together on
their stiff sweet legs toward heaven.

Hardware

My father always knew the secret
name of everything—
stove bolt and wing nut,
set screw and rasp, ratchet
wrench, band saw, and ball
peen hammer. He was my
tour guide and translator
through that foreign country
with its short-tempered natives
in their crew cuts and tattoos,
who suffered my incompetence
with gruffness and disgust.
Pay attention, he would say,
and you'll learn a thing or two.

Now it's forty years later,
and I'm packing up his tools
*(If you know the proper
names of things you're never
at a loss)* tongue-tied, incompetent,
my hands and heart full
of doohickeys and widgets,
watchamacallits, thingamabobs.

The Friday Night Fights

Every Friday night we watched the fights.
Me, ten years old and stretched out on the couch;
my father, in his wheelchair, looking on
as Rocky Marciano, Sonny Liston, Floyd Patterson
fought and won the battles we could not.
Him, twenty-nine, and beat up with disease;
me, counting God among my enemies
for what he'd done to us. We never touched.

But in between the rounds we'd sing how we'd
Look sharp! Feel sharp! & Be sharp! with Gillette
and Howard Cosell, the Bela Lugosi of boxing.

Out in the kitchen, my mother never understood
our need for blood, how this was as close as we'd get
to love—bobbing and weaving, feinting and sparring.

FIELDING

I like to see him out in center field
fifty years ago, at twenty-two,
waiting for that towering fly ball—
August, Williamsburg, a lazy afternoon—
dreaming how he'd one day be a pro
and how he'd have a wide-eyed son to throw
a few fat pitches to. An easy catch.
He drifts back deeper into a small patch

of weeds at the fence and waits. In a second or two
the ball is going to stagger in the air,
the future take him to his knees: wheelchair,
MS, paralysis, grief. But for now
he's camped out under happiness. Life is good.
For at least one second more he owns the world.

THE MCPOEM

I must confess that I, too, like it:
the poem that's fried up flat and fast with condiments
on a sesame seed bun. Steamy, grease-spattered,
and juicy, fluent with salt, piping hot
from the grill, glazed with bubbling oil.
A poem you can count on always to be
the same—small, domestic, fun for the whole
family. Economical. American. Free

of culinary pretension. I used to have to ride
ten miles or so out to the suburbs to find
one back in 1956 when poems were
more expensive, reserved for connoisseurs.
Now everyone is welcome to the griddle.
(I also like toads, and all this fiddle.)

Blessings

occur.
Some days I find myself
putting my foot in
the same stream twice;
leading a horse to water
and making him drink.
I have a clue.
I can see the forest
for the trees.

All around me people
are making silk purses
out of sows' ears,
getting blood from turnips,
building Rome in a day.
There's a business
like show business.
There's something new
under the sun.

Some days misery
no longer loves company;
it puts itself out of its.
There's rest for the weary.
There's turning back.
There are guarantees.
I can be serious.
I can mean that.
You can quite
put your finger on it.

Some days I know
I am long for this world.
I can go home again.
And when I go
I can
take it with me.

Toads, and All This Fiddle: Wallace on Music, Metaphor, and Mirth

When asked his definition of a good poem, Howard Moss, the great poetry editor of *The New Yorker*, was purported to have said, "One I like." Which is maybe what it comes down to. Of course, Howard Moss's likes and dislikes were informed by his vast reading, and by his own experience of writing poetry over a lifetime. Now, faced with selecting my own "best" poems, I find myself falling back on the simple criterion of "ones I like."

One poem that both Howard Moss and I have liked (it was originally published in *The New Yorker*) is "Oranges." In fact, as is often the case with my best work, I remember vividly the circumstances surrounding the writing of the poem. It was 1975. I was on leave from the University of Wisconsin, writing a book on humor in American literature and working on my first book of poetry. My wife, Peg, and I had only been in Wisconsin for three years, having moved from St. Louis where I grew up, to take a job teaching creative writing.

"I remember saying a little prayer, to God or the muse or my subconscious or whatever was generating the poem, to let me finish it. Just then my wife walked in downstairs and my heart sank. Would she interrupt me? Would I lose the poem? But what happened instead was that SHE WALKED INTO THE POEM."

It was a bitterly cold winter—the kind one never sees in St. Louis—and I had just bicycled home from my office. The wind off the lake was fierce, my eyes were watering, and my eyelash had frozen to my parka hood zipper—I had to stop and warm the eyelash between my thumb and forefinger to free it. When I arrived home, my wife was out, and when I sat down to write about the ride and the cold and the eyelash, the image of an orange came to me, and the poem took off, seemingly writing itself. I remember saying a little prayer, to God or the muse or my subconscious or whatever was generating the poem, to let me finish it. Just then my wife walked in downstairs and my heart sank. Would she interrupt me? Would I lose the poem? But what happened instead was that *she walked into the poem*, which became, in effect, a love poem to her. Rather than interrupting the poem, she pointed it in the direction it wanted to go.

Part of what I like about the poem is my sense of its communal generation—my wife, the weather, the conventions of poetry, and I all came together to produce it. Partly I like its celebratory nature and its sensory quality and the fact that, even after the poem was published, it continued to surprise me. As I was closing the poem I was thinking more of tactile and olfactory than of visual imagery—the touch, the smell, of oranges on the lips. It wasn't until a reader later pointed out the visual image of the ending—lips look like orange slices—that I saw that element of the poem.

"Oranges" was a gift, a poem that seemed to write itself, that was "inspired." Of course, it was also the culmination of years of work, reminding me of Dylan Thomas's observation that although he only wrote when he was inspired, he found that the more he wrote, the more inspired he got. Did "Oranges" take thirty minutes to write? Or thirty years?

"The Facts of Life" also seemed to come effortlessly. Having explored the brief sensory lyric in my first book, I found myself moving toward narrative and humor in my second. Humor has been a defining characteristic of American poetry since Walt Whitman, with his hyperbolic self-celebration, and Emily Dickinson, with her witty self-deprecation, provided the models for subsequent generations of poets. When my six-year-old daughter asked where babies came from, and my wife, having read an article in a popular magazine recommending full disclosure, began telling her the whole wonderful story, it seemed more awkward and embarrassing than funny to me. But as I began writing about it later the situation seemed funnier and funnier, and even the rhymes participated in the joke on us. What starts as a free-verse poem shifts to the surprising couplet in the middle ("*penis, vagina, sperm, womb,* and *egg.*/ She thinks we're pulling her leg.") with its near rhyme of "*penis va-*"/ "She thinks we're" and its exact rhyme of "*egg*" and "leg"—wordplay that always evokes laughter at a public reading. Like "Oranges," "The Facts of Life" is a love poem, in this case the humor leading us to an embrace of the "truth" of metaphor, symbolism, and tale, over the "lie" of literalism.

"ORANGES' was a gift, a poem that seemed to write itself, that was 'inspired.' Of course, it was also the culmination of years of work, reminding me of Dylan Thomas's observation that although he only wrote when he was inspired, he found that the more he wrote, the more inspired he got."

Perhaps I feel a special affection for these two poems because they are personal (though I hope not private) poems drawing directly on my own intimate experience. "At Chet's Feed & Seed" is, perhaps, less obviously personal, being more an observation of a public scene. But, like "Oranges" and "The Facts of Life," it is a kind of love poem, drawing on humor and sound for its effects. Sound has, in fact, been a central element in my work—often words, or lines, or entire poems are generated more by sound than by sense. In *Alice in Wonderland,* Lewis Carroll has Humpty Dumpty advise Alice to "take care of the sounds and the sense will take care of itself" (a play on the English maxim, "take care of the pence and the pounds will take care of themselves"). Robert Frost similarly insisted, "subject matter is important, but sound is the gold in the ore." One of my earliest influences, in addition to Emily Dickinson and Dylan Thomas, was Gerard Manley Hopkins who argued that you should read a poem not with your eyes but with your ears.

"At Chet's Feed & Seed" was written with my ears. The rich variety of sound—alliteration, assonance, consonance, internal rhyme—is meant to evoke a sense of buoyancy, exuberance, and sufficiency in the scene, and (as a kind of in-joke on the chicken man and myself) aurally to reflect the animal imagery. The repetition of "t," "ch," "k," "b," and "blk" in words like "each," "scratch," "clabber," and "scutter," suggest a chicken's clucking to me, while the vowels in "stupid," "approval," and "do," suggest a cow's "moo."

The reference to the Vietnam War in "At Chet's Feed & Seed" introduces a political dimension into the poem. "The Hell Mural" presents an even more clearly political agenda, using the rigid, repeating form of the sestina to explore issues of nuclear armament and the ethics of mass annihilation. The poem had its genesis in a short documentary film I saw about Iri and Toshi Maruki, two Japanese artists whose life project has been to paint what they call "the bomb," by which they mean all evil and war and atrocity. They paint in the nude, on huge canvases on the floor that are displayed in a museum dedicated to their work. Their statements about art were very moving, including, among other things, the idea that they wanted to pass their work on to others who would keep it alive in different forms. The form I decided to pass their work along in, the sestina, seemed especially appropriate for reflecting their method. The six stanzas and envoi consider the repeating end-words from multiple angles, which is what the Marukis' art does—looks at the same horrors from every angle. I was active in the nuclear freeze movement, and "The Hell Mural" was my attempt to contribute to the ongoing political dialogue.

As "The Hell Mural" is my best effort to depict hell, "In the Amish Bakery" is my best effort to depict heaven. The image of the staid Amish family jumping on their trampoline is what stays with me here, the various incongruities in the poem evoking the kind of surprise and whimsy and humor that would have to be present in any heaven I'd want to spend the afterlife in. When I was writing the poem I really didn't know the answer to the question I opened the piece with about why the image of the trampoline came to mind in the context of the imagined deaths of my wife and daughters. I'm still not sure I know, though it probably has something to do with the power of celebration and humor and memory and sensory evocation to provide Frost's "momentary stay against confusion" in the face of loss and mortality.

My speculations on heaven and hell and mortality began at an early age, generated in part by my father's illness. Paralyzed with multiple sclerosis for most of my life, my father appears in each of my books, often in multiple poems. When my first book was accepted and I realized that my father would be seeing the poems about him for the first time (and they didn't always present him or our relationship in the best light), I asked him, in the nursing home where he spent his last years, whether he'd prefer that I remove them from the book. He said something that has been very important for my writing. He said, "I've felt so useless to anyone over the years that if I can be of some use to you in your writing it would make me happy."

Appropriation of other people's stories, and the exposure of friends' and family's lives, has always been a vexing problem for writers, so my father's permission was liberating. In the poem "Hardware," written after my father's death, I acknowledge his importance for me as a kind of "tour guide" and "translator" of the foreign country of adulthood, suggesting that no words are finally sufficient to accommodate the enormity of his loss. Faced with such sorrow, the heart has only "doohickeys and widgets, watchamacallits and thingamabobs" with which to try to make do.

Two poems about my father, "The Friday Night Fights" and "Fielding," are from the title sequence of my book of one hundred sonnets, *The Uses of Adversity*. The book resulted from my decision to write a sonnet a day for a year, a project which was an outgrowth of my interest in traditional forms and their revival in recent poetry. Although I wanted my sonnets to be fairly rigorous, with a clear gesture, at least, to iambic pentameter, to a consistent rhyme scheme, to a structure built on a central contrast whether in the Petrarchan octave and sestet or the Shakespearian quatrains and couplet or in some hybrid, I also wanted the sonnets to read as conversationally as free verse, employing common diction, slant rhyme, speech rhythms, and a liberal use of enjambment and caesura.

"The Friday Night Fights," perhaps more accessible to older readers who remember the ABC sports show from the 1950s, aims to explore the affinities of conflict and caring, how even fighting can be an expression of affection and love. "Fielding" aims to fix in the memory a moment of happiness and exhilaration before a lifetime of frustration and struggle ensues.

Ever since its invention in 1230 by Giacomo da Lentino in the court of Frederick II of Sicily, the sonnet has, in its length and intensity, leant itself to serious poems about love and death such as these. It has also, in its structural resemblance to the joke (the Shakespearian couplet can be something of a punch line), leant itself to humor. "The McPoem" draws on Donald Hall's humorous label dismissing the kind of poetry sometimes referred to as "the workshop poem"—"the McPoem, fifty billion served." My answer to Hall echoes, of course, Marianne Moore's poem entitled "Poetry" that begins, "I, too, dislike it. There are things that are important beyond all this fiddle" and ends by defending poetry as an art that can "present for inspection imaginary gardens with real toads in them."

Burgers and boxing, oranges and eyelashes, good fairies, and God, Hell murals and Amish bakeries, conflict and affection, watchamacallits and thingamabobs—these are some of the things that poetry can incorporate and celebrate, and, if the poems are good poems, translate from the commonplace and the mundane to the miraculous and the extraordinary. Even a list of clichés, like those in my recent poem "Blessings," can have their day.

"Burgers and boxing, oranges and eyelashes, good fairies, and God, Hell murals and Amish bakeries, conflict and affection, watchamacallits and thingamabobs—these are some of the things that poetry can incorporate and celebrate."

Are the poems included here good poems? I guess it's not up to me, finally, to say. I do know that I like them. But then, I also like toads, and all this fiddle.

Writing Suggestions

1. For a real change of pace in your writing, construct a collage poem. Photocopy text from a variety of sources (*USA Today* sports section front page, *Esquire*, dust jacket of a historical biography, back of a box of breakfast cereal, church bulletin, and so on) and then scan for lines and words that appeal to you. Cut them out and begin to arrange them on paper in lines. Work entirely from the photocopies you've made, or introduce a poem you've been working on and extract lines from that, too. Once you're done, either keep the poem in collage form and let part of its "art" be its look on the page, or type it up like your regular poems. Does this poem vary in tone, structure, voice, mood, and imagery from your usual poems? What questions of ownership of a text does this sort of poem bring up?

2. Go to a highly public place (library, shopping mall, Super Wal-Mart) and find a spot where you can sit and write. Begin a poem about *anything except being where you are*. When you find yourself taking a mental pause after you've written a few lines, a few stanzas, look up and find someone who catches your eye. Let them, as Wallace did, "walk into the poem." Connect the present with the past, the "there" with the "here," the "what if" with the "what is." These sort of wildly intuitive leaps (Billy Collins, Wanda Coleman, and many, many others do these too) are risky but wonderfully rewarding moments in poetry that often result in little epiphanies that surprise a reader without necessarily draining all of one's blood.

3. Select a poem draft of yours that you've been having trouble with, that you can't get exactly right yet. Perform surgery on it—amputate the head (first few lines, or whole first stanza), or perhaps the feet (last few lines), or even the stomach (middle stanza). Do you need to patch up the hole with a line or two? Do these changes put new emphasis and/or musicality into what you have left? If you're still not satisfied with the poem, put on your journalist's cap and ask the six big questions: Who, What, When, Where, Why, and How. If you can't answer them directly from the poem, add in those details. Does answering these questions help clarify the poem, at least in your own mind? What's the biggest three problems you encounter with revision?

4. Walk (or imagine yourself walking) into a ma-and-pa store or family business. Note all body language and invent the family's mission. Write a poem about it, á la Wallace's "At Chet's Feed & Seed." Let your poem be an

eclectic gathering of elements—listen to Wallace's selections on the audio CD for examples of making surprisingly disparate elements work together. Let the rhythms and cadences of language work the images in the poem. Pay particular attention to the specifics—the exactness of detail.

"I'm not trying to tell people what to do or what to think or none of that. I'm not a leader. I'm not a guru. I'm just a poet looking at the world."

—Nikki Giovanni

Afaa Michael Weaver

The Picnic, an Homage to Civil Rights

We spread torn quilts and blankets,
mashing the grass under us until it was hard,
piled the baskets of steamed crabs
by the trees in columns that hid the trunk,
put our water coolers of soda pop
on the edge to mark the encampment,
like gypsies settling in for revelry
in a forest in Rumania or pioneers
blazing through the land of the Sioux,
the Apache, and the Arapaho, looking guardedly
over our perimeters for poachers
or the curious noses of fat women
ambling past on the backs of their shoes.
The sun crashed through the trees,
tumbling down and splattering in shadows
on the baseball diamond like mashed bananas.
We hunted for wild animals in the clumps
of forests, fried hot dogs until the odor
turned solid in our nostrils like wood.
We were in the park.

One uncle talked incessantly, because he knew
the universe; another was the griot[1]
who stomped his foot in syncopation
to call the details from the base of his mind;
another was a cynic who doubted everything,
toasting everyone around him with gin.
The patriarchal council mumbled on,

[1]African tribal storyteller

while the women took the evening to tune
their hearts to the slow air and buzzing flies,
to hold their hands out so angels could stand
in their palms and give dispensation,
as we played a rough game of softball
in the diamond with borrowed gloves,
singing Chuck Berry and Chubby Checker,
diving in long lines into the public pool,
throwing empty peanut shells to the lion,
buying cotton candy in the aviary
of the old mansion, laughing at the monkeys,
running open-mouthed and full in the heat
until our smell was pungent and natural,
while the sun made our fathers and uncles
fall down in naps on their wives' laps, and
we frolicked like wealthy children on an English estate,
as reluctant laws and bloodied heads
tacked God's theses on wooden doors,[2]
guaranteed the canopy of the firmament above us.

SUB SHOP GIRL
FOR JAMES MANN

She is lovely. Her eyes are big almonds
floating over the electronic cash register.
She puts magic dust in my mayonnaise,
hoochie-koochie notes in my fries.
There is no other reason to order
tomatoes, lettuce, hot peppers, onions,
and french fries in a suit and tie.
I come nearer the shop tiptoeing in Florsheims.
With a quarter I set the mood on the jukebox.
"What do you want today?" she asks. "What is it, Baby?"
I am probably the only man who puts strategy
in a Saturday night foray to the sub shop.
I line my cologne up carefully on the dresser,
the Parisian designer bottle for cheese steak,
for pizza the cheaper, less subtle aromas,
laying my clothes out to match each meal.

---

[2]tacked . . . theses: As did Martin Luther, beginning the Protestant Reformation

She puts the change in my palm a coin at a time,
measuring the contours of the lines in my hands.
I think I lost my sanity a long time ago
on the way to buy a foot-long and fries.
The essence of Sango fires my red urge
longing to meld with the small greasy apron
that throws frozen steak portions with expertise.
How could the heavens have wasted such youth
on me and this corner sub shop and vagrants
and the empty neon in after-hours streets,
and the music from old Smokey Robinson 45s
I play on my boom box the nights I want to serenade?
Have you ever listed the extras on a cold cut with
"Tracks of My Tears" or "Second That Emotion"?
When the shop is closed some Sundays I melt
in the afternoon apparitions in the empty windows,
the deserted counters, the cold ovens, the silence.
There are blessings for noble spirits confined
to ordinary lives, the dribble of an oba like me
and a great spirit like my sub shop Osun slicing pickles.
There are blessings as we dazzle the ordinary universe,
pervert the threadbare perceptions of doldrums
with our elegant affair at night, our perfect love,
me in an all-leather racing jacket and Gucci loafers.

One night after work I'll coax her and we'll pretend
to be Marvin Gaye and Tammi Terrell on the parking lot.
I'll caress her around the waist and spin her softly.
A dark night sky laden with stars will crack,
the moon will pour love's essence on the earth,
truth will overcome us on the voices of the orisas—
"Ain't Nothing Like the Real Thing," or maybe
"You're All I Need to Get By," but most of all the song
the world needs to hear—"You Ain't Livin Till You're Lovin."
I am probably the only man who sees the answer
in a cheese-steak hoagie with all the fixins and fries,
music from my boom box or the jukebox nearby,
two almond eyes as deep as canyons over the counter,
and my Gucci and Florsheim shoes doing a soft tap,
the mania and danger of an insecure world hanging out
like a florid design in the curtain of the night.

African Jump Ball
for E. Ethelbert Miller

Can you dribble? Aw man, you can't dribble.
Do you know travelling ain't going to the West Side
    to see your woman?
Dribble, man! This ain't no Amtrak Metroliner!
Don't bogarde me, trying to roll off to the left.
Your layup ain't that tough. Don't try the sky hook.
Give me that ball, partner. Give me that ball.
                                        This is *friendship one on one*.
I'll cut you some slack. Go back to half court
and just run here to the foul line. Do a jumper.
I'll even let you do a set shot and won't even smack
it back to where you buy them dirty sneakers
every Saturday, the *You Was Here Yesterday Store*.
Tell you what. We'll play for African-American Trivia.
Tell me where William Wells Brown stopped running.
                        I'll spot you six points.
This one is even better. Who is bigger and what
the hell is the big that they got? Chamberlain or Jabbar?

You sweatin, man. See, you sweatin. I ain't
busted a bead nowhere, as dry as when my honey
wiped down this morning with that terry towel
and called me love, called me sweetness.
You and me got trickster hearts,
but I know a foul ain't no fried chicken, cuz.
                        Bert, enough with the bum rush, man.
                        See there, we done set the net on fire.

The lead opened so wide it was
too hard for The Poets to keep from
laughing. They slapped their hands
and did the slow jazz of black boys
walking away from an easy game.
In the streets, we watched them stride
away in Florsheims to get high,
too brilliant to live, too brilliant to die.

Cities of Experience: Weaver on the Poetry of Self

My life changed dramatically in 1985. Leaving fifteen years of factory work and writing to enter the formal world of letters and literati, I made a stop in Paris, France. Visiting the Impressionist collection at the Jeu de Paume that spring, I gazed at Renoir's painting *The Picnic* and loved both memories of home and being so far from home. I wanted to fill my life with new experiences in a faraway place, only to find that I was full of memories. In the moment in which I stood gazing into Renoir's picnic, I saw my family on the many treks we made to Druid Hill Park in Baltimore, a park that was once segregated, as most of Baltimore was as a southern city. So "The Picnic, an Homage to Civil Rights" is a big place in my poet self, and I like to think of the poet self as a city, among other things, the city of life, the city of experience.

Paris was so far from the factory. I walked in the main buildings of the Louvre so much one day that my eyes began to ache. There was so much to see, so much to feel connected to in Paris, a city that is made for walking, made for spring. In my sight the poem has a painterly progression, assembling itself through the accumulation of detail. Renoir gives way to Bosch in the image of women holding angels in their hands. Constructing lines is much like bricklaying for me in poems like this. I set the pacing and length in the first line by looking to touch the emotions in the experience. In getting inside the experience this way, I build the poem and the structure of what I know about myself by exploring memory and experience in visual ways. For me sound in language emerges from imagery in language. Certain moments in a line depend upon their intended meaning on emphasis when read aloud, on intonation. For example, I give heavy weight to "we" in "We were in the park." I sometimes fear making the poem that dependent on me is similar to what I am critical of in what people call "spoken word" poetry, but in other ways I think that kind of signature is inevitable.

"In my sight the poem has a painterly progression, assembling itself through the accumulation of detail. Renoir gives way to Bosch in the image of women holding angels in their hands. Constructing lines is much like bricklaying for me in poems like this."

The poem's progression takes as its thesis that the private makes the public possible and vice versa. As much as the private and public are two parts of a whole, I wanted two long stanzas for this poem. The first stanza is the private self and the second stanza is the public mask. For synthesis I chose the image of the two Martin Luthers, one critiquing religious oppression and the other critiquing segregation and racism. I worried when writing the poem that my hand was too "heavy" in showing my family as perhaps not quite conscious of why they are in the park, but I abandoned revision of the poem in the hope that the speaker's consciousness speaks for everyone.

Someone once remarked that my poems accumulate a weightiness that forces a resolution in the closure as opposed to it happening gradually along the way. This was intended as a positive remark, but it continues to cause me anxiety. However, in this poem I surrender to that kind of closure in the poem that I wanted to be one moment's whole view of life.

In my early years as a poet in the factory, I scanned my lines to study metrics, influenced as I was by the whirring sound of conveyor lines. In doing this scansion I sometimes practiced the iambic, while at other times I tried to identify my natural meter. It seems my natural meter is a *natural blues*.

My two-month stay in Europe that year was the beginning of my journey to writing about myself, for looking into myself with what I call the investigative lyric. At the time that I was gazing into Renoir, I was entering the world of visual art in my marriage to Aissatou Mijiza, a Philadelphia-born artist I met as I was leaving Baltimore. A painter and mixed-media sculptor, Aissatou lived in the world of the tangible, of things, and she often talked fondly of Mr. Funk's junk shop, a mecca I could only envision as I had not the pleasure of going there. But it was this world of Baltimore's bohemia that fuels "The Picnic, an Homage to Civil Rights," one of my favorite poems, one which E. Ethelbert Miller has said is one of my best. I trust his voice, and I trust Helen Vendler's choice, as she included the poem in a text of hers entitled *Poems, Poets and Poetry*.

My amour in "Sub Shop Girl" lived in the neighborhood that was the center of Baltimore's bohemia, an area near Johns Hopkins University, the old Memorial Stadium, and Johnny Unitas's Sportsman's Lounge. It was a sub shop that later became Tugboat Annie's before becoming a pizza parlor—again. The site seems to have its own karmic cycle of birth and rebirth, but the excitement of poetry in Baltimore in the early to mid-eighties, of great times with my poet friends and the infamous Poetry Wars between factions of poets has not come again. It was the energy of a time in a way that time becomes history, and in writing this poem I thought of sixties rhythm and blues music as well as hoagies and subs. Philadelphians call subs "hoagies," and I have always found that interesting. It seems like a footballish way of naming the submarine. Also, I had come to know the word "hoagie" while an undergraduate at the University of Maryland from 1968 until 1970, when I went into the factory and the U.S. Army Reserves.

My city of experience was filling with an assortment of structures, as complex as a hoagie with all the fixings and fries, a delight that was fixed forever when I looked into the eyes of this cashier, a lovely woman I admired in a brief but magical moment that inspired me to go and write what I see now as this frolicking dispensation on romantic love. If the music of "The Picnic, an Homage to Civil Rights" is Milt Jackson's vibraphone in the Modern Jazz Quartet, it is Stevie Wonder's "My Cherie Amour" in this poem to the cashier in the sandwich shop. The lines are expansive. I was reading Allen Ginsberg and Ntozake Shange at the time I composed this piece. I was also taking acting lessons. In addition I was still under the influence of projective verse, the idea of the line as exhalation of breath. The breathing here is deep and long, but deep breathing does not mean greater seriousness in tone. The moment was more one of a crush that I felt for her, but it inspired a gazing back over the idea of what it might mean to know love, which can be a pure serenity.

This poem has always been fun at readings, and I have loved the response of audiences to it, especially when I can get to a place where none of us are taking ourselves quite so seriously. So I take its success to be affirmed by the responses of audiences over the years since the first draft. In later drafts I changed Aurora to Osun, gave the cosmic references African locations in the city of experience. I have often taken poems to task, even after publication. My habit of revision owes much to my Baltimorean poet friend James Taylor, who did his graduate work in the Hopkins Seminars. He helped me understand the *joie* of revision is as much joy as the first draft. I like the long lines in the poem and have not tampered with them. I let them take me where they wish, even as I read the poem today. I would be remiss if I did not cite Thulani Davis's ode to the Commodores in her poem "Zoom" as a major influence in my sub shop fixing onto romance. I read Thulani's poem in her early book *All the Renegade Ghosts Rise*.

"I felt so guilty about writing about the factory, the warehouse, the truck driver's lore, but when I came to accept that poetry is everywhere, as my friend Rodger Kamenetz told me I had to do, I was free to go everywhere in my writing."

In the years that I was working in the factory and writing poetry, my biggest challenge came to be to find the poetic value in writing about things around me. I felt so guilty about writing about the factory, the warehouse, the truck driver's lore, but when I came to accept that poetry is everywhere, as my friend Rodger Kamenetz told me I had to do, I was free to go everywhere in my writing. So "Sub Shop Girl" is filled will all kinds of things, as is "African Jump Ball," a poem that celebrates a friendship.

"African Jump Ball" takes Ethelbert's favorite way of naming the game as its title. He knows much more about basketball than I do, and my favorite basketball poem of all time may be Quincy Troupe's "Poem for Magic." However, I have had my own court life. I have made some memorable stop-and-go jump shots and had my most active time as a fan and player back when Kareem Abdul Jabbar was Lou Alcindor and played for Coach John Wooden's legendary UCLA team. It was when Earl Monroe was Earl the Pearl for the Baltimore Bullets and Pete Maravich was Droopy Socks and Pistol Pete. I know those basketball tropes, so I decided to play the dozens, the African-American ritual of boasting and teasing, in this offering to years of a literary friendship, even as Ethelbert or "Bert" as many of us know him, has passed his top dribbling phase, just as I have. We are now in the free-throw zone known as middle age.

The assumption, of course, is that I win this man-on-man battle at half-court, and it begins with my critical assault on his ability to dribble. The poem looks to run freely through African-American vernacular speech, as a more formal usage of the language would give the dozens its much deserved justice. I wanted a percussive roll in the poem, one that would give the feel of the ball tapping the court's surface in rhythm with the pushing of the challenges and taunting between players that is as much the temper of the jock world as it is playing Afro-American dozens. This poem was as much fun to write as "Sub Shop Girl" and grew out of the spirit of an e-mail exchange Ethelbert and I have had in recent years where we write in personas. He is *Big* G to my *Micky* as we do our takeoff on *The Godfather,* and in our vintage African-American folk play he is *Papa B* while I am *Papa D,* as we name our own selves as repositories of having seen and therefore knowing everything. We are veteran players become coaches of the game.

Big G *and Micky move gracefully down the court, turning, spinning in mid-air. The score is for poetry.*

Writing Suggestions

1. Take a piece of fruit from your refrigerator (a lemon, a bunch of grapes, an apple) and look closely at it. Smell it. Touch it. Taste it. Listen to it. Record your impressions on paper. Does the fruit stir up any personal memories? Any associations, symbolic or otherwise? Write a poem from your list of impressions, memories, and associations.

2. Use a line from "The Picnic, an Homage to Civil Rights" or "African Jump Ball" as an epigraph for a poem of your own. (Variation: Write a response poem to either "The Picnic, an Homage to Civil Rights" or "African Jump Ball" that reflects the same structure, or style, or voice. Is it easier to follow someone else's structure, style, or voice, or is it easier to use your own? Why?)

3. Take a poem you've already written and perform a radical revision on its language. Shift the tone from humorous to deadly serious, or alter the diction from the very formal to a slangy, colloquial voice. Which version is more effective? What is the relationship between diction and meaning? Tone and meaning? Is it possible to shift tone or voice in a poem in such a way the end is far different than the beginning? Do Afaa Michael Weaver's poems change tone from poem to poem? Within the same poem? Reread Lee Ann Roripaugh's selections for more examples.

4. Look up reviews of Afaa Michael Weaver's poetry collections on Amazon.com or via an Internet search engine. What sort of concerns do people have when reviewing a poetry collection? Do these concerns change when the review is done by a literary critic or a layman? What claims might you make

about what we value in contemporary American poetry? Read an entire book by Weaver or any writer included in this book. Post your own review on Amazon.com.

"There is a lively history of poetry, and poetry keeps engaging, fulfilling, and transgressing that history."

—Edward Hirsch

Miller Williams

A Poem for Emily

Small fact and fingers and farthest one from me,
a hand's width and two generations away,
in this still present I am fifty-three.
You are not yet a full day.

When I am sixty-three, when you are ten,
and you are neither closer nor as far,
your arms will fill with what you know by then,
the arithmetic and love we do and are.

When I by blood and luck am eighty-six
and you are someplace else and thirty-three
believing in sex and god and politics
with children who look not at all like me,

sometime I know you will have read them this
so they will know I love them and say so
and love their mother. Child, whatever is
is always or never was. Long ago,

a day I watched awhile beside your bed,
I wrote this down, a thing that might be kept
awhile, to tell you what I would have said
when you were who knows what and I was dead
which is I stood and loved you while you slept.

Ruby Tells All

When I was told, as Delta children were,
that crops don't grow unless you sweat at night,
I thought that it was my own sweat they meant.
I have never felt as important again
as on those early mornings, waking up,
my body slick, the moon full on the fields.
That was before air conditioning.
Farm girls sleep cool now and wake up dry
but still the cotton overflows the fields.
We lose everything that's grand and foolish;
it all becomes something else. One by one,
butterflies turn into caterpillars
and we grow up, or more or less we do,
and, Lord, we do lie then. We lie so much
truth has a false ring and it's hard to tell.

I wouldn't take crap off anybody
if I just knew that I was getting crap
in time not to take it. I could have won
a small one now and then if I was smarter,
but I've poured coffee here too many years
for men who rolled in in Peterbilts,
and I have gotten into bed with some
if they could talk and seemed to be in pain.

I never asked for anything myself;
giving is more blessed and leaves you free.
There was a man, married and fond of whiskey.
Given the limitations of men, he loved me.
Lord, we laid concern upon our bodies
but then he left. Everything has its time.
We used to dance. He made me feel the way
a human wants to feel and fears to.
He was a slow man and didn't expect.
I would get off work and find him waiting.
We'd have a drink or two and kiss awhile.
Then a bird-loud morning late one April
we woke up naked. We had made a child.

She's grown up now and gone though God knows where.
She ought to write, for I do love her dearly
who raised her carefully and dressed her well.
Everything has its time. For thirty years
I never had a thought about time.
Now, turning through newspapers, I pause
to see if anyone who passed away
was younger than I am. If one was
I feel hollow for a little while
but then it passes. Nothing matters enough
to stay bent down about. You have to see
that some things matter slightly and some don't.
Dying matters a little. So does pain.
So does being old. Men do not.
Men live by negatives, like don't give up,
don't be a coward, don't call me a liar,
don't ever tell me don't. If I could live
two hundred years and had to be a man
I'd take my grave. What's a man but a match,
a little stick to start a fire with?

My daughter knows this, if she's alive.
What could I tell her now, to bring her close,
something she doesn't know, if we met somewhere?
Maybe that I think about her father,
maybe that my fingers hurt at night,
maybe that against appearances
there is love, constancy, and kindness,
that I have dresses I have never worn.

After All These Years of Prayer and Pi R Square

How sweet a confusion that science, that creed of the creature,
that earthly philosophy of numbers in motion,
so distrusted by rabbi, sheik, and preacher
who have clothed its nakedness in flame,
should quietly introduce us to the notion
of something weightless within us wanting a name.

Waking from a Dream

There was a nothingness, an impulse, a quark
flittering around existence in a place
of purest emptiness, no light, no dark,
a flicker of mathematics in manifold space,

less a movement than a moment. Still,
less a moment than numbers, that slowly start
folding into others the way they will,
like, say, on a checking account and a credit card.

Then moving to build toward everything we've been,
the quarks became the cores of electrons,
flying formations like clouds around their kin
who sit at the center of atoms like toy suns.

Already there were forces weak and strong,
the seeds of war and empire and molecules.
There were such clear signs all along
with no one to read them. Molecules in pools

complicated themselves into protoplasm
then suddenly into Mary Beth and Sam,
both looking dimly backward across a chasm
to numbers that somehow came to give a damn,

that one day would look an hour for a simile,
that one day would cry almost as one for the One
who might have been there when there was nowhere to be,
whose thought might be how universes run—

thoughts we perceive as shoestrings, crickets, and bread
and car keys and a maple leaf and a kiss.
So what is a thought? Better ask instead
what is not? Think of a thought as this:
A table. A dog. A door. A footstool. A fire.
And Sam and all his looks at Mary Beth.
Headaches and birthdays and glass. Failure and fear.
It isn't fact or fantasy. It's both.

Circling circles, I wonder why God should beguile
a thought of God into thinking I am me,
but this will do—you and some jazz a while
with a dog at your feet, or one that seems to be;

the senses of ourselves, of sense, of stuff;
the lifelong impression that we live;
what we believed was wine; what feels like love;
your shapes I touch. These are convincing enough

to a man from a small town, not too quick,
who doesn't know a lot of arithmetic.

Love Poem with Toast

Some of what we do, we do
to make things happen,
the alarm to wake us up, the coffee to perc,
the car to start.

The rest of what we do, we do
trying to keep something from doing something,
the skin from aging, the hoe from rusting,
the truth from getting out.

With yes and no like the poles of a battery
powering our passage through the days,
we move, as we call it, forward,
wanting to be wanted,
wanting not to lose the rain forest,
wanting the water to boil,
wanting not to have cancer,
wanting to be home by dark,
wanting not to run out of gas,

as each of us wants the other
watching at the end,
as both want not to leave the other alone,
as wanting to love beyond this meat and bone,
we gaze across breakfast and pretend.

Williams on Structure and Lineation

A Poem for Emily

This is one of my poems that I feel particularly good about. I wanted to write a poem in a prosodic pattern in such a way that the pattern would seem not to be a vessel into which the statement of the poem was poured, or one imposed on what the poem says, but a form the statement naturally takes as it moves forward.

It's interesting to note that the editor of one of the textbooks in which the poem appears says in a note below it that it "was written as the poet stood at the crib of his granddaughter on the day of her birth." No poem, of course, was ever written as the poet stood anywhere. I got the idea for the poem as I stood there, but it was finished five weeks and a full yellow legal pad later.

"Some poems are very much the soul of the poet, given words; in writing a dramatic monologue, the poet makes an attempt to give voice to the soul of another. Both sorts of poetry have their places in our heads and hearts."

Ruby Tells All

Some poems are very much the soul of the poet, given words; in writing a dramatic monologue, the poet makes an attempt to give voice to the soul of another. Both sorts of poetry have their places in our heads and hearts.

I've never felt inclined, though, to see how deeply mine I could make a poem. On the other hand, I've often felt the impulse to see how far removed from myself I could get in the writing of one—to see how thoroughly I could become stenographer for a voice far removed from my own. A few women have offered me this opportunity; Ruby is one of them.

After All These Years of Prayer and Pi R Square

The energy giving life to any work of art is created when two forces move in opposite directions. Irony is the embodiment of this fact. That I have a son who drives an eighteen-wheeler is not remarkable, nor is it remarkable that I have a son who plays piano in a jazz combo. It becomes a matter of some interest, though, when I mention that this is the same son.

The work of quantum theorists brushing increasingly against the questions of religion (suggesting that there's more there than simply the questions—given the suspicion with which science has traditionally been viewed by most religious leaders) cried out to find expression in a poem.

Waking From a Dream

As one whose formal education is in the sciences and who was raised in a Methodist parsonage, I've long been intrigued—in terms of philosophy, religion, and natural history—by the concept of the nature of God, and feel most comfortable thinking of God as energy that knows itself, and of every particle in existence as a thought of God. This draws my upbringing and my education together and begins to give me some comfort, until I realize finally that all this doesn't much matter. Whatever unknowable there is will not be known by us, but there's still something to know. What does matter is that we learn the joy of loving our moments together—our shapes, a dog or a cat, maybe a little wine, some jazz a while.

Love Poem with Toast

A discussion of *how* a poem means is most effective, it seems to me, against a backdrop of *what* it means. What this one means, in the simplest terms, is that while our lives are driven by the tension created between opposing forces within and around us, forces that generally cancel each other out, we decide to live as if one force—in this case romantic love—will prevail.

My formal education is in the sciences—mostly physiology. In working toward my doctorate, I took preclinical courses in medical school. The perspective of that education stays with me, and I continually find parallels between the sciences and the humanities. I know, for instance, how much a dissection leaves unsaid about the dissected. Still, it's useful. One of the parallels between science and the humanities can be observed in those forces that keep us going by undoing each other, as the stretching of a heart muscle initiates its contraction, which pushes blood through the body and back into the heart; as production of an enzyme is inhibited by the enzyme's end product; as we move on foot by falling forward, catching ourselves in the fall, and falling forward again; as death is the mother not only of beauty but of religion. If we as individuals were to live forever on this planet, we would surely not be driven by a need for eternal salvation by faith. So death gives us religion, which then overcomes death. Also, it's difficult to think how there would be romantic love if there were no death. These thoughts, turning about in my mind, took shape as "Love Poem with Toast."

> *"The energy giving life to any work of art is created when two forces move in opposite directions. Irony is the embodiment of this fact. That I have a son who drives an eighteen-wheeler is not remarkable, nor is it remarkable that I have a son who plays piano in a jazz combo. It becomes a matter of some interest, though, when I mention that this is the same son."*

The structure of a poem's argument is a part of this turning. In this case, the four strophes set forth in sequence a positive, a negative, the balance of the two, and the personal and spiritual implications and resolution of that balance. This progression—the shape of the poem, apart from but in support of what it says—is something for a reader taking part in the poem to recognize as an enhancement of the statement, though the recognition may not be on a conscious level.

Another function of structure that helps to carry the poem's argument is lineation; each line is a unit at the same time of rhythm, sense, and syntax, meant to allow the reader to move forward with a momentary sense of satisfaction line by line, in addition to which the first line of each strophe raises an implicit question which is answered by the following line, driving the reader's attention forward. For instance, the question "Some of what we do, we do *why?*", is answered by "to make things happen"; "like the poles of a battery *how?*" is answered by "powering our passage through the days." Then the next-to-last line in the poem raises the larger question—"wanting to love, we do *what?*"

"The role of lineation . . . is to help imbue the poem with a sense of form . . . and a heightened sense of forward motion."

The role of lineation, then, is to help imbue the poem with a sense of form—an endoskeleton, if you will, since it doesn't have a prosodic or other external form—and a heightened sense of forward motion. Also, moving from the deductive to the inductive, from specific to broader realms, to the future, to imagination itself, gives the reader a sense of deepening significance as the poem moves forward, then the reader is invited to help take the poem wherever it might go by at least subliminally completing the final statement—"pretend *what*, exactly?"

Something else that the reader comes to as part of the experience of the poem, of how it means, is the way the repeated patterns, as a kind of incantation—as, for instance, beginning six lines in sequence with the word "wanting"—suggest the rituals of our lives, the repeated concerns and decisions that tie our days together. The reader is first invited into the poem by the elements of a beginning—"wake up," "coffee," and "start"—then moves into the body of the poem among ordinary individual and social concerns—aging skin, a rusting hoe, the state of the rain forest, boiling water, getting home in the evening—and finally into a closing strophe where resolution is brought about by a number of devices.

As one such device, "love" and "toast" look back at the title, creating a sense of having come full circle. Then there is a change in tone from impersonal to intimate. Then the introduction of "closing words" in *end* and *leave*. There is a shift from the use of "we" to "us" and back to "we," a break in a pattern and then a return to it being one of the most convincing signals of resolution. There is a shift to pentameter for the last three lines, the only three consecutive lines of equal length. There is an introduction of terminal rhyme in the last four lines, hearkening back to Shakespeare's rhymed couplet as resolution to a scene.

Further heightening the sense of resolution is—at the end of the penultimate line—what John Ciardi called the central silence and John Nims called the emotional fulcrum, at which point the reader pauses and the reader's voice (heard or not) drops and slows down as the import of what has gone before is confronted.

It's never enough for a poet simply to say what has to be said: a poem doesn't work unless the reader takes part in the saying of it. How a poem means is the sum of all the ways, beyond paraphraseable content, by which a reader is brought to do this. That's what makes writing the poem one wants to write always impossible, always a joy.

Writing Suggestions

1. Write your own short version (twenty to thirty lines) of "Love Poem with _________" and fill in the title's blank with something meaningful to the speaker of the poem. Use images and refrain from commenting or expanding on them—let the reader's associative powers carry much of the load. Use details to suggest context and a recent as well as deep past.

2. The next time you find yourself with the infamous curse of writer's block (feeling as if you're unable to write), use that very block as the source for new work. Write a list (grocery style, if you need to) of all the things you *can't* write about. Look around you and jot down whatever you eye falls on (TV, picture window, shag carpet) and add that to the piece, perhaps, too, lamenting that you wish you could write about it. Write down all the people you've spoken with over the last three days, and add the most memorable lines from those conversations. Once you've got a page or two of material, go back and hone it all into a poem. Call it "Against Writer's Block" or whatever else you like.

3. Miller Williams wrote a poem for President Clinton's second inauguration. Find a copy of that poem (entitled "Of History and Hope") either on the Internet or in hard copy in one of his books or through government/newspaper archives. How does this poem fit in with those he's selected for this book? Does occasional verse necessarily mean writing outside of your regular style and thematic concerns? Why/why not? Imagine that you were asked to write a poem for the next president's inauguration. What might the topic and theme(s) of your poem be? Write the first stanza of that poem.

4. Write a poem that has both yin and yang, two forces moving in opposite directions that Miller Williams talks about in "After All These Years of Prayer and Pi R Square." Some examples: Darwinism versus Adam and Eve, Reincarnation versus One-Life-And-Out, McDonald's versus Burger King—there's plenty of other choices. In your poem, support both, or neither, or one at first, then later the other. Keep your poem in flux throughout. Let details and images work on multiple levels. Listen to "After All These Years of Prayer and Pi R Square" on the audio CD for inspiration.

"Poetry is liberative language, connecting the fragments within us, connecting us to others like and unlike ourselves, replenishing our desires. It's potentially catalytic speech because it's more than speech: it is associative, metaphoric, dialectical, visual, musical; in poetry, words can say more than they mean and mean more than they say."

—Adrienne Rich

Appendix A—Poet Biographies

The poets' biographies are given here so that readers can enter the poems without an "introduction," so to speak. An easy mistake for readers to make is to conflate the writers' lives with their work. Many of these bios offer so much information about the poet that they run the risk of steering how one reads the poetry selections, and may even suggest that the historical facts of a writer's life can be (should be?) plugged into their work. This can quickly become something of an Easter egg hunt, trying to find references to the writer's personal life in the poem. Though many poems do in fact begin in reality (historical happenings in a writer's life), *every* poet also uses a good dose of imagination to create a purposeful, rich poem that goes beyond the reportorial.

The biographical information below, contributed by the poets, might offer enrichment to your understanding of a writer's life as easily as it offers blueprints for success as a creative writer. Take from it what you will.

Kim Addonizio was born in 1954 in Washington, D.C., and grew up in suburban Bethesda, Maryland in a sports family (tennis champion mother, sportswriter father). At an early age she discovered books and fell in love with reading. Her favorite books were *The Chronicles of Narnia* by C. S. Lewis, and the Nancy Drew mysteries. Her first writing project was a mystery novel, which she began at the age of ten, and stalled after ten pages. In high school she began to read a variety of genres, though she didn't discover poetry until her late twenties. Her poetic influences include John Keats, Walt Whitman, Sylvia Plath, and many others. She has also been influenced by the spirit of the blues and rock and roll, and has studied several musical instruments (flute, guitar, and most recently, blues harmonica) which have influenced her poetry and have sometimes been used as subject matter. Her main obsessions as a writer are—like most writers—suffering, evil, love, and death.

Addonizio's awards include the Great Lakes New Writers Award, a Commonwealth Club Poetry Medal, two National Endowment for the Arts Fellowships, and the Pushcart Prize. Her books include three collections of poems: *The Philosopher's Club, Jimmy & Rita,* and *Tell Me,* which was a finalist for the 2000 National Book Award; a collection of stories, *In the Box Called Pleasure,* and *The Poet's Companion: A Guide to the Pleasures of Writing Poetry,* co-authored with Dorianne Laux. She has also recently coedited, with Cheryl Dumesnil, an anthology of writing on tattoos, entitled *Dorothy Parker's Elbow.* Currently, Addonizio spends her time working on both fiction and poetry, teaching private writing groups in the San Francisco Bay Area, and playing the blues.

As for how she became a poet, Addonizio writes: "I think poetry found me. I read some poetry that blew me away, and then I started trying to write it, and I've been writing every since. There are two secrets I know about writing: You must love to read as much as write, and you must keep going no matter what people tell you or what obstacles are in your way."

Dick Allen writes: "I can't remember ever not writing poetry and not considering myself a poet. I think hundreds of thousands of people have the 'poetic calling' but very few listen to it. I just kept listening.

"Most artists try to do in their particular art form what they have great desire but no ability to do in another art form. Working in the wrong art form, as we attempt to do the impossible, creates a major usable tension. Poetry was the sole way I could come close to being able to paint and sing and tell fictional stories.

"As for specific facts, I was born at the tail end of a decade, on August 8, 1939, in Troy, New York. I grew up in the tiny upstate New York village of Round Lake—a poverty-ridden place of pine trees, winterized vacation camps, squirrels, and rowboats. My father was postmaster there, a gas station attendant, and in his forties became a well-published writer of Americana, especially on covered bridges and early aviation history. I wrote my first poems in second grade, then wrote vague poems about hills and lakes throughout high school, and kept writing in college. Early voracious reading of science fiction led my poetry to science, especially physics and technology. Experience in journalism and politics helped me feel a writer's duty is to write more of others than of self. These outer concerns, along with eclectic musical tastes (rock and roll, jazz, country, classic, you name it), would lead me to be one of the founders of the Expansive Poetry movement (the expansion of poetry into and beyond New Formalism and New Narrative).

"After a long while, listening to the calling and stubbornly writing, I met W. D. Snodgrass and from him finally learned how to trust specific imagery. Somewhere between the end of my Syracuse University years (A.B., 1961) and the beginning of my Brown University years (M.A., 1963), my poetic forms seemed to start catching up with the visions I'd always had. Maybe then, and with a first poem acceptance from *The New York Times,* I actually became what I'd always thought I was.

"I taught literature and creative writing for thirty-three years at the University of Bridgeport. In 2001, I took early retirement from an endowed chair professorship and directorship of creative writing to devote my life completely to this 'terrible' calling. Between Brown and now, I've published hundreds of poems, won some of the usual awards, including N.E.A. and Ingram

Merrill fellowships, and published six volumes of poetry, including *Ode to the Cold War: Poems New and Selected,* from Sarabande Books. My seventh collection, *The Day Before,* also from Sarabande, will be published in Spring 2003.

"The only things in my life that constantly have seemed real to me have been poetry and Zen. Currently, somewhat hermetic, I live with my wife, L. N. Allen, in a small cottage near the shores of Thrushwood Lake, in Trumbull, Connecticut. Every year, we drive 10,000 miles around the country. Our two children have grown up, but they visit sometimes."

David Baker was born in Bangor, Maine, in 1954 and grew up in Jefferson City, Missouri. He started writing poems as an undergraduate at Central Missouri State University in the mid-1970s, and has since published eight books of poetry and poetry criticism, most recently *Changeable Thunder* (2001, poems), and *Heresy and the Ideal: On Contemporary Poetry* (2000, essays). For his writing he has received awards and fellowships from the John Simon Guggenheim Memorial Foundation, National Endowment for the Arts, Poetry Society of America, Ohio Arts Council, and Society of Midland Authors. Baker's recent poetry and criticism have appeared in many important periodicals, including *The Atlantic Monthly, The Nation, The New Yorker, The Paris Review, Poetry,* and *The Yale Review.*

For many years Baker taught guitar and played in various bands, from jazz and rock to country and swing. His wide experience in music continues to shape his lyrical skills. As a young man he spent much time fishing, hunting, and hiking in the Missouri woods and fields; his devotion to nature remains a primary subject in his poems, along with his abiding fascination with people—their families, politics, neighborhoods, and their most intimate engagements.

Since 1983 Baker has made his living as a college professor. He has taught as Kenyon College, the University of Michigan, and the M.F.A. program for writers at Warren Wilson College. He currently lives in Granville, Ohio, where he is Professor of English and holds the Thomas B. Fordham Chair of Creative Writing at Denison University. He also serves as Poetry Editor of *The Kenyon Review.* David Baker is married to the poet Ann Townsend, and their daughter is Katherine Baker.

Robert Bly writes: "A beautiful high school teacher interested me in poetry. I think I wrote a poem for her saying that Tojo was a bad person. In the Navy, I met the first person I'd known who actually wrote poetry, a man named Eisy Eisenstein. We conspired to flunk out of the radar program on the grounds that we were poets who couldn't be bothered with science. We didn't succeed. Once out of the Navy, I entered St. Olaf College, which is an old Norwegian Lutheran hangout—a Bly was a dean there. My freshman English teacher, to my amazement, excused me from freshman English when I turned in my first piece. That was a generous move; I joined an underclassmen creative writing group. A woman my age wrote poetry; I fell in love with her, and I wrote a poem to her. I had the strangest sensation. I felt something in the poem I hadn't intended to put there. It was as if 'someone else was with me.'

"A year or two later, I transferred to Harvard. The literary magazine, *The Harvard Advocate,* had just started up again, with its memories and mementos of Eliot and Stevens, who had written for it. An amazing group of writers were at Harvard at that time. Because of the war, several classes were bunched up along with the class of 1950. Archibald MacLeish had been hired away from his job as Director of the Library of Congress; the student writers gathered around him and Albert Guerard, a fine teacher of essay and fiction writing. The group I remember included Donald Hall, Frank O'Hara, John Hawkes, Kenneth Koch, John Ashbery, Adrienne Rich, George Plimpton, and many others. Richard Wilbur, a bit older, was a Fellow of some sort, and Robert Frost stayed in Boston during the spring and fall.

"By the time I graduated, I had used up my available capitol for extroversion, and I wanted to be by myself. I intended to be alone for a year, but it turned out to be four. At the start I lived in a small cabin in northern Minnesota and got part of my food by shooting partridge out of season. In the summer of 1951, I moved to New York City, where I lived for three more years excessively or extremely alone. I lived in tiny rooms—the better ones had a hot plate—and was determined to write twelve hours a day for six days a week. And did. I worked one day a week as a file clerk or a typist and, for a while, a painter, carrying around my painter's bag with the coveralls. New York was lonely then. Poets were reading only at the Y. I lived in a room I rented from an old portrait painter from the South on West 67th Street. He painted portraits there every day faithfully, and was disappointed because the Salmagundi Club wouldn't hang his paintings in the front room anymore. He was 65 or 70 years old; I was 26. Together we would walk five or six blocks west and buy three-day-old bread from a bakery and then walk home again. We were on both sides of success—too old and too young."

Michael J. Bugeja has published hundreds of poems in such magazines as *Antioch Review, Harper's, The Kenyon Review, Michigan Quarterly Review, Poetry, TriQuarterly, The Sewanee Review,* and *Shenandoah.* His writing has been anthologized in *Contemporary Literary Criticism* and *Anthology of Magazine Verse & Yearbook of American Poetry,* among others. His autobiography appears in the Contemporary Authors series by Gale Research.

Bugeja has authored seven collections of poetry, including *Millennium's End* (Archer) and *Talk* (Arkansas), along with ten texts, including *Living Without Fear: Understanding Cancer and the New Therapies* (Whitston); *Guide to Writing Magazine Nonfiction* (Allyn & Bacon); *Living Ethics: Developing Values in Mass*

Communication (Allyn & Bacon); *Poet's Guide* (Story Line Press); and *Art and Craft of Poetry* (Writer's Digest Books), which has sold more than 30,000 copies.

His writing awards include a National Endowment for the Arts fellowship, fiction; a National Endowment for the Humanities grant, culture; Ohio Arts Council fellowship, poetry; Associated Writing Programs anniversary award, poetry; an Academy of American Poets award; *Writer's Digest* Grand Prize, fiction; The Strousse Award, poetry, *Prairie Schooner;* the Theodore Christian Hoepfner Award, poetry, *Southern Humanities Review;* and Poet of the Year, Ohio Poetry Day Association, for *After Oz*. In 1997, Bugeja was unanimously selected honorary chancellor by the National Federation of State Poetry Societies, to succeed Tess Gallagher and to promote poetry in America.

Wanda Coleman

home to liquor stores & churches on every corner
to dark red & gold wall-papered holes of refuge
to stark welcoming envelopes of
food stamps & government stipends
to mom & pop stores with their counters of
stinking meat & overripe fruit

i am a haint here

Coleman writes: "My major aesthetic love is form. I abandoned visual art as teenager; and dance, as a young adult, deferring to creative writing. I live the poetic, although I enjoy script writing and performance. I willed myself to be a poet/writer—hard work, long hours, ongoing study and introspection, with goo-gobs of stubborn belief. I am thrilled by the printed word. Peer recognition such as fellowships from the National Endowment for the Arts, and from the Guggenheim Foundation, and a Djerassi artists' residency has reinforced my writer's will. With *Bathwater Wine*, I was the first African-American woman to receive the Lenore Marshall Poetry Prize in 1999, presented by the Academy of American Poets for the most outstanding book of poems the previous year. My books of poetry and prose include *Imagoes, Heavy Daughter Blues, A War of Eyes & Other Stories, African Sleeping Sickness, The Dicksboro Hotel, Hand Dance, Native in a Strange Land, American Sonnets, Mambo Hips & Make Believe* (a novel), and *Mercurochrome,* which was a finalist for the 2001 National Book Award. They document mastery coming dearly, my observations of life, my empathizing with others, my troubled pursuit blessed by those who declare one poem inspired creativity, lifted a soul, or prolonged a life. What sustains me is the faith and needs of my children. My husband, poet-painter Austin Straus, and I are wedded twenty years. His only rival is my birthplace, Los Angeles—a carnivorously ambivalent affair:

it looks worse every time i come here it looks worse
all the new shine gone
nothing left but rust, dust
and the cracked bones of a dream
—from "Region of Deserts" (African Sleeping Sickness)

Billy Collins was born in New York City in 1941. His recent books include *Picnic, Lightning* (University of Pittsburgh Press, 1998), *The Art of Drowning* (University of Pittsburgh Press, 1995), and *Questions About Angels* (William Morrow, 1991), which was selected by Edward Hirsch for the National Poetry Series and reprinted by the University of Pittsburgh Press in 1999. He is a recipient of the Bess Hokin Prize, the Levinson Prize, the Frederick Bock Prize, the Oscar Blumenthal Prize, and the Wood Prize—all awards from *Poetry* magazine. Collins is the recipient of a Guggenheim fellowship, a New York Foundation for the Arts Fellowship, and a grant from the National Endowment for the Arts, among other awards and honors. He is professor of English at Lehman College, CUNY, and a visiting writer at Sarah Lawrence College. Collins is currently the U. S. Poet Laureate.

Denise Duhamel's most recent poetry collection is *Queen for a Day: Selected and New Poems* (University of Pittsburgh Press, 2001). Her other titles include *The Star-Spangled Banner* (winner of the Crab Orchard Award in Poetry, Southern Illinois University Press, 1999); *Kinky* (Orchises Press, 1997); and *Oyl* (a collaborative chapbook with Maureen Seaton, Pearl Editions, 2000). Her work has been widely anthologized, including four editions of *The Best American Poetry* (2000, 1998, 1994, and 1993).

Duhamel has read her work on National Public Radio's "All Things Considered" and Bill Moyer's PBS special "Fooling with Words." A winner of a 2001 National Endowment for the Arts Fellowship in Poetry, she is an assistant professor at Florida International University in Miami.

She first started writing at the age of ten—novels, mostly. She would make her one-of-a-kind creations for which she also designed covers and used ribbons as binding and bring them to Big Joe's Supermarket to slip in the magazine racks hoping that someone would buy them. She wrote prose exclusively until her freshman year in college when she began reading contemporary poetry. Her first poetry loves were Kathleen Spivack and Sharon Olds.

Stephen Dunn is the author of eleven collections of poetry, including *Different Hours* (Pulitzer Prize, 2001) and *Loosestrife* (National Book Critics Circle Award finalist, 1996), both published by W. W. Norton. His other Norton books are *New & Selected Poems: 1974–1994*, *Landscape at the End of the Century*, *Between Angels*, and *Riffs & Reciprocities: Prose Pairs*. *Local Time* (William Morrow & Co.) was a winner of the National Poetry Series in 1986. Four other poetry collections were published by Carnegie-Mellon University Press. A new and expanded version of *Walking Light: Memoirs and Essays on Poetry*, was issued by BOA Editions, Ltd. in 2001.

Dunn has received fellowships from the Guggenheim and Rockefeller foundations, three National Endowment for the Arts Creative Writing Fellowships, and a Distinguished Artist Fellowship from the New Jersey State Council on the Arts. He also has received the Academy Award in Literature from the American Academy of Arts & Letters, the Levinson and Oscar Blumenthal Prizes from *Poetry*, the Theodore Roethke Prize from *Poetry Northwest*, the James Wright Poetry Prize from *Mid-American Review*, and many others.

Dunn is Distinguished Professor of Creative Writing at Richard Stockton College of New Jersey. As for how he became a poet, he claims: "I've written rather extensively about the factors that might have precipitated it, all half-truths at best. The fact is that I don't know. Maybe none of us do."

Stuart Dybek is the author of a book of poems, *Brass Knuckles* (University of Pittsburgh Press) and a chapbook of prose poems and short-short stories, *The Story of Mist* (State Street Press). He has also published two prize-winning collections of short stories. His work appears regularly in magazines such as *American Poetry Review*, *Poetry*, and *TriQuarterly*, and is frequently anthologized. His awards include Guggenheim and National Endowment for the Arts fellowships, a Whiting Writer's Award, and a Lannan Literary Award. He has been a visiting professor at Princeton, the University of California at Irvine, and the University of Iowa Writers' Workshop, and is currently on the faculties at Western Michigan University and the Prague Summer Seminar.

Dybek writes: "For me, writing poetry began with the reading of verse. As a child, I loved the Mother Goose rhymes, and poems like 'Charge of the Light Brigade,' 'The Highwayman,' and Poe's 'The Raven' and 'Bells.' When I actually began to write poems—at around age sixteen—it was in response to reading the Beat poets. I was playing the saxophone then, loved jazz, and the connection between jazz and poetry that I saw in the Beat writers inspired me (and gave me permission) to try a little improvising of my own in words."

Ray Gonzalez is a poet, essayist, and editor born in El Paso, Texas. He is the author of *Memory Fever* (University of Arizona Press, 1999), a memoir about growing up in the Southwest, and *Turtle Pictures* (University of Arizona Press, 2000), which received the 2001 Minnesota Book Award for Poetry. He is the author of six other books of poetry, including three from BOA Editions—*The Heat of Arrivals* (1997 PEN/Oakland Josephine Miles Book Award), *Cabato Sentora* (2000 Minnesota Book Award Finalist), and *The Hawk Temple at Tierra Grande*. Creative Arts Books published his collection of short-short fictions, *Circling the Tortilla Dragon*, and Arizona Press released his second collection of essays, *The Underground Heart: Essays from Hidden Landscapes* in 2002. His poetry has appeared in the 1999 and 2000 editions of *The Best American Poetry* (Scribners) and *The Pushcart Prize: Best of the Small Presses 2000* (Pushcart Press). His nonfiction is included in the second edition of *The Norton Anthology of Nature Writing* (W. W. Norton). He received an M.F.A. from Southwest Texas State University and is the editor of twelve anthologies, most recently *Touching the Fire: Fifteen Poets of the Latino Renaissance* (Anchor/Doubleday Books, 1998). He has served as Poetry Editor of *The Bloomsbury Review* for twenty years and founded *Luna*, a poetry journal, in 1998. Among his awards are a 2000 Loft Literary Center Career Initiative Fellowship, a 1998 Illinois Arts Council Fellowship in Poetry, a 1993 Before Columbus Foundation American Book Award for Excellence in Editing, and a 1988 Colorado Governor's Award for Excellence in the Arts. He is an Associate Professor in the M.F.A. Creative Writing Program at the University of Minnesota in Minneapolis.

Bob Hicok was born in Michigan in 1960. His books include the poetry collections *The Legend of Light* (University of Wisconsin Press)—which Carolyn Kizer chose as the winner of the Felix Pollak Prize in poetry and which was an ALA Booklist Notable Book of the Year—*Plus Shipping* (BOA Editions), as well as *Animal Soul* (Invisible Cities Press). His poetry has appeared in *The New Yorker*, *Poetry*, and *American Poetry Review*, as well as *Best American Poetry* (1997, 1999) and the Pushcart Prize anthology (XXIV, XXV). He received a fellowship from the National Endowment for the Arts in 1999. He owns a die design firm in Ann Arbor, Michigan.

About his start in poetry, he says, "I have little to say about how I got started, except the truth. I began writing by accident at nineteen and never corrected my mistake."

Born and raised in New York City, **Jane Hirshfield** is the author of five volumes of poetry, *Alaya* (QRL Series, 1982), *Of Gravity & Angels* (Wesleyan University Press, 1988), *The October Palace*, *The Lives of the Heart*, and most recently *Given Sugar, Given Salt* (all Harper Collins, 1994, 1997, 2001). She has also edited and co-translated two now-classic collections of poetry by women poets of the past, and is the author of a collection of essays, *Nine Gates: Entering the Mind of Poetry* (Harper Collins, 1997). Her work has appeared in *The Atlantic Monthly*, *The Nation*, *The New Republic*, *The New Yorker*, and many literary publications and anthologies. Recipient of fellowships from the Guggenheim and Rockefeller foundations, and of awards including the Poetry Center Book Award, the Bay Area Book Reviewers Award, and multiple selections in the *Best American Poems* and *Pushcart Prize* anthologies, Hirshfield lives in the San Francisco Bay Area and currently teaches in Bennington College's low-residency M.F.A. program.

David Lehman was born in New York City and grew up there, attending Stuyvesant High School and Columbia University. After two years of studying English and French literature at Cambridge University in England as a Kellett Fellow, he returned to New York City where he worked as Lionel Trilling's research assistant. He also taught at Brooklyn College and Hamilton College while completing his dissertation—on the subject of the prose poem—for his Ph.D. in English from Columbia. In 1982 he left academe to set up shop as a freelance writer. He has never regretted this decision. He feels it is important for poets to derive their gratification, and if possible their income, from sources outside of academe. In 1983 he began writing book reviews and literary articles for *Newsweek*. He also wrote for the *New York Times Magazine*, the *Washington Post*, the *Wall Street Journal*, and *Partisan Review*. In 1986 his first book of poems, *An Alternative to Speech*, was published by Princeton University Press. In 1988 he launched *The Best American Poetry* annual anthology, and he continues as the general editor of this series. His other books include such prose works as *The Perfect Murder* (on mystery novels and movies) in 1989 (The Free Press), *Signs of the Times* (on deconstruction and the Paul de Man scandal) in 1991 (Simon & Schuster), and *The Last Avant-Garde* (about the New York School of poets) in 1998 (Doubleday). His recent poetry books include *Valentine Place* in 1996 and *The Daily Mirror* in 2000. *The Daily Mirror* includes 150 of the daily poems he wrote after embarking on the project of writing a poem a day. A second collection of daily poems, *The Evening Sun*, was published by Scribner in 2002. He has taught in the graduate writing programs at Bennington College and at the New School since the inception of both programs, in 1994 and 1996 respectively. Since 1997 he has taught a "Great Poems" course for NYU freshmen. He succeeded Donald Hall as the general editor of the University of Michigan Press's Poets on Poetry Series. He lives primarily in New York City.

Born in 1965 in San Jose, CA, **Timothy Liu** recently celebrated the third return of his Chinese birth sign, the Year of the Snake. In the first twelve years of his life, he was basically dead to poetry. In the second twelve years, he had an awakening as a freshman at UCLA where a dormie addicted to coke recommended that Liu read Sylvia Plath's *Ariel*, an experience that led Liu out of the realm of rock-and-roll lyricists (Peter Gabriel, Rickie Lee Jones, Robert Plant, and Pete Townshend) and into the land of poesy. His first mentor, the Welsh poet Leslie Norris, was in residence at Brigham Young University where Liu completed his B.A. in 1989 after serving a Mormon mission to Hong Kong. Liu inaugurated his most recent cycle of the Chinese zodiac as a graduate student at the University of Houston (M.A., 1991), working with Richard Howard, Edward Hirsch, and Adam Zagajewski among others, launching an apprenticeship that has culminated in four books of poems (*Vox Angelica,* Alice James Books; *Burnt Offerings,* Copper Canyon Press, 1995; *Say Goodnight,* Copper Canyon Press, 1998; *Hard Evidence,* Talisman House, 2001) and an anthology that he edited, *Word of Mouth: An Anthology of Gay American Poetry.*

Liu has received the 1992 Norma Farber First Book Award from the Poetry Society of America, and his journals and papers have been acquired by the Berg Collection at the New York Public Library. He has also served as the 1997 Holloway Lecturer at U.C. Berkeley and has served as the Visiting Poet at UNC Wilmington as well as the University of Michigan in the 2001–02 school year. A frequent contributor to such review magazines as *Art Papers, New Art Examiner,* and *Publishers Weekly,* Liu is an Assistant Professor at William Paterson University and makes his home in Hoboken, NJ. As for how he became a poet, he writes: "Poets are born, not made, though I was indeed made in the image of the One who called me to the task and so shall abide until I again return to dust."

Adrian C. Louis was born and raised in Nevada and is an enrolled member of the Lovelock Paiute Tribe. From 1984 to 1998, he taught at Oglala Lakota College in Pine Ridge Reservation in South Dakota. Prior to this, Louis edited four Native newspapers, including a stint as managing editor of *Indian Country Today*. He currently teaches at Southwest State University in Marshall, Minnesota.

Louis has written nine books of poems and two works of fiction: *Wild Indians & Other Creatures*, short stories, and *Skins*, a novel. *Skins* was filmed as a feature movie, directed by Chris Eyre, in the summer of 2001 and was released in the spring of 2002.

Louis has won various writing awards, including a Pushcart Prize and fellowships from the Bush Foundation, the National Endowment for the Arts, and the Lila Wallace-Reader's Digest Foundation. In 1999, he was elected to the Nevada Writer's Hall of Fame.

Campbell McGrath was born in Chicago in 1962, grew up in Washington, D.C., and has since lived primarily in Chicago, New York, and Miami. He currently lives in Miami Beach and spends most of his time watching reruns with his children and writing poems about American culture and landscape in the Imperial Present in all its griefs and splendors. His fifth and most recent collection of poetry, *Florida Poems*, details his ambivalent relationship with his current home state, while his earlier volumes—*Capitalism, American Noise, Spring Comes to Chicago, Road Atlas*—examine likewise the world as he found it. His awards include the Kingsley Tufts Prize and fellowships from the MacArthur and Guggenheim foundations. He teaches in the Creative Writing Program at Florida International University. He became a poet the same way most people do—by fortunate accident.

Peter Meinke writes: "I agree with Ben Jonson that a 'poet's made, as well as born,' and in my case it took a while in the making. Although I wrote poetry from the time I was a child in Brooklyn (born 1932) I never heard of a workshop, never read contemporary poetry, and never knew another poet until I had graduated from Hamilton College and was in the Army. Growing up in blue-collar Flatbush, I was a closet poet, majoring in stickball. Poetry was a secret vice, the secrecy adding to the pleasure. Like almost every poet, over the years I showed some poems to a few chosen teachers, who encouraged me—but I remained steadfastly in the closet.

"The first poetry reading I ever attended—by Donald Hall and X. J. Kennedy—was in 1961 when I returned to graduate school at the University of Michigan, after teaching two years of middle-school English. My poetry up to then had been imitations of John Donne and Wordsworth, poets I liked to read (and still do). With an M.A. in English Literature I went to teach at Hamline University in St. Paul, while working on my Ph.D. There I met and heard Allen Tate, James Wright, and John Berryman, all teaching and drinking at the University of Minnesota—these were the alcoholic days of American poetry (though decadent and bad for us, I miss them). My advisor talked me into doing my thesis on a living writer; he was tired, he said, of reading rehashed discussions of long-dead famous writers. I picked Howard Nemerov, because of his Donne-like mixture of wit, passion, and formal ability. A shortened version of my thesis was my first 'book,' and the first published study of Nemerov (1968). I remember the moment while I was studying Nemerov's writing, almost syllable by syllable, that I first thought, 'Oh, I see why he's doing that. I see why he ends or breaks the line there." Soon after that my poems began getting published in magazines like *The New Republic, The Antioch Review, The Carleton Miscellany*, and others.

"After Hamline, I spent, and enjoyed, my teaching career at Eckerd College, St. Petersburg, Florida (1966–1993), taking early retirement in order to write more. Since then I've been writer-in-residence at UNC/Greensboro, the University of Hawaii, Davidson, Austin Peay, Converse College, and elsewhere. The University of Pittsburgh Press published my first collection in 1977, *The Night Train & the Golden Bird*; and has published another one every four or five years since. My most recent book, *Zinc Fingers,* received the 2000 Southeast Booksellers Association Award.

"My wife, the artist Jeanne Clark, and I have lived in the same house in St. Petersburg, Florida for over thirty years; we have four children. Though I've occasionally felt out of the loop working so far from the nexus of literary power and activity, it's made for a quiet, pleasant life—and on our wedding anniversaries (now past the forty-fourth) we often go to New York and stay at the Algonquin for a few days. That seems to suffice."

Lisel Mueller has published six volumes of poetry, most recently *Alive Together: New and Selected Poems,* which was awarded the 1997 Pulitzer Prize. Awards for Lisel Mueller's previous books include the 1980 National Book Award for *The Need to Hold Still* and the Lamont Poetry Selection Award from the Academy of American Poets for *The Private Life. Waving the Shore* received the Carl Sandburg Prize of the Chicago Public Library, and many of her individual poems have been honored with awards.

Mueller came to the United States from Germany at age fifteen. Her work has appeared in the major literary journals and in numerous anthologies and textbooks. She is also the translator of four volumes of German poetry and fiction. Mueller has taught in a number of graduate and undergraduate writing programs. She lives in Chicago.

About her start in poetry, she writes, "About a year after I came to this country from Germany, a friend at school introduced me to the poetry of Carl Sandburg. I was delighted by his vigorous, accessible free verse, his down-to-earth subjects, and his plain, idiomatic language—so much so that I felt encouraged to try my hand at writing some poems of my own in my new language. Some time later I took a wonderful college course in modern American poetry ranging from Whitman to Muriel Rukeyser (born in 1913), which exposed me to the exciting and innumerable possibilities for making poems and sent me to the library for further reading. Many of the poems I wrote during those college years, which were also the years of World War II, were love poems written for my husband-to-be, who was serving overseas in the armed forces.

"After his return we entered into a full and busy life, in which other interests took over and I wrote no poetry for the next seven years, nor did I think much about writing. But then my mother died suddenly at age fifty-four. A few weeks after her death I suddenly felt an overwhelming urge to express my grief in what I knew had to be a poem. I went outside into our landlord's beautifully landscaped backyard, and there, surrounded by flowers, I wrote the poem I needed to write. (Years later I described this occasion quite literally in a poem called "When I Am Asked.") Writing this poem opened the floodgates. It was my second beginning, and what I think of as my real one. The year was 1953, and I've been writing poems ever since."

Sharon Olds was born in San Francisco, CA, and raised in Berkeley, CA. She has written six books: *Satan Says* (University of Pittsburgh Press), *The Dead and the Living, The Gold Cell, The Father, The Wellspring,* and *Blood, Tin, Straw* (Alfred A. Knopf). She teaches in the Graduate Program in Creative Writing at New York University, and helps run the N.Y.U. writing workshop at a state hospital for the severely physically challenged. She was New York State Poet Laureate from 1998 to 2000. She has received the Lamont Award from the Academy of American Poets, the New York Critics Circle Award, and the Harriet Monroe Poetry Prize. She lives in New York City. As to how she became a poet, she writes: "From reading poems, from loving rhyme and rhythm, from need and desire, from the great good fortune of education—all those passionate and devoted teachers!"

Lee Ann Roripaugh was born and raised in Laramie, Wyoming. Her degrees include an M.M. in music history, a B.M. in piano performance, and an M.F.A. in creative writing, all from Indiana University. Her first volume of poetry, *Beyond Heart Mountain* (Penguin Books, 1999), was selected by Ishmael Reed for the National Poetry Series and was also a finalist for the 2000 Asian American Literature Awards. Other honors include an Academy of American Poets Prize, an Associated Writing Programs Intro Award, and the 1995 Randall Jarrell International Poetry Prize. Her poetry has appeared in numerous journals and anthologies, including *Black Warrior Review, Cream City Review, Crab Orchard Review, New England Review, Parnassus: Poetry in Review, Phoebe,* and *Seneca Review.* Her poetry has also been selected for inclusion in the anthologies *American Identities: Contemporary Multicultural Voices* (eds. Robert Pack and Jay Parini, 1994), *American Poetry: The Next Generation* (eds. Gerald Costanzo and Jim Daniels, 2000), and *Waltzing on Water: Poetry by Women* (eds. Norma Fox Mazer and Marjorie Lewis, 1989). Roripaugh is an Assistant Professor of English at the University of South Dakota.

Kay Ryan is author of five books of poems, most recently *Say Uncle* (Grove Press, 2000). Her awards include a National Endowment for the Arts fellowship, an Ingram Merrill Award, the Union League Poetry Prize (*Poetry* Magazine), the Maurice English Poetry Award, and two Pushcart Prizes. Her work was selected for *The Best American Poetry* in 1995 and again in 1999, as well as for *The Best American Poetry 1988–1997*. She was born in California in 1945 and grew up in small towns in the San Joaquin Valley and the Mojave Desert. Since 1971 she has lived in Marin County. She did not begin to publish until she was in her thirties. A number of her poems appeared in *The New Yorker. Entertainment Weekly* magazine named Kay Ryan its favorite poet for 2001.

Vivian Shipley, editor of *Connecticut Review,* is the Connecticut State University Distinguished Professor. In 2000, she won the Marble Faun Award for Poetry from the William Faulkner Society, the *Thin Air Magazine* Poetry Prize from Northern Arizona University, and was named Faculty Scholar at Southern Connecticut State University where she teaches creative writing. She has also won the Lucille Medwick Award from the Poetry Society of America, the Ann Stanford Prize from the University of Southern California, the Reader's Choice Award from *Prairie Schooner,* the *Sonora Review* Poetry Prize from the University of Arizona, the *So To Speak* Poetry Prize from George Mason University, and many other awards and prizes.

Shipley has published eight books of poetry, including *Devil's Lane* (Negative Capability Press, 1996), which was nominated for a Pulitzer Prize in 2000; *How Many Stones?,* winner of the *Devil's Millhopper* chapbook contest (University of South Carolina–Aiken, 1998); *Crazy Quilt* (Hanover Press, 1999); *Fair Haven* (Negative Capability Press, 2000), which has been nominated for the Pulitzer Prize; and *Echo and Anger, Still* (Southeastern Louisiana University Press, 2000). Her most recent book is the poetry collection *A Cormorant in the Tree* (Red Hen Press, 2001).

Shipley writes: "My best poems explore why some voices surface and others do not. My interest in writing poems about silences comes from a personal experience I had twenty-seven years ago when I was thirty years old. Right after the birth of my second son, doctors discovered I had a brain tumor the size of a baseball. After it was removed from my right frontal lobe, most of my skull was replaced with an acrylic plate. Prior to Todd's birth, I had completed my dissertation on Robert Louis Stevenson for my Ph.D. in English from Vanderbilt University. However, after months of recovering from surgery, I started writing poetry and never returned to the study of Victorian literature. Believe it or not, there has been no outcry from scholars! The awareness of how frail life is and how suddenly it can end has stayed with me, fueling my need to write. A passage from Dana Gioia's translation of Jakob and Wilhelm Grimm's *Godfather Death* where Death shows the life lights of people to a doctor in an underground cavern haunts me: *Some were tall, other medium-sized, and others quite small. Every moment some went out and others lit up so that the tiny flames seemed to jump to and fro in perpetual motion.* My fear of death created by the brain tumor remains and injects emotion into my poems about how other people are silenced."

Elizabeth Spires—born in 1952 in Lancaster, Ohio—is the author of five collections of poetry: *Globe* (Wesleyan UP, 1981); *Swan's Island* (Henry Holt & Company, 1985; Carnegie-Mellon UP, 1997); *Annonciade* (Viking Penguin, 1989); *Worldling* (W. W. Norton, 1995); and *Now the Green Blade Rises* (W. W. Norton, 2002). She also edited and introduced *The Instant of Knowing: Lectures,*

Criticism, and Occasional Prose of Josephine Jacobsen (University of Michigan Press, 1997).

Spires has been the recipient of a Whiting Award, a Guggenheim Fellowship, the Amy Lowell Traveling Poetry Scholarship, and two fellowships from the National Endowment for the Arts. In 1998 she received the Witter Bynner Prize for Poetry from the American Academy of Arts and Letters, and the Maryland Author Award from the Maryland Library Association. Her poems have been featured on National Public Radio and have appeared in *American Poetry Review, The New Criterion, The New Yorker, Poetry,* and in many anthologies.

Her books for children include *The Mouse of Amherst* (Farrar, Straus & Giroux, 1999); *I Am Arachne* (Farrar, Straus & Giroux, 2001); *With One White Wing* (Simon & Schuster, 1995); and *Riddle Road* (Simon & Schuster, 1999).

She lives in Baltimore with her husband, the novelist Madison Smartt Bell, and their daughter Celia, and is Professor of English at Goucher College where she holds a Chair for Distinguished Achievement.

Virgil Suárez was born in Havana, Cuba, in 1962. He is the author of four novels, five anthologies, and five books of poetry, including most recently *Banyan* (LSU Press, 2001) and *Palm Crows* (University of Arizona Press, 2001). The University of Illinois published his latest poetry collection, *The Guide to the Blue Tongue,* in 2002. His poetry, stories, translations, and essays continue to be published in journals and reviews including *Cimarron Review, Field, The Kenyon Review, New England Review, Ploughshares, Salmagundi,* and *TriQuarterly,* and many others in the United States and abroad.

Suárez became a poet early in his young adult life after his first girlfriend broke his heart, causing him to spend the next three years writing bad love poetry, which lead him to college and the mentorship of Eliot Fried at California State University at Long Beach. For the next twenty-five years, he wrote poetry secretly, focusing his publishing efforts on fiction, that is until a few poems were published and he grew more confident that his poetry mattered. Currently he is at work on a new poetry collection titled *E(x)it Jesus: The Exegesis Poems,* from which some of the poems in this book are taken.

Ron Wallace was born on February 18, 1945 in Cedar Rapids, Iowa, and grew up in St. Louis, Missouri. He has spent his life circling the upper Midwest, starting in Iowa, moving to St. Louis, attending college in Ohio and graduate school in Michigan, and spending the past thirty years at the University of Wisconsin-Madison where he codirects the creative-writing program and edits the University of Wisconsin Press poetry series. The landscape, ecology, flora and fauna, and people of the Midwest have figured centrally in his work. His wife, Peg, and his daughters, Molly and Emily, have been influential in focusing his domestic themes, as was his father's multiple sclerosis which prompted him to explore issues of illness and mortality.

He currently divides his time between Madison and a forty-acre farm in Bear Valley, Wisconsin, which provides the setting and inspiration for a number of his poems. In addition to seven books and five chapbooks of poetry (most recently *Long for This World: New & Selected Poems*), Wallace has published one book of interconnected short stories, *Quick Bright Things*, and three critical books on humor in American literature, *Henry James and the Comic Form*, *The Last Laugh*, and *God Be with the Clown*. His coed volleyball team, The Grapes of Wrath, has been together for twenty-five years, and continues to win trophies.

Afaa Michael Weaver (born Michael S. Weaver) was born in Baltimore, Maryland, in 1951 and is the author of nine collections of poetry, most recently *Multitudes* (Sarabande Books, 2000), *The Ten Lights of God* (Bucknell UP, 2000), and *Sandy Point* (The Press of Appletree Alley, 2000). Afaa worked in factories in Baltimore for fifteen years after two years of college at the University of Maryland, and he returned to academia in 1985 when he went to Brown University and also finished his bachelor's at Excelsior College. His time in the factory was his literary apprenticeship. In his free time on the job he worked at his poetry and, with his friend the poet Melvin Brown, started a small press entitled Seventh Son Press. Afaa and Melvin published *Blind Alleys*, a journal of poetry, for several years before he left factory life.

For twenty-two years, Afaa has also been a student of the Chinese internal arts of Tai Chi Chuan and Hsing I Chuan, which are the products of Taoist studies over long periods of Chinese history. He has written on the subject of Tai Chi for several publications, including the Baltimore *Sunpapers* in the early eighties. Afaa credits Taoist philosophy for helping him accept the varied nature of his experience, especially what has often seemed like huge distances between parts of that city of experience. He has received major fellowships for his poetry and teaches at Simmons College in Boston.

Afaa lives in Somerville, Massachusetts.

". . . the poet's eyes are washed
in the common spring."
—Ni'yi Osundare

"Our senses are the doorways.
The borders are our body."
—Alberto Blanco

Miller Williams is the author, editor, or translator of thirty books, including fourteen volumes of poetry. Recognition for his work has included the Amy Lowell Traveling Scholarship in Poetry from Harvard University; the Prix de Rome for Literature and the Academy Award for Literature, both from the American Academy of Arts and Letters; the Poets's Prize; the Charity Randall Citation for Contribution to Poetry as a Spoken Art from the International Poetry Forum; the John William Corrington Award for Excellence in Literature; honorary doctorates from Lander College and Hendrix College; and designation as a member of *The Circle of Distinguished Citizens of the World* by the Trilussa Center of Rome. He was inaugural poet for the second presidential inauguration of Bill Clinton. His *Patterns of Poetry: An Encyclopedia of Forms* is a standard in the field. A collection of essays on his work, *Miller Williams and the Poetry of the Particular,* edited by Michael Burns, is available from the University of Missouri Press.

A multinational board of the journal *Visions International* has named Williams one of the world's twenty best poets now writing in English, and his poems are included on a CD from the Roth Publishing Company entitled *Poetry of Our Time,* featuring work by the world's 500 best poets of the twentieth century in all languages, as selected by an advisory board of teachers, librarians, and writers. The body of his best poetry over the years, gathered under the title *Some Jazz A While: The Collected Poems,* was published by the University of Illinois Press in 1999.

Appendix B—Further Readings

Books on Poetry Writing and Poetics

Addonizio, Kim, and Dorianne Laux. *The Poet's Companion: A Guide to the Pleasures of Writing Poetry*. New York: W. W. Norton & Company, 1997.

Behn, Robin, and Chase Twitchell. *The Practice of Poetry*. New York: Harper Perennial, 1992.

Bugeja, Michael J. *Poet's Guide: How to Publish and Perform Your Work*. Brownsville, OR: Story Line Press, 1995.

Corn, Alfred. *The Poet's Heartbeat: A Manual of Prosody*. Brownsville, OR: Story Line Press, 1997.

Drury, John. *Creating Poetry*. Cincinnati, OH: Writer's Digest Books, 1991.

Friebert, Stuart, David Walker, and David Young, eds. *A Field Guide to Contemporary Poetry and Poetics*, 2nd ed. Oberlin, OH: Oberlin College Press, 2001.

Fulton, Alice. *Feeling as a Foreign Language*. St. Paul, MN: Graywolf, 1999.

Fussell, Paul. *Poetic Meter and Poetic Form*. Paperback rev. edition. New York: McGraw Hill, 1979.

Hollander, John. *Rhymes Reason: A Guide to English Verse*. New Haven: Yale UP, 1989.

Kowit, Steve. *In the Palm of Your Hand*. Gardiner, ME: Tilbury House, 1995.

Rosenthal, M. L. *The Poet's Art*. New York: W. W. Norton & Company, 1989.

Wallace, Robert, and Michelle Boisseau. *Writing Poems*, 5th ed. New York: Addison Wesley Longman, 2000.

Wooldridge, Susan Goldsmith. *poemcrazy: freeing your life with words*. New York: Crown, 1997.

Writing Reference Books

Abrams, M. H. *A Glossary of Literary Terms*, 7th ed. Cambridge, MA: International Thomson Publishing, 1999.

Aristotle. *Aristotle's Poetics*, ed. Stephen Halliwell. Chicago, IL: University of Chicago Press, 1999.

Packard, William. *The Poet's Dictionary: A Handbook of Prosody and Poetic Devices*. New York: HarperCollins, 1994.

Padgett, Ron, ed. *The Teachers and Writers Handbook of Poetic Forms*, 2nd ed. New York: Teachers and Writers Collaborative, 2000.

Preminger, Alex, and T. V. F. Brogan, eds. *The New Princeton Encyclopedia of Poetry and Poetics*. Princeton, NJ: Princeton UP, 1993.

Turco, Lewis. *The New Book of Forms: A Handbook of Poetics*. Hanover, NH: University Press of New England, 1986.

Books Containing Essays, Interviews, and/or Critical Perspectives on Poetry

Chappell, Fred. *A Way of Happening: Observations of Contemporary Poetry*. New York: Picador USA, 1998.

Des Pres, Terrence. *Praises and Dispraises: Poetry and Politics, the 20th Century*. New York: Penguin, 1989.

Gioia, Dana. *Can Poetry Matter?* Minneapolis, MN: Graywolf Press, 1992.

Hass, Robert. *Twentieth Century Pleasures: Prose on Poetry*, reprint edition. Hopewell, NJ: The Ecco Press, 1997.

Hirsch, Edward. *How to Read a Poem and Fall in Love with Poetry*. New York: Harcourt Harvest, 2000.

Hirshfield, Jane. *Nine Gates: Entering the Mind of Poetry*. New York: Harper Perennial, 1998.

McDowell, Robert, ed. *Poetry After Modernism*. Brownsville, OR: Story Line Press, 1998.

Paz, Octavio. *The Other Voice: Essays on Modern Poetry*, trans. Helen Lane. New York: Harvest Books, 1992.

Walcott, Derek. *What the Twilight Says: Essays*. New York: Farrar, Straus and Giroux, 1999.

The Writing Life: A Collection of Essays and Interviews. New York: Random House, 1995.

Books on Creative Writing in General

Bishop, Wendy. *Working Words: The Process of Creative Writing*. New York, McGraw Hill, 1991.

Burke, Carol, and Molly Best Tinsley. *The Creative Process*. New York: St. Martins, 1993.

Burroway, Janet. *Imaginative Writing: The Elements of Craft*. New York: Addison Wesley Longman, 2003.

Dillard, Annie. *Living by Fiction*, revised edition. New York: HarperCollins, 1988.

Lamott, Anne. *Bird by Bird: Some Instructions on Writing and Life*. Landover Hills, MD: Anchor, 1995.

Mueller, Lavonne, and Jerry D. Reynolds. *Creative Writing: Forms and Techniques*. Lincolnwood, IL: NTC Publishing Group, 1990.

Rico, Gabriele Lusser. *Writing the Natural Way: Using Right Brain Techniques to Release Your Expressive Powers*, revised edition. Los Angeles: J. P. Tarcher Inc., 2000.

Smith, Michael C., and Suzanne Greenberg. *Everyday Creative Writing: Panning for Gold in the Kitchen Sink*. Lincolnwood, IL: NTC Publishing Group, 2000.

Books on Creativity and the Psychology of Writing

DiTiberio, John K., and George H. Jensen. *Writing Personality*. Palo Alto, CA: Davies-Black Publishing, 1995.

Jung, Carl Gustav. *Psychological Types*, ed. Gerald Adler, Michael Fordham, and William McGuire. Princeton, NJ: Princeton UP, 1976.

Myers, Isabel Briggs. *Introduction to Type: A Guide to Understanding Your Results on the Myers-Briggs Type Indicator.* Gainesville, FL: Center for Applications of Psychological Type, 1998.

Rank, Otto, Charles Francis Atkinson, and Anais Nin. *Art and Artist: Creative Urge and Personality Development*. New York: W. W. Norton & Company, 1989.

Rothenberg, Albert. *Creativity and Madness*. Baltimore, MD: Johns Hopkins UP, 1994.

Appendix C—Other Resources for Writers

Poetry Market Listings

CLMP Directory of Literary Magazines (Council of Literary Magazines and Press, 154 Christopher Street, Suite 3C, New York, NY 10014-2839). A listing of literary journals nationwide that contains brief descriptions and a useful state-by-state breakdown. This publication is less comprehensive than *Poet's Market* or *The International Directory of Little Magazines and Small Presses*, but since it focuses exclusively on literary journals, it might be more useful to the student writer.

The International Directory of Little Magazines and Small Presses (published annually by Dustbooks, P.O. Box 100, Paradise, CA 95967). Although this annual guide contains thousands of publishing opportunities, many are for fiction, nonfiction, or reviews. Entries are listed alphabetically and contain specific information about the publishing format, submission guidelines, and editorial interests of each.

Poet's Market and *Writer's Market* (published annually by Writer's Digest Books, 1507 Dana Avenue, Cincinnati, OH 45207). Readily available books that contain a wealth of information on commercial markets and writing contests, though both also have sections on small presses, university presses, and literary markets. Both also contain How-I-Made-My-First-Big-Sale success stories.

Some Good Writer's Magazines

Poets & Writers (P.O. Box 543, Mt. Morris, IL 61054). A bimonthly publication that has interviews, reviews, articles, and essays, as well as contest and publishing information. This is a professional publication, so it may be of more use to the intermediate and advanced writer than the novice.

The Writer (Kalmach Publishing Co., 21027 Crossroads Circle, P.O. Box 1612, Waukesha, WI 53187-1612). Web site: http://www.writermag.com. *The Writer,* founded in 1887, is a monthly magazine about writing for writers. It features how-to and inspirational articles focusing on the writing of fiction, nonfiction, poetry, and children's and young adult literature. It also offers limited market and contest information.

Writer's Digest (1507 Dana Avenue, Cincinnati, OH 45207). Web site: http://www.writersdigest.com. *WD* is a monthly magazine that includes how-to articles, market reports, technique discussions, and contest information. Their editorial mission is to be a monthly handbook for writers who want to get more out of their writing. Because their subscription base is so large (200,000), many of the articles and information is geared to the intermediate and beginning writer.

Other Useful Books for Poets

A Directory of American Poets and Fiction Writers (Poets & Writers, Inc., P.O. Box 543, Mt. Morris, IL 61054). Published annually, this book lists contact information and writing interests of amateur and professional poets and fiction writers.

Writer's Guide to Copyright (Poets & Writers, Inc., P.O. Box 543, Mt. Morris, IL 61054). An inexpensive booklet that clearly explains current copyright laws.

Useful Writer's Organizations

Academy of American Poets (588 Broadway, Suite 1203, New York, NY 10012-3210). Web site: http://www.poetry.org. This organization is the largest in the country dedicated specifically to the art of poetry. Their Web site is one of the most useful for poets. They also publish *American Poet*, a biannual journal that contains poetry, literary essays, news of Academy activities, and listings of new and noteworthy books of criticism and poetry.

Associated Writing Programs (Tallwood House, Mail Stop 1E3, George Mason University, Fairfax, VA 22030). E-mail: awp@gmu.edu. Web site: http://www.awpwriter.org. AWP is a nonprofit organization of writers and (mostly graduate) creative writing programs. It publishes *The AWP Chronicle* bimonthly, which includes interviews, articles, essays, reviews, and useful information on conferences, publishing opportunities, contests, and writing colonies.

PEN American Center (568 Broadway, New York, NY 10012-3225). Web site: http://www.pen.org. Among the activities, programs, and services sponsored by the Headquarters and the five Branches are public literary events, literary awards, outreach projects to encourage reading, assistance to writers in financial need, and international and domestic human rights campaigns on behalf of the many writers, editors, and journalists censored, persecuted, or imprisoned because of their writing. All PEN members receive the quarterly PEN Newsletter, the literary journal *PEN America*, and qualify for medical insurance at group rates.

Poetry Society of America (15 Gramercy Park, New York, NY 10003). Web site: http://www.poetrysociety.com. PSA is an organization that sponsors classes and literary events throughout the United States. It publishes *PSA News* three times a year, which includes articles, interviews, and information on PSA events. PSA also offers a number of yearly poetry awards.

SPAWN (Small Publishers, Artists, & Writers Network) (P.O. Box 2653, Ventura, CA 93002-2653). Web site: http://www.spawn.org. SPAWN is a Web resource that has information relevant to writers, publishers, editors, illustrators, artists, booksellers, and photographers at all points in their career. SPAWN also has local chapters which focus on career success, professional seminars, and networking.

Writers's Colonies

Artists & Writers Colonies: Retreats, Residencies, and Respite for the Creative Mind, by Gail Hellund Bowler (Poets & Writers, Inc., P.O. Box 543, Mt. Morris, IL 61054).

Online Directory of Writer's Colonies: http://www.poewar.com/articles/colonies.htm

CD-ROMs

American Poetry: The Nineteenth Century. This CD-ROM that presents 1,000 poems by almost 150 poets is edited by John Hollander and issued by Voyager and The Library of America. The poems range from Walt Whitman to folk songs to Native American texts to outlaw ballads. This CD-ROM is supported by photographs and audio recordings.

The Columbia Granger's World of Poetry on CD-ROM 3.0. This CD-ROM indexes over 250,000 poems and also offers commentaries, biographies, bibliographies, and a glossary. It's designed more with the scholar in mind than the creative writer, though poets might find the full-text searchability of 10,000 poems in their entirety a useful feature.

The Norton Poetry Workshop CD-ROM. A useful CD-ROM that's designed for the creative writer. For more information, go to Norton's Web site that has illustrations and examples of what this CD-ROM has to offer: http://www.wwnorton.com/college/english/npwcdr.htm

Poetry in Motion. Twenty-four award-winning poets perform their work to accompany printed poems. To name just a few: Amiri Baraka, Charles Bukowski, Jim Carroll, Diane DiPrima, Ted Milton, and Anne Waldman. It's important to note that director/producer Ron Mann set out with the idea of making a performance film, so he chose selections mainly on how well the poets performed.

Web Information

Literary Leaps is a comprehensive resource site that has thousands of literary links for editors, writers, publishers, and literary agents. www.literaryleaps.com

The Favorite Poem Project is Robert Pinsky's greatest contribution as U.S. Poet Laureate. This Web site includes a database of people's favorite poems and their responses, video documentaries, and audio files of people reading their favorite poems.
www.favoritepoem.org

Poetry Daily highlights a recent contemporary American poem each day and also offers many poetry-related resources, including links to many book publishers, literary journal Web sites, and writers' own home pages.
www.poems.com

Wed Del Sol is a "literary arts new media complex" that publishes original poetry and fiction, as well as columns, reviews, essays, interviews, and hypermedia.
www.webdelsol.com/solhome.htm

WritersNet is the Internet directory of writers, editors, publishers, and literary agents. This site includes market information, articles, essays, and discussion forums.
http://www.writers.net

The Zuzu's Petals Literary Resource is an award-winning Web site that "seeks to unearth and present the best resources for creative people on the Internet."
www.zuzu.com/index.htm

Particularly Good E-zines

The Blue Moon Review is an on-line literary magazine featuring first-rate poetry, fiction, and creative nonfiction.
www.bluemoonreview.com

The Cortland Review is an on-line literary magazine which features poetry, interviews, reviews, essays, and many Real Audio recordings of poems.
www.cortlandreview.com

The Exquisite Corpse is a very different type of on-line literary magazine that one needs to experience to fully understand.
www.corpse.org/index.html

Appendix D—Web Information

Elizabeth Bishop always told her students that if they enjoyed a poet's work, they ought to read everything they could by or about that poet. The availability of information on the Internet provides people with that opportunity. A word of warning, though—information on the Internet is unstable, meaning that anyone with the right know-how and inclination can alter what's there. For more reliable and consistent information, always seek books and reputable journals. But the Internet is a good place to begin research, so use the listings below as a leaping-off point.

Also, the URLs (Universal Resource Locator) listed below are accurate and up-to-date as of this writing, but they may change or disappear completely at some point in the future. For updated links or more information on these and other poets, see www.ryangvancleave.com where a comprehensive links page is updated and maintained regularly.

Kim Addonizio

Personal home page:
addonizio.home.mindspring.com/

Interview with Jessica Ball:
www.sanfranciscoartmagazine.com/February/kimaddonizio/kimaddonizio.html

Biographical information/Academy of America Poets:
www.poets.org/poets/poets.cfm?prmID=784

Electronic chapbooks:
www.alsopreview.com/addonizio/addonizio.html
www.geocities.com/billiedee2000/anth-addonizio.html
www.webdelsol.com/LITARTS/kim/

Dick Allen

Two poems:
www.cortlandreview.com/issue/10/allen10.htm

Interview:
www.sarabandebooks.org/interv/allen/SBalleni.html

Review of *Ode to the Cold War* (Sarabande Books, 1997):
home.earthlink.net/~arthur505/rev0497a.html

Colloquim on contemporary poetry:
www.csf.edu/countermeasures/colloquium7-4.html

David Baker

General information:
members.aol.com/poetrynet/month/archive/baker/intro.html

Review of *After the Reunion:*
members.aol.com/nsp97/cafe.htm

Robert Bly

Personal home page:
www.mrs.umn.edu/~cst/html/robert_bly.html

PBS interview:
www.pbs.org/kued/nosafeplace/interv/bly.html

Enc.com information:
www.encyclopedia.com/articles/01598.html

Various poems and essays:
www.english.uiuc.edu/maps/poets/a_f/bly/bly.htm

Interview with *M.E.N. Magazine:*
www.vix.com/menmag/bly-iv.html

Michael J. Bugeja

University home page:
oak.cats.ohiou.edu/~bugeja/

Poems and audio files of poems:
www.tcom.ohiou.edu/books/poetry/bugeja/

AWP Essay by Bugeja:
awpwriter.org/bugeja1.htm

Three poems:
www.aboutmalta.com/grazio/kor.html

Five poems:
www.poetrymagazine.com/archives/2000/August00/bugeja.htm

Short essay:
www.apoetborn.com/tc-archive%5Ctc-Bugeja.cfm

Wanda Coleman

General information:
poetry.about.com/library/weekly/aa040301a.htm

General information/Academy of American Poets:
www.poets.org/poets/poets.cfm?prmID=119

Essay by Scott Carlson:
www.daily.umn.edu/~online/ae/Print/ISSUE8/fewanda.htm

Four sonnets:
www.thing.net/~grist/l&d/lcoleman.htm

Billy Collins

Personal home page:
www.bigsnap.com/billy.html

His literary agency:
www.barclayagency.com/collins.html

Two poems:
www.cortlandreview.com/issue/7/collinsb7.htm

Essay on Collins:
www.bookwire.com/bbr/interviews/billy-collins.html

Denise Duhamel

Fan Web page:
www.geocities.com/SoHo/Square/3911/

General information/Academy of American Poets:
www.poets.org/poets/poets.cfm?prmID=34

The Woman with 2 Vaginas (whole book):
capa.conncoll.edu/duhamel.ww2v.html

Smile (whole book):
capa.conncoll.edu/duhamel.smile.html

Two poems:
www.cortlandreview.com/issue/11/duhamel11.html

Poem and audio file:
arts.endow.gov/explore/Writers/duhamel.html

Stephen Dunn

Poems and general info:
www.geocities.com/blightj/dunn.html

Ploughshares information:
www.pshares.org/Authors/authordetails.cfm?prmauthoriD=426

Interview by Philip Dacey:
www.cortlandreview.com/features/00/03/

Two poems:
www.woodstockpoetryfestival.com/dunn.htm

Stuart Dybek

University home page (with samples):
www.wmich.edu/english/fac/Dybek.html

Interview by James Plath:
titan.iwu.edu/~jplath/dybek.html

Short story ("Bottle Caps"):
www.earthtalk.org/bookmark/dybek.html

Review of *The Coast of Chicago* (stories):
www.pandorasbox.com/archive/dybek.html

Ray Gonzalez

University home page:
english.cla.umn.edu/faculty/GONZALEZ/Gonzalez.htm

Two poems:
www.hartnell.cc.ca.us/homestead_review/sp01/gonzalez.html

One poem:
www.colorado.edu/journals/standards/V7N1/MMM/gonzalez.html

Bob Hicok

Poetry Daily feature:
www.poems.com/anim2hic.htm

One poem:
www.geocities.com/billiedee2000/anth-hicok.html

One poem:
english.fsu.edu/southeastreview/hicok.htm

Three poems:
www.cohums.ohio-state.edu/english/journals/the_journal/archive/21.2/fall97.htm

Jane Hirshfield

Her literary agency:
www.barclayagency.com/hirshfield.html

Interview by Katie Bolick:
www.theatlantic.com/unbound/bookauth/jhirsh.htm

Interview by Judith Moore:
www.poems.com/hirinter.htm

One poem:
www.middlebury.edu/~nereview/hirshfield.html

One poem:
www.uaa.alaska.edu/aqr/15_3&4/clock.htm

David Lehman

General information/Academy of American Poets:
www.poets.org/poets/poets.cfm?prmID=41

Excerpts from *The Last Avant-Garde:*
www.randomhouse.com/boldtype/0998/lehman/

Interview with Judith Moore:
www.poems.com/lehm_bio.htm

Three poems from *The Daily Mirror:*
www.cortlandreview.com/issue/7/lehman7.htm

Two poems from *The Evening Sun:*
www.drunkenboat.com/db2/lehman/lehman.html

Timothy Liu

University home page:
euphrates.wpunj.edu/faculty/liut/

General information/POEM FINDER:
www.rothpoem.com/timothy.html

Interview by Andrena Zawinski:
www.poetrymagazine.com/archives/1999/sept99/interview.htm

Five poems:
www.poetrymagazine.com/archives/1999/sept99/liu.htm

Adrian C. Louis

General information:
www.english.uiuc.edu/maps/poets/g_l/louis/louis.htm

Two poems:
www.cortlandreview.com/issuethree/poetlouis3.htm

One poem:
www.hypertxt.com/sh/no5/louis.html

One poem:
www.und.nodak.edu/org/ndq/louis.html

Campbell McGrath

University home page:
www.fiu.edu/~crwritng/mcgrath.htm

One poem from *The Chicago Review:*
humanities.uchicago.edu/orgs/review/462/McGrath.html

Various poems:
www.poetrysociety.org/mcgrath.html

Peter Meinke

University home page:
www.eckerd.edu/academics/cra/writing/peter_meinke.htm

Interview by James Plath:
titan.iwu.edu/~jplath/meinke.html

One poem from *The Literary Review:*
www.webdelsol.com/tlr/poems/meinkepoem.html

Essay by Patricia Lieb and poems by Meinke:
www.geocities.com/evmanak/authors.html

Lisel Mueller

General information and two poems:
www.wiu.edu/foliopress/illinois/poetmueller.htm

General information:
www.poets.org/poets/poets.cfm?prmID=86

One poem from *Alive Together:*
www.bio.brandeis.edu/~sekuler/senpro/topic_1_stuff/what_the_dog_hears_perhaps.html

Sharon Olds

Home page:
www.wilmington.org/poets/olds.html

General Information:
www.english.uiuc.edu/maps/poets/m_r/olds/olds.htm

Interview by Dwight Garner:
www.salon.com/weekly/interview960701.html

One poem:
www.poetrymagazine.org/featured_poet_0704.html

Lee Ann Roripaugh

Her cyber-salon and on-line bookstore:
www.angelfire.com/wy/heartmountain/

One poem:
www.webdelsol.com/Quarterly_West/excerpts/poetry/roripaugh.html

Kay Ryan

Essay by Dana Gioia:
www.danagioia.net/essays/eryan.htm

Poetry Daily feature:
www.poems.com/sayunrya.htm

One poem:
bostonreview.mit.edu/BR21.3/Ryan.html

Review of *Elephant Rocks* (poetry collection):
www.ablemuse.com/premiere/cmuse_review.htm

Vivian Shipley

One poem:
www.city-net.com/~tpq/perennial.html

One poem:
www.ohiou.edu/~quarter/submission9.html

One poem:
www.glimmertrain.com/iadsizofgrie.html

Elizabeth Spires

General information/Norton Poets Online:
www.nortonpoets.com/spirese.htm

One poem:
www.newcriterion.com/archive/18/nov99/spires2.htm

Virgil Suárez

Personal home page:
www.virgilsuarez.com/

University home page:
www.english.fsu.edu/faculty/vsuarez.htm

Four poems:
www.barcelonareview.com/12/e_vs.htm

One poem and audio files/N.E.A.:
arts.endow.gov/explore/Writers/suarez.html

Three poems:
www.crazyhorseweb.org/virgilsuarez.htm

Interview of Suárez:
www.valpo.edu/english/vpr/vprsideframe.html

Ron Wallace

Review of short-story collection *Quick Bright Things:*
www.midlist.org/Mid-ListPressFiction.html

Afaa Michael Weaver

General information (with poetry samples):
www.pewarts.org/98/Weaver/

Two poems:
www.canwehaveourballback.com/weaver.htm

Miller Williams

President Bill Clinton's inaugural poem:
vcepolitics.com/usa/clinton/speeches/miller.shtml

Critical response to the inaugural poem:
www.toad.net/~andrews/inaug.html
www.blockhead.com/williams.htm

One poem:
www.hsu.edu/dept/alf/2000/williams3.htm

Appendix E—Sample Poet Groupings

These categories are by no means exhaustive, nor are they intended to make the claim that the entire body of a poet's work vividly exhibits these particular areas. Poets listed in each category merely are quite strong in this particular aspect of poetry and much of their work offers prime examples for enjoyment, study, and discussion.

Use the commentary by the poets included in this book as a leaping-off point to engage other poets of like (and unlike) strengths. You are in a position of privilege to know the behind-the-scenes information on a wide range of contemporary American poets—revisit their commentary and see how it applies or doesn't apply to the work of others.

Formal Poetry

- Dick Allen
- Michael J. Bugeja
- Peter Meinke
- Ron Wallace
- Miller Williams

Free Verse

- Wanda Coleman
- Denise Duhamel
- Bob Hicok
- Campbell McGrath
- Virgil Suárez
- Afaa Michael Weaver

Experimental Poetry

- Wanda Coleman
- Timothy Liu

Use of Persona

- Kim Addonizio
- Bob Hicok
- Lisel Mueller

Structure ***(including use of space)***

- Wanda Coleman
- Campbell McGrath
- Peter Meinke
- Lee Ann Roripaugh
- Kay Ryan
- Elizabeth Spires

Sound

- David Baker
- Robert Bly
- Billy Collins
- Stephen Dunn
- Jane Hirshfield
- Sharon Olds
- Ron Wallace

Metaphor

- Billy Collins
- Stephen Dunn
- Ray Gonzalez
- Campbell McGrath
- Sharon Olds
- Miller Williams

Narrative Poetry

- Kim Addonizio
- Stuart Dybek
- Bob Hicok
- David Lehman
- Adrian C. Louis
- Vivian Shipley
- Virgil Suárez

Glossary

Abstract words—words that denote things we understand the meaning of, but cannot feel or see, or apprehend by any of the five senses. Examples: love, beauty, justice, soul.

Alliteration—the repetition of like initial sounds (not letters), vowels, or consonants. *See* **assonance** and **consonance.** Example: Zebras xeroxed zestily.

Allusion—reference in a poem to a historical event, cultural artifact, or another literary work.

Anapest—a metrical foot consisting of three syllables, with the stress only on the final syllable.

Anaphora—a rhetorical device where several lines, phrases, or sentences in a row begin with the same word or phrase. Example: I remember eating poppy seeds beneath the golden sun/I remember bursting my brother's balloons/I remember . . . . For a classical example, look at Part 42 of Walt Whitman's "Song of Myself" where "Ever" begins each new line.

Ars Poetica—a poem that presents, explores, or challenges the poet's view on what poetry is as well as how one should write it. *See* Michael J. Bugeja's "Ars Poetica: The Influence of Lady Mary Wroth" or Stephen Dunn's "Ars Poetica." For other examples, *see* Norman Dubie's "Ars Poetica" or a similarly titled poem by Archibald MacLeish.

Assonance—the repetition of a vowel sound within a line or verse of poetry, usually internally. Examples: The orange owl opened its mouth on demand. An extra repetition betters the sound.

Ballad—a narrative poem which uses the **ballad stanza.** For some classic examples, *see* Samuel T. Coleridge's "The Rime of the Ancient Mariner," John Keats's "La Belle Dame Sans Merci," or Robert Hayden's "The Ballad of Nat Turner."

Ballad stanza—a four-line stanza where the first and third lines have four stresses each and the second and fourth lines have three stresses each. So for each stanza, the pattern of stress is 4-3-4-3. The ballad stanza also uses rhyme, but only in the even-numbered lines, so the pattern is XaXa XbXb, where X=lines that don't rhyme, though if they do in addition to the "a" and "b" rhyming lines, this is a specific type of ballad stanza called a hymn stanza.

Close reading—a fundamental technique used in literature interpretation. "Reading closely" means developing a deep understanding and a precise interpretation of a literary work that is based first and foremost on the words themselves—it involves embracing larger themes and ideas evoked or implied by the passage itself.

Concrete words—words that denote things we can actually feel, see, or apprehend via one or more of our senses in some way. Examples: cat, grass, cloud, sister, sun.

Confessional poetry—a term M. L. Rosenthal coined in his book *The New Poets* which dealt with John Berryman, Robert Lowell, Anne Sexton, and Sylvia Plath, all American poets of the mid-twentieth century who use private, personal details from their lives in their work. Prior to these writers, this sort of material was thought inappropriate and too embarrassing to use in poetry.

Consonance—the repetition of a consonant sound within a line or verse of poetry that can be internal and/or final. Examples: Frankie's friend wanted a frog. And wait to hear the water.

Dactyl—a metrical foot composed of three syllables, stressing the first syllable only.

Dramatic monologue—a poem in which the speaker (often a persona) addresses a specific listener or listeners and relates a dramatic moment in their life. Because of the nature of dramatic monologues (someone is telling a story), these poems are primarily narrative poems and they often reveal much about the speaker's desires, fears, and flaws.

Dramatic poetry—one of the three major subdivisions of poetry (as opposed to **lyric** or **narrative**). Dramatic poetry is poetry written for a performance as a play. For contemporary examples, look at the serious verse plays of T. S. Eliot, Federico Garcia Lorca, and William Butler Yeats.

Duende—a term coined by Federico Garcia Lorca that refers to the charisma of art in general, and, specifically, its ability to seduce. Lorca calls it a mysterious power that's inexplicable but tangible, powerful, and undeniable. The late jazz critic George Frazier claims that works with duende have soul, style, grace under pressure, charisma, panache, and passion to the nth power.

Elegy—a poem of mourning, especially one that laments a person who has died. Many poets write elegies to other poets who have died, such as W. H. Auden's "In Memory of W. B. Yeats." For classic examples, *see* Walt Whitman's "When Lilacs Last in the Dooryard Bloom'd" and Ben Jonson's "On My First Son."

End-stopped line—a line of poetry in which both the grammatical structure and the sense are complete. Example: *See* Dick Allen's "Veterans Day" or the last three lines of David Baker's "Snow Figure." *See also* **enjambed line.**

Enjambed line—a line of poetry in which the grammatical structure and the sense are not complete but are continued in the following line.

Example: "On a Tuesday I learned I'd never sit" is an enjambed line because the following line is "with my father on a curb and chuck" (from Bob Hicok's "The Wish"). *See* Timothy Liu's "In Flagrante Delicto," for an example. See also **end-stopped line.**

Envoi—a brief ending which contains a summary and rounding off of the subject. Envois are short (usually no more than four lines) and are used most often in the **ballad** and the **sestina.**

Epigraph—a quotation or informative note that precedes the body of some poems. Epigraphs can acknowledge sources of material and/or present relevant information to the poem that doesn't fit within the poem itself. *See* Michael J. Bugeja's "Ars Poetica: The Influence of Lady Mary Wroth" and Stephen Dunn's "John & Mary."

Epistolary poem—a type of poem written in the form of letters. They can, but do not necessarily have to include salutations ("Dear ____") or closings ("Sincerely").

Figure of speech—a type of rhetoric device used to achieve special effects. *See* **hyperbole, metaphor, metonymy, paradox, simile, synaesthesia, synecdoche,** and **understatement.**

Foot—a rhythmical unit in poetry. *See also* **anapest, datcyl, iamb, spondee** and **trochee.** Poetry is not only described by the type of foot, but also by the number of feet in a line (monometer=one, dimeter=two, trimeter=three, tetrameter=four, pentameter=five, hexameter=six, heptameter=seven, and so on).

Form poetry—poems that follow a set pattern of one or more of the following: meter, line length, poem length, and rhyme scheme. Examples: **ballad, pantoum, sonnet,** and **villanelle.**

Free verse—poems that do not follow a set pattern of meter, line length, poem length, or rhyme scheme. Free verse tends to approximate the rhythms and cadences of regular speech. *See also* **form poetry.**

Hyperbole—an extravagant overstatement used for effect. Example: Her eyes were wide as dinner plates. Also called **overstatement.** The opposite of **understatement.**

Iamb—a metrical foot composed of an unstressed syllable followed by a stressed syllable. An iamb is the opposite of a **trochee.**

Image—a descriptive representation of any of the five sensory impressions: sight, sound, smell, touch, or taste.

Imagism—a movement in early twentieth-century poetry that emphasized concrete, succinct language while de-emphasizing abstract commentary. One of the most famous examples of an Imagist poem is Ezra Pound's "In the Station of the Metro."

Irony—(1) a discrepancy between actual circumstances and those that would seem appropriate (situational irony), (2) a rhetorical figure by which a speaker means something other than what he says (verbal irony), or (3) a device by which the writer implies a different meaning from that intended by the speaker (dramatic irony). One example of verbal irony is sarcasm, saying one thing and meaning another.

Line—the basic compositional unit of a poem written in verse. A row of words that constitutes an element in the form of poetry.

List poem—a poem that enumerates or names a series of things. As opposed to the catalogue of ships in Homer's *Iliad,* a list poem tends to use list specific details and images. *See* David Lehman's "The Gift and "February 10." Much of Walt Whitman's poetry is in a list form, as is much of Allen Ginsberg's "Howl."

Lyric poem—one of the three major subdivisions of poetry (as opposed to **narrative** or **dramatic**). Lyric poetry is poetry in which music and musicality over drama or story. Modern lyric poetry tends to be quiet, meditative, inward, and emotional.

Meditation—a poem that focuses closely, without distraction, upon an object or person. Meditation poems move from the concrete to the abstract through association and levels of meaning.

Metaphor—a comparison between unlike things that does not use the word *like* or *as*. Examples: (a) My father is an ogre. (b) Walter Payton's a great running back—he's a machine.

Meter—the predominant rhythmic measure of a line of verse.

Metonymy—a figure of speech in which the name of one closely related thing is substituted for that of another. Example: referring to "the White House" when you mean the President, or referring to "the Crown" when you mean the monarchy.

Narrative poem—one of the three major subdivisions of poetry (as opposed to **dramatic** or **lyric**). Narrative poetry is poetry in which a story is told using chronological organization. Two examples of narrative poetry are the epic and the **ballad.** Narrative elements (story, action, chronology) are often incorporated into lyric poems.

Narrator—the speaker, or voice, in a poem.

Neologism—a newly made word or phrase (usually meaningless).

Objective correlative—T. S. Eliot's term that refers to a situation or an object that evokes a particular set of emotions in a reader.

Onomatopoeia—the use of words that imitate sounds, which also suggests their meaning. Example: crack, hiss, pop, sizzle, thump, whirr.

Pantoum—a Malay form written in quatrains (four-line stanzas) in which the second and fourth lines of each stanza become the first and third lines of the next one. The poem usually ends with the second and fourth lines repeating lines one and three from the first stanza. For contemporary examples, look at John Ashbery's "Pantoum."

Paradox—an apparent self-contradiction that possesses some quality of truth or sense.

Persona—the implied author or "second self" created by an author and through whom the poem is told. A persona poem's "second self" is often a person different than the author. Persona is a term that's sometimes used broadly to mean any first-person narrator.

Personification—a manner of speaking that endows things, abstractions, or ideas with human qualities.

Prose poem—poetry written in the form of prose. Most prose poems are compact, rhythmic, and imagistic, and do not utilize line breaks in the manner nonprose poems do. Prose poems challenge the very idea of what poetry is—in this capacity, many prose poems are experimental or surreal in nature.

Refrain—a phrase, line, or group of lines that is repeated at intervals.

Rhyme—the repetition of sounds in poetry, one of the characteristics commonly associated with poetry. In conjunction with rhythm, repetition, and various word sounds, rhyme gives poetry its musical quality. The six main types of rhyme are: (1) vowel rhyme (example: so/go), which is the repetition of only the vowel sound or sounds in words, (2) slant rhyme (example: brake/spoke), which is an inexact rhyme, (3) feminine rhyme, which is a rhyme with an unstressed final syllable, (4) masculine rhyme, which is a rhyme with a stressed final syllable, (5) end rhyme, which occurs at the end of a line, and (6) internal rhyme, which occurs within the line.

Additionally, rhymes can be either half or full. Half rhymes use either assonance (example: gleam/creed/easy) or consonance (example: thin/man/glean). Full rhyme is the repetition of the final vowel or vowel and consonant sound.

Sentimentality—mawkish tenderness, or being overly emotional. In most poems, this would be discouraged.

Setting—the place, time, scenery, and background details of a story or poem.

Simile—a comparison between two unlike things using the word *like* or the word *as*. Examples: (a) Joe was as angry as a wounded elephant. (b) His shouting was like thunder.

Sonnet—a rhyming poem of fourteen lines. The Italian (Petrarchan) sonnet has a rhyme scheme of abba | abba | cdc | cdc | or abba | abba | cde | cde. The English (Shakespearean) sonnet has a rhyme scheme of abab | cdcd | efef | gg. *See* Kim Addonizio's "First Poem for You," Dick Allen's "Lost Love," Michael J. Bugeja's "Ars Poetica: The Influence of Lady Mary Wroth," Peter Meinke's "Rage" and "The Poet, Trying to Surprise God."

Spondee—a metrical foot composed of two stressed syllables.

Stanza—a structural unit in a poem usually with a pattern of **rhyme** and **meter** that is repeated throughout the poem. Stanza literally means "station" or "stopping place."

Style—the distinctive way writers express themselves; style includes the words they choose as well as the rhythm, structure, rhyme, meter, and voice used.

Symbol—an action, object, image, or word that radiates meanings beyond itself. These meanings may be hard to express in other words, but are accessible on an intuitive level. A symbol is like a metaphorical vehicle without a clearly definable subject.

Synaesthesia—the technique of interpreting one kind of sensory impression in terms of a different sense. Examples: (a) an ear-shattering stink. (b) a blinding sweetness.

Synecdoche—the technique of referring to a person or thing in terms of only one part of that person or thing. Example: saying to a buddy "Nice wheels!" when you mean you like the entire car. Or telling someone to "Get your butt over here!" when you clearly want the whole person to come over.

Syllabics—a meter in which the number of syllables in a line is counted, ignoring the accents or syllable lengths. Syllabics is the predominant meter of Japanese and French poetry. For classic examples, *see* the work of Dylan Thomas or Marianne Moore.

Theme—a unifying concept or idea of a literary work.

Tone—the attitude conveyed by the voice of the narrator in a poem; the emotional coloring of a literary work.

Trochee—a metrical foot of two syllables composed of a stressed syllable followed by an unstressed syllable. A trochee is the opposite of an **iamb**.

Ubi sunt—a phrase often appearing in medieval poems, which roughly translates from Latin into English as "where are [they]?" Poems with an *ubi sunt* theme lament life's ephemeral nature, the inevitable passing of time.

Understatement—a figure of speech that consists of saying less than one means, or of saying what one means less strongly than the occasion warrants. The opposite of **hyperbole.**

Verisimilitude—the appearance or semblance of being true. In poetry, verisimilitude means providing the specific, significant details that make the poem seem realistic versus fanciful.

Villanelle—a nineteen-line, closed form poem. Villanelles have five stanzas, each of which are three lines long, though the final stanza has four lines. The first line of the first stanza is repeated as the last line of the second and fourth stanza. *See* Dick Allen's "Veterans Day" and Peter Meinke's "Meditation on You & Wittgenstein."

Voice—a term used since the 1980s that has two meanings: (1) voice simply refers to **style,** or (2) voice is synonymous with **persona,** the characteristic speech (and thought) patterns of any narrator or speaker of a poem.

Credits

Kim Addonizio, "The Way of the World" appeared in *Five Points*. Reprinted by permission of the author. "Onset" and "Night of the Living, Night of the Dead" from *Tell Me*. Copyright © 2000 by Kim Addonizio. Reprinted with the permission of BOA Editions, Ltd. "First Poem for You" from *The Philosopher's Club*. Copyright © 1994 by Kim Addonizio. Reprinted with the permission of BOA Editions, Ltd.

Dick Allen, "Cities of the Fifties (A Glose)," and "Still Waters" from *Ode to the Cold War: Poems New and Selected* by Dick Allen, © 1997. Reprinted with the permission of Sarabande Books. "Being Taught" appeared in *Poetry*, "The Cove" appeared in *The Hudson Review*, and "Then" appeared in *The New Republic*. All reprinted by permission of the author. "Veterans Day," "Dignity," and "Lost Love" from *Flight and Pursuit* by Dick Allen, copyright © 1987. Reprinted by the permission of the author.

David Baker, "Starlight" and "Patriotics" reprinted from *Sweet Home, Saturday Night*, by permission of the University of Arkansas Press. Copyright © 1991 by David Baker. "Snow Figure" reprinted from *After the Reunion* by permission of the University of Arkansas Press. Copyright © 1994 by David Baker. "Benton's Cloud" and "Forced Bloom" reprinted from *Changeable Thunder* by permission of the University of Arkansas Press. Copyright © 2001 by David Baker.

Robert Bly, "Snowbanks North of the House" from *Eating the Honey of Words* by Robert Bly. Copyright © 1999 by Robert Bly. Reprinted by permission of HarperCollins Publishers Inc.

Michael J. Bugeja, "Ars Poetica: The Influence of Lady Mary Wroth" reprinted by permission of the University of Arkansas Press. Copyright © 1997 by Michael J. Bugeja.

Wanda Coleman, "Hand Dance," "Neruda," and "All of That" copyright © 1993 by Wanda Coleman. Reprinted from *Hand Dance* with permission of Black Sparrow Press. "In Search of the Mythology of Do Wah Wah" and "The California Crack" copyright © 1983 by Wanda Coleman. Reprinted from *Imagoes* with the permission of Black Sparrow Press. "Mr. Lopez," "Prove It Why Don't You," and "You Judge a Man by the Silence He Keeps" copyright © 1990 by Wanda Coleman. Reprinted from *African Sleep Sickness: Stories & Poems* with the permission of Black Sparrow Press.

Billy Collins, "Questions About Angels" and "A History of Weather" from *Questions About Angels* by Billy Collins, copyright © 1991. Reprinted by permission of the University of Pittsburgh Press. "Osso Buco" and "Nightclub" from *The Art of Drowning* by Billy Collins, copyright © 1995. Reprinted by permission of the University of Pittsburgh Press.

Denise Duhamel, "Id," "Ego," and "Superego" from *Queen for a Day: Selected and New Poems* by Denise Duhamel, copyright © 2001. Reprinted by permission of the University of Pittsburgh Press.

Stephen Dunn, "Knowledge." Reprinted with permission of the author. "Something Like Happiness," "Desire" from *New and Selected Poems 1974–1994* by Stephen Dunn. Copyright © 1994 by Stephen Dunn. Used by permission of W. W. Norton & Company, Inc. "The Guardian Angel," "Tenderness" from *Between Angels* by Stephen Dunn. Copyright © 1989 by Stephen Dunn. Used by permission of W. W. Norton & Company, Inc. "Midwest" from *Landscape at the End of the Century* by Stephen Dunn. Copyright © 1991 by Stephen Dunn. Used by permission of W. W. Norton & Company, Inc. "The Postmortem Guide," "John &

Mary" from *Different Hours* by Stephen Dunn. Copyright © 2000 by Stephen Dunn. Used by permission of W. W. Norton & Company, Inc. "Ars Poetica," "Imagining Myself My Father" from *Loosestrife* by Stephen Dunn. Copyright © 1996 by Stephen Dunn. Used by permission of W. W. Norton & Company, Inc.

Paul Durcan, "The Mayo Accent" from *A Snail in My Prime* © Paul Durcan, 1993. Reproduced by permission of the Harvill Press.

Stuart Dybek, "Sirens" appeared in *The Iowa Review*. "Windy City," "Today, Tonight," and "Overhead Fan" appeared in *Poetry*. "Three Nocturnes" appeared in *American Poetry Review*. "Inspiration" appeared in *TriQuarterly*. All reprinted with permission of the author.

Ray Gonzalez, "Under the Freeway in El Paso" and "White" from *Cabato Sentora*. Copyright © 1999 by Ray Gonzalez. Reprinted with the permission of BOA Editions, Ltd. "Kiva Floor at Abo," "I Am Afraid of the Moon," "Federico Garcia Lorca's Desk," and "Kick the Heart" from *The Hawk Temple at Tierra Grande*. Copyright © 2002 by Ray Gonzalez. Reprinted with the permission of BOA Editions, Ltd.

Bob Hicok, "The Wish," "Bottom of the Ocean," "Radical Neck," and "To Err is Humid" reprinted with permission of the author. "Process of Elimination" and "Other Lives and Dimensions and Finally a Love Poem" from *Plus Shipping*. Copyright © 1998 by Bob Hicok. Reprinted with the permission of BOA Editions, Ltd.

Jane Hirshfield, "In Praise of Coldness," "Tree," and "The Envoy" from *Given Sugar, Given Salt* by Jane Hirshfield. Copyright © 2001 by Jane Hirshfield. Reprinted by permission of HarperCollins Publishers Inc. "Three Foxes by the Edge of the Field at Twilight" and "The Poet" from *The Lives of the Heart* by Jane Hirshfield. Copyright © 1997 by Jane Hirshfield. Reprinted by permission of HarperCollins Publishers Inc. "The Love of Aged Horses" and "The Weighing" from *The October Palace* by Jane Hirshfield. Copyright © 1994 by Jane Hirshfield. Reprinted by permission of HarperCollins Publishers Inc. "For What Binds Us" reprinted from *Gravity & Angels* (Wesleyan University Press, 1988). Copyright © 1988 by Jane Hirshfield. Reprinted by permission of the author and Wesleyan University Press.

David Lehman, "February 10" reprinted with the permission of Scribner, a Division of Simon & Schuster, Inc., from *The Daily Mirror: A Journal in Poetry* by David Lehman. Copyright © 2000 by David Lehman. "Sestina," "Corrections," "Wittgenstein's Ladder," and "The Gift," copyright © by David Lehman, appear here by permission of Writer's Representatives, Inc. and the author.

Timothy Liu, "In *Flagrante Delicto*," first published in pieces in *Denver Quarterly*, *Rhizome*, and *Talisman*, and subsequently in its entirety in *Hard Evidence* (Talisman House, 2001). Copyright © 2001 by Timothy Liu. Reprinted with permission of the author.

Adrian C. Louis, "Indian Summer Gives Way to the Land of the Rising Sun," and "Adios Again, My Blessed Angel of Thunderheads and Urine" from *Bone & Juice*. Evanston: Northwestern University Press, 2001, pp. 76–86.

Campbell McGrath, "Capitalism Poem #5" from *Capitalism* (The Ecco Press, 1990). Copyright © 1990 by Campbell McGrath. Reprinted with permission of The Ecco Press. "Almond Blossoms, Rock and Roll, the Past Seen as Burning Fields" from *American Noise* (The Ecco Press, 1993). Copyright © 1993 by Campbell McGrath. Reprinted with permission of The Ecco Press. "Delphos, Ohio" from *Spring Comes to Chicago* (The Ecco Press, 1996). Copyright by Campbell McGrath. Reprinted with permission of The Ecco Press. "The Prose Poem" from *Road Atlas* (The Ecco Press, 1999). Copyright © by Campbell McGrath. Reprinted with permission of The Ecco Press. "The Orange" from *Florida Poems* (The Ecco Press, 2002). Copyright © 2002 by Campbell McGrath. Reprinted with permission of The Ecco Press.

Peter Meinke, "Liquid Paper," "Ode to Good Men Fallen Before Hero Came," and "The Poet, Trying to Surprise God" from *Liquid Paper*, by Peter Meinke, copyright © 1996. Reprinted by permission of the University of Pittsburgh Press. "Rage" from *Night Watch on the Chesapeake*, by Peter Meinke, copyright © 1996. Reprinted by permission of the University of Pittsburgh Press. "Scars" and "The Secret Code" from *Scars*, by Peter Meinke, copyright © 1996. Reprinted by permission of the University of Pittsburgh Press. "Assisted Living," "A Meditation on You & Wittgenstein," "Seven & Seven," and "Zinc Fingers" from *Zinc Fingers* by Peter Meinke, © 1996. Reprinted by permission of the University of Pittsburgh Press.

Lisel Mueller,"The Triumph of Life: Mary Shelley" from *The Need to Hold Still* (Louisiana State University Press, 1980). Copyright © 1980 by Lisel Mueller. Reprinted with permission of Louisiana State University Press. "When I Am Asked" from *Waving from Shore* (Louisiana State University Press, 1989). Copyright © 1989 by Lisel Mueller. Reprinted with permission of Louisiana State University Press.

Sharon Olds, "5¢ a Peek" appeared in *The New Yorker* (November 6, 2000). "His Costume" appeared in *The New Yorker* (September 11, 2000). "The Space Heater" appeared in *The New Yorker* (January 22, 2001). "Silence, With Two Texts" appeared in *The New Yorker* (April 9, 2001). All reprinted with permission of the author. "I Go Back to May 1937" and "Little Things" are reprinted from *The Gold Cell* by Sharon Olds, copyright © 1987 by Sharon Olds. Used by permission of Alfred A. Knopf, a division of Random House. Inc. "The Missing Boy" reprinted from *The Dead and the Living* by Sharon Olds, copyright © 1987 by Sharon Olds. Used by permission of Alfred A. Knopf, a division of Random House. Inc. "The Race" reprinted from *The Father* by Sharon Olds, copyright © 1992 by Sharon Olds. Used by permission of Alfred A. Knopf, a division of Random House. Inc. "The Promise" and "The Knowing" reprinted from *Blood, Tin, Straw,* by Sharon Olds, copyright © 1999 by Sharon Olds. Used by permission of Alfred A. Knopf, a division of Random House. Inc.

Lee Ann Roripaugh, "Octopus in the Freezer," first published in *The North American Review,* appears here by permission of the author. "Pearls" and "The Woman Who Loves Insects" from *Beyond Heart Mountain* by Lee Ann Roripaugh, copyright © 1999. Reprinted by permission of Penguin/Putnam, Inc.

Kay Ryan, "The Hinge of Spring," "Turtle," and "Impersonal" from *Flamingo Watching* (Copper Beech Press, 1994). Copyright © 1994 by Kay Ryan. Reprinted with permission of the author and Copper Beech Press. "Swept Up Whole," "Mirage Oases," and "Crustacean Island" from *Elephant Rocks* (Grove Press, 1996). Copyright © 1996 by Kay Ryan. Reprinted with permission of the author and Grove/Atlantic, Inc. "The Excluded Animals," "Blandeur," "Star Block," "The Pass," and "Failure" from *Say Uncle* (Grove Press, 2001). Copyright © 2001 by Kay Ryan. Reprinted with permission of the author and Grove/ Atlantic, Inc.

Vivian Shipley, "Black Hole" from *Devil's Lane* (Negative Capability Press, 1996). Copyright © 1996 by Vivian Shipley. Reprinted by permission of the author. "May 17, 1720: Superiour Court Justice Counsels Elizabeth Atwood in His Chambers Before Sentencing Her to Hang," "Number Fifty-Two: Winifred Benham, Hartford, Connecticut, October 7, 1697," "Kachino, Russia: Perm 36," and "Barbie, Madame Alexander, Bronislawa Wajs" from *When There Is No Shore* (Word Press, 2002). Copyright © 2002 by Vivian Shipley. Reprinted by permission of the author.

Elizabeth Spires, "Cemetery Reef," appeared in *Poetry*. Reprinted with permission of the author. "Easter Sunday, 1955" from *Worldling* by Elizabeth Spires. Copyright © 1995 by Elizabeth Spires. Used by permission of the author and W. W. Norton & Company, Inc.

Virgil Suárez, "Psalm of the Boy Cartographer," "Those Lost Souls: Florida Strait Tragedy #1," "*Aguacero*," "Women Who Carry Water from the River," and "*Carterista*/Pickpocket." Reprinted with permission of the author. "In the House of White Light" from *You Come Singing* (Tia Chucha Press, 1998). Copyright © 1998 by Virgil Suarez. Reprinted by permission of the author and Tia Chucha Press. "Bitterness" from *Garabato Poems* (Wings Press, 1999). Copyright © 1999 by Virgil Suarez. Reprinted by permission of the author and Wings Press.

Ronald Wallace, "Blessings" appeared in *Poetry Northwest* and subsequently in a limited edition chapbook, *Blessings*. Reprinted with permission of the author and Silver Buckle Press. "Oranges" from *Plums, Stones, Kisses & Hooks* (University of Missouri Press, 1981). Copyright © 1981 by Ronald Wallace. Reprinted by permission of the author and the University of Missouri Press. "The Friday Night Fights," "Fielding," and "The McPoem" from *The Uses of Adversity* by Ronald Wallace, copyright © 1998. Reprinted by permission of the University of Pittsburgh Press. "The Hell Mural: Panel 1" and "In the Amish Bakery" from *The Making of Happiness* by Ronald Wallace, copyright © 1991. Reprinted by permission of the University of Pittsburgh Press. "At Chet's Feed and Seed" from *People and Dog in the Sun* by Ronald Wallace, copyright © 1987. Reprinted by permission of the University of Pittsburgh Press. "Hardware" from *Time's Fancy* by Ronald Wallace, copyright © 1994. Reprinted by permission of the University of Pittsburgh Press. "The Facts of Life" from *Tunes for Bears to Dance to* by Ronald Wallace, copyright © 1983. Reprinted by permission of the University of Pittsburgh Press.

Afaa Michael Weaver, "The Picnic, an Homage to Civil Rights" from *My Father's Geography* by Afaa Michael Weaver, copyright © 1992. Reprinted by permission of the University of Pittsburgh Press. "Sub Shop Girl" from *Timber and Prayer* by Afaa Michael Weaver, copyright © 1995. Reprinted by permission of the University of Pittsburgh Press. "African Jump Ball" from *Multitudes: Poems Selected and New* by Afaa Michael Weaver, copyright © 2000. Reprinted by permission of Sarabande Books.

Miller Williams, "After All These Years of Prayer and Pi R Square," first published in Arts and Letters (#4), reprinted here with permission of the author. "Waking from a Dream" reprinted from *Some Jazz a While: Collected Poems*. Copyright © 1999 by Miller Williams. Used with permission of the poet and the University of Illinois Press. "Love Poem with Toast" reprinted from *Some Jazz a While: Collected Poems*. Copyright 1999 by Miller Williams. Used with permission of the poet and the University of Illinois Press. "Ruby Tells All" and "A Poem for Emily" from *Imperfect Love* (Louisiana State University Press, 1986). Copyright © 1986 by Miller Williams. Reprinted with permission of Louisiana State University Press.

General Index

Index of Authors, Titles, and First Lines

Authors are indexed in **bold,** titles in *italic*, and first lines in roman.